D1488131

CLASSICS
IN ECONOMICS

CLASSICS IN ECONOMICS

A Course of Selected Reading
by Authorities

*

Particular attention is directed to the
Introductory Reading Guide by
G. D. H. COLE, M.A.

KENNIKAT PRESS
Port Washington, N. Y./London

CLASSICS IN ECONOMICS

Copyright, 1960, Cultural Publications (I.U.S.), Ltd.
Reissued in 1971 by Kennikat Press by arrangement
with Philosophical Library, Inc.
Library of Congress Catalog Card No: 70-122972
ISBN 0-8046-1353-2

Manufactured by Taylor Publishing Company   Dallas, Texas

ESSAY AND GENERAL LITERATURE INDEX REPRINT SERIES

CONTENTS

BOOK I

PRODUCTION AND DISTRIBUTION

BOOK II

MONEY AND TRADE

v

CONTENTS

BOOK III

WORK AND WELFARE

INTRODUCTORY READING GUIDE

G. D. H. COLE, M.A.

***

WHAT ECONOMICS IS ABOUT

ECONOMICS is the study of the conditions which govern the production and distribution of wealth. " Wealth ", in the sense here implied, consists of anything that is an object of human desire, and is either naturally scarce (*e.g.* diamonds, or uranium) or costs effort to produce, so that the resources used up in producing it are not available for producing other things. Only a few things, such as air, are normally to be had in such quantities without effort in producing or collecting them that people can have as much as they want of them without either depriving any-one else of what he wants or using scarce resources in supplying them. Even water is so distributed that a great deal of effort has to be used up in making it available where it is wanted—*e.g.* for consumption in large towns or for the irrigation of arid tracts of land. Most of the materials of industry have to be dug up out of the earth or grown by the applica-tion of effort and scarce resources to the cultivation of land, and then have to be transported by further effort to the places where they are required for use in the production of finished goods. Similarly, though some food is yielded by nature without human effort in growing it, most foodstuffs have to be produced by applying scarce resources to the cultivation of land and have to be carried, often over long distances, to where they are needed. For practical puposes we can in modern communities ignore those " gifts of nature " which can be had without effort either in producing them or in transporting them to the places where they are to be consumed, and can concentrate our attention on things which use up scarce resources either in production or in moving them from where they are produced to where they are worked up into more finished products, or consumed.

The Factors of Production. The scarce resources which are applied to the production of goods and services for meeting human wants, either directly or indirectly, are basically of three kinds. Economists call them the " factors of production ", and usually classify them under three heads—Land, Labour and Capital. Some economists add a fourth factor, which they call " Enterprise " ; but Enterprise is really only a kind of labour—that of scientists and inventors who devise improved methods of production or find out new ways of harnessing natural resources to the service of human wants, or that of business organizers or managers who undertake the organization of the productive processes or launch out on new enterprises or new ways of meeting the consumers' needs. For some purposes it is necessary to consider Enterprise as a special " factor " of production, or at any rate as a special kind of labour ; but, in general, it is most convenient to treat the " factors of production " as the three defined by the classical economists—Land, Labour, and Capital.

Land. All these factors are *scarce*. There is, indeed, much more land in the world than has been, or is ever likely to be, put to productive use ; but land that is worth using as a productive factor is scarce in the sense that there is much less land that is usable for productive purposes than would be used if anyone could have as much productive land as he wanted without having to pay anything for the use of it. Much of the earth's surface is *arid* and could be used for production, if at all, only after much effort had been spent on it—for example, by irrigation. Much more is so situated that little or no use could be made of it until much effort had been expended on providing means of transporting its produce to the places where it is wanted. Moreover, land differs greatly in quality and in capacity to produce wanted things even if it were improved by human effort : so that one patch of land is " worth " much more than another. This " worth " depends partly on the land itself, and on the local climate ; but it also depends largely on situation in relation to markets and on the things consumers want. Very infertile land can be very valuable if it is situated where men want to erect buildings—for example, in the neighbourhood of growing cities ; and the " value " of land depends also on the demand for the crops that can be grown on it or for the minerals which lie beneath its surface. The value of land is also affected by the amount of effort that is required to make it yield a particular crop or to extract each ton of coal or some other mineral that it can supply.

Rent. Thus, every patch of land has its own value, which depends partly on its natural properties and partly on the intensity of the demand for the products it can be made to yield. The greater the yield, in terms of what people are prepared to give for the product, the higher the value of the land is—of course, after allowing for the varying cost of transporting the product to where it is wanted. Economists call the value of land, measured in terms of the annual net yield, after the costs incurred in cultivation or mining have been met, its *Rent*, which, under conditions of private ownership, is what a farmer or a mining concern or a town developer can be expected to be prepared to pay for the right to use it. Thus Rent is essentially a *differential* payment for the right to use a particular patch of land because of its

LAND-RENT AS DIFFERENTIAL SURPLUS

A–G are 7 equal land-areas. A1, B1, etc., are the yields of, say, wheat to be got from each area in an average year by equal applications of labour and capital. A2, B2, etc., are the additional yields to be got by doubling the amounts of labour and capital used. D2 and E2 and G2 show *Increasing Returns*: B2, C2, and F2 show *Diminishing Returns*. X–X shows the returns needed to make the land worth cultivating *if no Rent is paid*. Everything to the *right* of X–X is the Rent (in terms of produce) that can be charged for the use of the land.

particular net advantages. There is some land so unproductive or so remote from markets that nobody is prepared to offer for it any payment at all. But in closely settled countries most land is worth something, if not for use in production then for the pleasure of possession, as in the case of unproductive parklands or forests.

Land and Capital. Land, strictly defined, is no more than a part of the earth's surface in the state in which nature has made it available for man's use. But, in settled countries, most cultivable land has been improved, in many cases over a number of generations, by human effort which has increased its fertility. In other cases, ill-directed human effort has destroyed the fertility which the land once possessed. Again, much of the present value of land is the result of its nearness to human settlements ; this applies not only to built-up land or to land needed for building development with the growth of towns but also to land which is well situated for the marketing of its produce because of good man-made communications with towns or ports, or merely because good natural communications by sea or river have acquired usefulness with the growth of available markets. It is impossible, nowadays, in most cases to distinguish the *natural* value of any particular piece of land from the value which it has acquired (or in some cases lost) because of these influences. A farm which has been farmed for centuries is mainly a man-made product both because of the effort that has been expended by successive generations upon it and because of the effect on its value of the secular growth of human settlements in its neighbourhood and of the means of transporting its produce to where it can be consumed or applied to the production of finished goods. Thus, Rent is only in small part attributable solely to natural fertility : it is in the main a social product. But it is essentially a *differential* payment, dependent on the expected net yield to be extracted from each particular parcel of land in view of its productive quality, natural or acquired.

Labour. The second " factor of production "—Labour—is also differentiated by its natural and acquired properties. Men differ in productive capacity, not only because some are more skilled or more energetic or better trained than others but also because different valuations are put upon different kinds of labour. Doctors are paid larger incomes than agricultural labourers, and usually, in any given occupation, men are paid more than women. A manager with a high reputation for efficiency is paid more than one whose reputation is lower, at any rate in many occupations ; and, under conditions of " payments by results ", a fast workman is paid more than a slow one. There is a double grading of rewards for productive effort, both *within* particular occupations and *between* them ; and even where wages or salaries are paid on a time basis, without direct relation to output, the better worker is likely to get more regular employment and to have more chance of promotion to a higher income grade than the less efficient. Similarly, when a man works " on his own " and not for an employer, his earnings are influenced by efficiency as well as by good or bad fortune.

The Reward of Labour. Within occupations, the reward of labour depends largely on relative efficiency, though there may be great variations in the general level from country to country or even from place to place within a single country. *Between* occupations, differences of reward depend on very complex factors. They are influenced by the state of demand for different products or services : thus, wages in a particular industry may rise or fall because the demand for its products rises or declines, at any rate until there has been time to adjust the number of trained workers to the changed state of demand. But *relative* rewards in different occupations are also greatly influenced by other factors, such as the cost or difficulty of securing training in or entry to a particular trade, and also according to the conventional estimation of the worth of different kinds of service.

Wages and Collective Bargaining: Wage Differences. In many occupations there are standard wage-rates, usually fixed nowadays by collective bargaining between Trade Unions and employing bodies. But earnings may vary widely even where time-rates are fixed ; and in many cases, even under time-working, there are grading systems which give the more skilled workers higher incomes than the less skilled. The extent to which collective bargaining destroys differences of reward according to differences of efficiency is often overestimated : indeed, fixed rates existed long before Trade Unions, and Trade Union bargaining has sometimes led to greater differentiation. It is, however, true that Trade Unionism has tended towards a standardization of wage-rates *over wider areas*, and also within particular grades of wage-labour. There has also been a strong tendency towards standardization of salaries in public services and in clerical and similar occupations, whereas no such tendency has appeared either in most types of managerial work (except in the public services) or among workers " on their own ", such as jobbing small employers or independent workers or professional consultants, lawyers, artists, writers, etc. In effect, the incomes derived from labour have a strong element that is derived from the personal quality of the worker, and to this extent resemble the " rents " paid for patches of land. Some economists have called this differential element " Rent of Ability " ; but the term has never passed into general use, and most economists have tended to concentrate attention rather on the differences *between* than on those *within* occupations and to treat the labour factor as a number of " lumps " of employable labour, each of a particular kind, of which employers hire more or fewer units according to their expectation of the profit, or net yield, to be derived from employing them.

Capital. The third " factor of production "—Capital—must be thought of, in this connexion, not as a sum of money, but as consisting of things that can be used either as instruments of production or in meeting human wants directly over a considerable time. To the first of these categories belong such things as factory buildings and equipment, ships, docks, railways, power-stations and a host of other " producers' goods " : to the second belong such things as houses and other " durable consumers' goods " which yield up their value by instalments over a longish period. There is no clear line between these latter and other consumers' goods : for example, a private motor car or a houseful of furniture can be looked at either as " capital " or as a consumers' good that lasts longer than, say, a leg of mutton. It is sometimes convenient to treat consumers' goods of these kinds as " capital " because they are often rented out by their owners and not owned by those who consume their services. For example, a house may be capital to its owner, whereas the annual rent of it is consumption from the standpoint of the family that lives in it. Another kind of " capital goods " consists of all the materials, partly-finished goods and finished goods that are in the hands of producers or traders and have not yet passed into the consumers' hands. Such things are part of the manufacturer's or trader's " capital stock " as much as the buildings or machines he uses in production or trade, and the holding of adequate stocks is an essential part of the real cost of making goods available for consumption.

All these " capital goods ", as distinct from unimproved land or minerals lying under land, are products of human effort. They have been made by men using the materials given by nature. Capital is distinguished by economists from Land, in the sense in which land is a gift of nature, as a product of human effort which, instead of being consumed at once, has been stored up, or saved, for use in further production. Some economists used to call it the result of " abstinence ", and to justify the rewards paid to the owners of capital goods as the " rewards of abstinence ", as in a sense they are. But the phrase has fallen out of use because so often the owner and the abstainer are not the same person, and the possession of capital is the result of inheritance, or good fortune, or the chances of the market, rather than of actual abstention by the owner from consuming anything he really wishes to consume.

Money Capital. Capital, as a " factor of production " side by side with Land and Labour, consists of real things. But in the modern world many people possess what they call " capital " in the form of ownership not of real things but of claims to receive *money*. This applies, for example, to holders of National Debt and to other creditors who have lent money at interest ; and with the growth of joint stock companies the investing shareholders in them have come to think of their property rather as a sum of money than as the ownership of a fraction of the real assets of the businesses in question. Money, however, is not a factor of production, but only a necessary lubricant of the real processes of production and distribution—one which has become more and more important with the growth of scale and complexity in business operations, so that " making money ", rather than making things, has come to be the principal incentive to productive effort for most people. The tendency to think of money as the main thing has also been fostered by the sub-division of productive processes, the development of standardized mass production, and the increase in the proportion of labour applied not to producing things but to moving them about, making book entries about them, selling them across counters, and so on. Most workers to-day have no complete product they can regard as their own : many have no physical product at all. They tend therefore more and more to regard themselves as producers of money-values rather than of things.

Interest. Money differs from Land, from Labour, and from Capital Goods in that, within each particular country at any rate, all units of it are alike, whereas each patch of land, each worker by hand or brain, and each factory, machine, or house has its own special quality. Accordingly, whereas the returns derived from the real factors of production are essentially *differential*, the return from lending money at interest tends to be the same for each unit lent. I do not mean that all money loans of equal amounts yield equal returns : the returns differ according to the conditions on which the loans are made. They differ according to the time-period over which the lent money is locked up ; in accordance with the risk that the interest will not be paid, or the principal not repaid when it falls due ; and in accordance with a number of other conditions. But, given the same conditions, one sum of £100 is as good as another, and tends, at any particular time, to command the same return. This is known as the Rate of Interest ; and there are a number of inter-related Rates of Interest, each tending towards uniformity, for particular kinds of loan (*e.g.* Government loans for short, medium and long periods ; bank loans for very short periods and ordinary bank overdrafts ; debentures or bonds in well-secured enterprises ; and so on). There is no one Rate of Interest ; but the various rates tend to some extent, though by no means completely, to move up and down together. They are greatly influenced by the supply of money, which used to be regarded by economists as in the main a self-regulating consequence of the volume of transactions needing to be financed, but is now commonly regarded as a matter for public regulation by Governments and Central Banks, in order to prevent inflation (too much money) or deflation (too little money) and to keep the supply of money at the level required to sustain full employment and to maintain prices at levels consistent with balancing the nation's international accounts.

The supply of money and the Rate of Exchange. This question of the international balance of payments is, however, more complex than the preceding paragraph suggests ; for except under an unalterable gold standard which settles the relative value of the monies of different countries, there is no absolutely fixed value of one national money in terms of another. A country can, as Great Britain did in 1949, alter the external value of its money in the hope of readjusting its balance of payments by making its exports cheaper (or dearer) to foreign buyers. Thus, if a country is suffering from " inflation " in the form of a rise in the prices of its goods above those charged for comparable products of other countries, it can seek to correct the inflation either by reducing the supply of money and thus forcing its own price-level down *in terms of its own money* or by altering the " rate of exchange " so as to leave its internal prices, broadly, as they were (except the prices of imports from countries which do not act in the same way) but at the same time make its goods cheaper in terms of the money of such countries.

Broadly speaking, when the supply of money—that is, of means of payment—in a country increases (or decreases) faster than its production increases (or decreases) prices will tend to rise (or fall) because there will be more (or less) money to offer in exchange for each unit of goods or services. The aim of monetary regulation is to prevent undesirable price-fluctuations arising from such causes, and to make the supply of money just adequate to render possible full employment of the available factors of production. This is, of course, a much more complicated matter than it sounds ; and it is the more complicated because the various national currencies are not isolated one from another, but have to be exchangeable for the conduct of international trade. The more dependent a country is on international trade, the more has it to take account of international price movements, either in regulating the supply of money or in varying the rates of exchange between its money and the monies of other countries.

Deflation and Disinflation. The case against trying to remedy a lack of balance by *Deflation* is that a reduction in the supply of money sufficient for this purpose usually causes widespread unemployment and thus makes the country in question poorer than it need be in real goods. There are, however, occasions when a reduction in the supply of money is necessary, and can be brought about without these disastrous results. In Great Britain, for example, after 1945, vast sums were piling up in profits that could not be spent without causing a sharp rise in prices, and these sums were being held unspent in business reserves in order to prevent this. In addition, the total of personal incomes, excluding these reserves, exceeded what could be spent on buying all the available goods and services at current prices. The Government therefore used high taxation to take this surplus spending power off the market, and built up a large budget surplus which was used to pay off government debt. This policy was called *Disinflation*, in order to distinguish it from the kind of *Deflation* that would have been inconsistent with the maintenance of full employment. It was accompanied by appeals for savings out of incomes and also for " restraint " in demands for higher wages or in the distribution of increased dividends by businesses out of their high profits.

The Balance of Payments. During the years after 1945 Great Britain, in common with many other countries, was struggling with a seriously adverse balance of payments, mainly the result of wartime dislocations. The most serious aspect of this situation was the " dollar shortage ", which persisted because the United States had become a great creditor country but had not increased its imports at all in proportion to its exports. The dollar shortage made it necessary for Great Britain and other countries, despite the concession of " Marshall Aid ", to restrict their purchases in dollar areas and to keep their money inconvertible into dollars, except under strict control. British production and exports alike made a remarkable recovery after 1945, but sales in dollar markets remained much too small to meet the need for dollars, even in 1950 when the British external accounts with the rest of the world as a whole balanced. In face of greatly increased American production and of limited American demand for imports the entire trade of the world was dislocated, and conditions in the United States acquired a preponderant influence on what happened throughout the world, except in the areas under Soviet control. This state of affairs rendered many of the normal workings of economic relations inoperative, and in particular twisted the shape of foreign trade because countries had to buy what they needed largely from other countries that were prepared to take their exports in exchange. This involved much *bilateral* bargaining (*i.e.* bargains between pairs of countries) instead of the *multilateralism* which existed in the nineteenth century and in some degree up to 1939.

International Trade. According to the classical theory of international trade, each country tends to specialize in producing those things which it can produce at the lowest cost and to exchange its surplus of such things for things which it can buy from abroad more cheaply than it can make them at home. This is what would tend to happen under conditions of universal free trade and competition ; but of course there would be under such a system no assurance that any country would be able to employ its whole population at a satisfactory standard of life. The rigid free trader argues that in such a case the surplus population should emigrate to countries which offer better prospects ; but this is not so easy as it sounds, especially since many countries restrict immigration. Protectionists have always argued that countries should protect home employment by keeping out imports which compete with home products ; and most countries do this nowadays to a considerable extent. But protection for high-cost industries, which could not compete with imports admitted without tariff or other restrictions, safeguards home employment only at the expense of making goods dearer for the consumers and in addition often raises the prices of exports and thus makes them harder to sell. The more a country depends on foreign trade, the less can protection meet its problems—though even such a country may of course be driven to restrict imports not so much in order to protect home industries as to prevent the purchase from abroad of goods for which it cannot afford to pay. The great extent of protectionism and restriction of imports in the world to-day is a result less of the desire to foster home employment (though this counts for something) than of the adverse balances of payments which threaten most countries except the United States.

NATIONAL INCOME AND CONSUMPTION

A nation must, under normal conditions, live within its national income—that is to say, it must consume less than it produces ; for it must set aside a part of its current production to replace capital goods as they wear out or become obsolete and also, at any rate when its population is increasing, to add to its supply of capital goods. A nation can consume as much as, or more than, it produces only if it is either receiving gifts from abroad (*e.g.* Marshall Aid), or borrowing from abroad by receiving investments of foreign capital. In the latter case, it has to pay interest to the lenders ; but as long as the flow of capital from abroad continues the interest may be much less than the sums borrowed, and to that extent the spending power of the borrowing country will be temporarily increased.

Consumption and Investment. Apart from gifts or borrowing, a country has to live by what it produces, either for its own use or for export in exchange for what it buys from abroad. If it owes debts to foreigners, or is lending to them, some of its exports will be " unrequited ", and will yield no imports in return. If these complications are left out, the nation's real income consists of its total current net production of goods and services *minus* its exports *plus* its imports. By net production is meant gross production *minus* the imported materials used in making it, and also *minus* what is needed to replace worn-out or obsolete capital goods. This income has to be used so as to cover both current consumption and additional investment over and above replacements of capital goods, including under each head both public and private expenditure. There is no fixed amount or proportion of the national income that has to be set aside for additional investment. That is a matter not only of changing needs but also of policy. The Soviet Union, in pursuit of very rapid industrial development, has been setting aside for the making of new capital goods a much higher proportion of its productive resources than any other country ; and Great Britain after 1945 tried to make up for wartime losses by a high level of investment until balance of payments difficulties caused it to slow investment down. Population increase and a high rate of technological development are normally the main reasons for high investment. A country already well equipped with capital goods and not increasing fast in population can usually afford to consume a higher proportion of its current output than countries which are less developed or are experiencing more rapid increase in numbers.

The Level of Investment. Under uncontrolled capitalist conditions, the amount of investment is left to be settled mainly by two factors— the willingness of income-receivers to save out of their incomes and the willingness of business men to take up money and use it for buying capital goods. A third factor comes in when the banking authorities expand or contract the supply of money by making loans more or less freely. If bankers increase the supply by lending freely to investors, the immediate effect is to expand the nation's *money* income and to create an additional demand for capital goods. But the sums paid out to the producers of such goods will be spent in part on consumption : so that before long the demand for consumers' goods will also increase. All will be well as long as the higher demand for both types of goods can be met by bringing previously unemployed resources into use or by higher productivity ; but when full employment has been reached and productivity cannot be raised further, additional emissions of money will be bound to have an inflationary effect on prices. Thus, additions to the supply of money may be useful in a situation in which usable productive resources are lying idle ; but they can do only harm if they are persisted in beyond what is required for full employment.

If bankers are not forcing the supply of money up or down, the level of investment depends mainly on what business men are prepared to take up and apply to the purchase of capital goods, within a maximum limit set by what the income-receivers are prepared to save and put at the business men's disposal. But the act of saving out of one's income does not of itself give rise to any investment of what is saved. If business men will not take up the money that is saved, and spend it on capital goods, the effect of saving will be to lessen the demand for consumers' goods and services without adding to the demand for capital goods. Where this occurs, unemployment is bound to follow ; and the discharge of workers whose labour is no longer wanted will depress the level of consumption, so that secondary unemployment in the industries making consumers' goods will be added to primary unemployment in the capital goods industries. This is what has happened in the past in every trade recession ; and the process is cumulative until a very low level of both production and consumption has been reached.

Public and Private Investment. The foregoing paragraphs refer to what happens under unregulated capitalist conditions. But, of course, public demand is just as effective as the demands of business men in providing outlets for production. When private investment sags, the State can, if it wishes, fill the void by public investment (including investment in publicly owned industries and services—*e.g.* roads, mines, railways, power-stations, houses, schools, hospitals, armaments). For these purposes the State can borrow the savings which private business men are unwilling to take up, thus preventing a fall in the level of total investment. Or the State can encourage consumption by tax remissions and borrow private savings to make up the consequent budget deficit ; or it can grant subsidies to either investment or consumption. Modern economists increasingly accept it as the obligation of the State to maintain total demand at a satisfactory level by one or other of these means, whenever recession is threatened. It was mainly the influence of Lord Keynes that was responsible for the revolution in economic theory that has occurred on this issue during the past twenty years ; though not a few " unorthodox " economists from Sismondi in the 1820s to J. A. Hobson in the 1900s had anticipated much of his doctrine without being listened to.

The Demand for Capital Goods. The older orthodox economists rejected this doctrine because they held that, in the absence of state intervention, unemployment of the factors of production could always be prevented by the lowering of the prices charged for their use to a point at which they would all be re-employed. Complete competition, they held, would bring about this result, if it were given unimpeded sway. They ignored both the tendency of unemployment to become cumulative and the fact that a fall in the consumers' incomes is liable to lead to a much sharper fall in the willingness of business men to spend money on capital goods. This happens because, if, say, capital goods last on the average for ten years, only 10 per cent of them need renewing each year in order to maintain productive capacity. If consumers' demand falls from one year to the next by 10 per cent, and 10 per cent of the capital goods wear out, the remaining 90 per cent of capital goods will be able to meet the whole of the reduced demands for consumers' goods even if *no new capital goods at all* are bought. In practice, the fall in the demand for capital goods is never so great as this suggests ; but a fall in consumers' demand does always result in a much more than proportionate fall in investment, unless the State steps in to restore the balance.

Stabilizing Investment. Modern economists, then, mostly lay stress on the need for keeping total demand reasonably steady, or rising as production can be increased, from year to year, and also on keeping reasonably steady each part of the demand, with special emphasis on the demand for capital goods because it is liable to the greatest fluctuation. Given such a policy, it should be possible to achieve a steadily rising national income *per head* as productivity rises with improving technical knowledge—provided only that progress is not upset by adverse international conditions, especially by the failure of other countries to keep their home demand in a progressively balanced condition.

THE DISTRIBUTION
OF THE NATIONAL INCOME

The national income, whether it be large or small, has to meet the claims of both consumption and investment. For this purpose, it has to be distributed among the various claimants, including both the owners of the " factors of production " and those members of the community who do not contribute either property or labour to its making. In capitalist societies, this distribution of incomes is brought about partly by the higgling of the market, partly by laws regulating incomes (*e.g.* minimum wage laws), and partly by redistributive taxation. The owners of the factors of production, including the labourers as owners of labour-power, all compete for shares in the total product, which cannot be sold for more than the buyers are able and willing to pay for it. We have here a circular process ; for the total the buyers can afford to spend is made up of the shares they are able to get out of this very total. Wages, interest, rent and (according to some economists) normal profit are all parts of the cost of production as well as of the incomes their recipients get for the services of the factors of production. In a balanced situation total incomes and total production can both be represented by the same circle, $\bigcirc$; for incomes which arise out of re-distribution through taxation have to come out of the incomes generated in the productive process. This circle, $\bigcirc$, can be divided up into segments, thus $\bigotimes$ —each segment representing the sum paid to a particular factor, or sub-factor. Thus, the national income of the United Kingdom in 1950 and in 1955 was analysed in the

HOW THE NATIONAL INCOME WAS EARNED IN THE UNITED KINGDOM IN 1950 AND 1955
(The figures show income *before taxation* in £ millions)

	1950	1955	Rise %
Wages	4,580 ⎱	10,040	46·1
Salaries	2,290 ⎰		
Pay of Armed Forces (Cash and kind)	230	351	52·6
Employers' contributions—			
To National Insurance	199	279	40·2
To other employee funds	244	380	55·7
TOTAL INCOME FROM EMPLOYMENT	7,543	11,050	46·5
Professional earnings	238	281	18·1
Farmers	340	381	12·1
Sole traders and partnerships	835	1,040	24·6
TOTAL INCOME FROM SELF-EMPLOYMENT	1,413	1,702	20·0
Gross trading profits of companies [a]	2,123	2,867	35·0
Gross surpluses of public corporations	194	297	53·1
Gross profits of other public enterprises	141	110	− 22·0
Rent of land and buildings	540	785	45·4
Net income from overseas	337	145	− 57·0
GROSS NATIONAL PRODUCT [b]	12,291	16,956	38·0

Note: [a] Including undistributed profits.
   [b] Not taking into account depreciation or changes in the value of stocks.

Government White Paper published in 1950 as consisting of the elements shown on p. xxii. This table shows the income *before taxation* and includes not only personal incomes but also company profits placed to reserve, profits of government enterprises, and other sums which did not get distributed as personal incomes. It does not show such incomes as those of old-age pensioners or recipients of cash benefits from the social services because these are not additional to the incomes derived from production but " transfers " made through deductions from such incomes by means of taxes and compulsory insurance contributions. Nor does it show income derived from ownership of the National Debt ; for this equally is a " transfer " income.

Re-distribution of Incomes. So far, the analysis of incomes has been in respect of their source and not of their amount. Another set of tables sets out the distribution of personal incomes by size, without respect to source ; and here again there are two sets of figures, the one before and the other after taking account of *direct* taxation. As *indirect* taxes produce large yields only when they are levied on things which are very widely consumed, and as, in general, poorer people spend a higher proportion of their incomes than richer people on current consumption, the figures of net income distribution after payment of direct taxes only will tend to overestimate the proportion of the real national income that goes to the relatively poor—though of course subsidies to consumption have opposite effects and may partly redress the balance.

DISTRIBUTION OF PERSONAL INCOMES BY SIZE (U.K.)

	No. of Incomes (thousands)		Gross Income before Taxation £m		Net Income minus Taxes on Income, £m		Proportion Retained %	
	1938	1955	1938	1955	1938	1955	1938	1955
Under £250	?	8,000	2,559	1,450	2,555	1,447	99·8	99·8
£250–£500	1,890	7,900	631	2,990	611	2,880	96·8	96·3
£500–£1,000	539	8,850	361	5,970	322	5,570	89·2	93·3
£1,000–£2,000	183	1,115	247	1,460	202	1,218	81·8	80·3
£2,000–£10,000	98	322	361	1,120	256	691	70·9	61·7
£10,000 and over	8	13	163	215	69	59	42·3	27·9

These figures exclude amounts of personal income which cannot be allocated to particular ranges of income. These are estimated at £630 million in 1938 and £1,460 million in 1949. The excluded income consists of interest on National Savings Certificates, Co-operative dividends, charity incomes from investments, incomes in kind, and a number of other items not subject to tax.

Gross and Net Incomes. There is undoubtedly in modern communities a considerable difference between the distribution of *gross* incomes and that of *net* incomes after allowance has been made for redistributive taxation. In Great Britain after 1939 there was a considerable narrowing of the gap between the real incomes of the rich and the poor, especially to the advantage of the very poor and to the disadvantage of the very rich, the middle ranges being, in general, less affected. These tendencies continued after 1945, as a consequence of extended social services and of the maintenance of rationing and of the policy of " fair shares " of limited total supplies. Moreover, greater regularity of incomes, owing to full employment and to the development of social services, eliminated a great deal of suffering and, above all, gave young children and old people a much improved position.

Substitution between Factors of Production. Social service incomes provided out of the yield of taxes or compulsory contributions depend on political decisions outside the economic system. Incomes derived from the ownership of factors of production, on the other hand, though they can be influenced by political agencies, depend mainly on the results of competition between the owners of the various factors. The older orthodox economists used to argue that the shares of the various factors were settled by the relative values of the contributions made by them to the value of the product and used to point to *substitution* of one factor for another in accordance with relative " productivity " as the means by which the distribution of incomes was brought about. Each business man was represented as seeking to achieve the most efficient (*i.e.* cheapest in relation to the value of the product) combination of the factors of production that was open to him, by using, for example, more (or less) labour to work on less (or more) land, or by substituting machines for workers or workers for machines according to the relative cost of different combinations of these factors in relation to a given output. There is, of course, no doubt that *substitution* of this kind is continually going on, and is of the greatest importance in connexion with changes in productive techniques. But modern economists are mostly a good deal more sceptical of the notion that the rewards of the factors correspond in any real sense to their relative contributions to production. Wage-rates, rates of interest, rents, and professional earnings are all influenced by many factors, including traditional standards, conditions and costs of training and education, government regulations, and many kinds of monopolistic control, so that the structure of relative incomes is at least as much an outcome of these other forces as of competition between the rival factors for employment. If all land could be put immediately to any use desired, if capital goods designed to produce railway engines could be turned over to making boots, if labour were perfectly fluid from place to place and from job to job, no matter how different, and if neither the State nor private groups intervened in any way to regulate the use or reward of any factor, matters might work out more or less as the older economists suggested. But in no actual economic system could conditions even remotely resembling these exist. The distribution of *gross*, as well as that of *net*, incomes is the consequence of many interacting forces, including government policy and the influence of many kinds of " pressure groups ".

Substitution by Consumers. Nevertheless, the economist's principle of *substitution* is of very great importance. It applies not only to business men seeking out the cheapest combinations of the factors of production, but also pre-eminently to consumers trying to make their limited incomes go as far as possible in meeting their wants. Consumers are always choosing between things—either choosing one thing at the penalty of going without something else, or choosing more of one thing at the penalty of having less of others. This choice can take place not only between obvious alternatives, such as butter and margarine, but also between quite unlike things, such as keeping a motor car and having another baby, or having a nicer house and going oftener to the pictures, or, again, saving more (say, by buying a life insurance policy) and spending more on current consumption. All these choices involve substitution of one form of expenditure for other possible forms ; and in many cases the substitution takes place at what economists call the " margin ". That is to say, the consumer does not cut off his or her whole expenditure on a thing—say, cigarettes—but buys a packet fewer in order to use the money saved for something else. This is like the kind of " marginal substitution " of one factor of production for another already described. Business men do not decide to buy machinery to replace *all* the labour they have been using : they dispense with some of the labour by installing machines that can turn out the same output (or a greater) with fewer workers. They dispense with the *marginal* labourers, just as the housewife dispenses with the *marginal* pound of tea in order to buy something else instead.

Substitution in Agriculture. Substitution is, of course, affected by relative prices. Where labour is cheap and capital dear, less mechanized processes will tend to be used than when the positions are reversed. Where there is plenty of land and labour is relatively scarce, there will be little intensive cultivation and yields per acre will tend to be lower than in countries where land is scarce. In the United States and Canada, wheat yields *per acre* are much lower than in Great Britain ; but the wheat costs less to produce, because land is cheap and much more machinery is employed. In backward peasant countries, however, yields are low both per acre and per worker because of lack of both capital and technical knowledge and also because of the existence of redundant populations on the land—so that production need not fall even if a number of the workers were taken away. That is why industrialization is so important as a means of raising standards of living in such countries.

Two Sorts of Capital Goods. In every country, as we saw, a part of the national product must be set aside for replacing worn-out or obsolete capital goods, and a further part for providing additional capital goods. These capital goods, we saw, are of two main kinds—means of production, and durable consumers' goods such as houses, schools, cinemas, and other constructional goods which yield up their value to the consumers over a considerable period. A country needs to apportion its investment among these various types of capital goods, as well as to decide what total investment to aim at. If it is sought to improve housing standards very rapidly, or to build a great many schools, something else will have to wait, not only because the total resources applicable to investment are limited by the consumers' demands for immediate satisfaction, but also because the capacity of such an industry as building is limited, and cannot be easily expanded (or contracted) at more than a moderate pace. Productive resources are not freely interchangeable : many of them are fixed to particular uses or can be shifted only within narrow limits, except over a long period of years.

PLANNING AND PRIVATE ENTERPRISE

The greatest disputed issue in Economics to-day is between the advocates of a " Planned Economy " and those of " Free Enterprise ". Both schools are agreed in wishing the consumers to have the widest possible range of choice between alternative ways of spending their money : that is not the issue. The question is whether this choice will be better exercised, and will yield a larger total of satisfactions, under a planned or an unplanned system of production. The " free enterprisers " argue that business men should be left to respond, under the stimulus of the profit motive, to the consumers' wants as far as they are expressed in " effective demand " (that is, offers to pay), without any attempt by the State to influence the course of production. The " planners " retort that, where this is allowed to happen, many productive resources are often left unused, so that the national income is less than it could be, and also that the demands of the rich, being backed by greater ability to pay, take priority over the wants of the poor. This latter objection is partly met where redistributive taxation is extensively used to redress the balance between rich and poor ; and such redistribution also tends to keep up the level of production, because the poor spend nearly all they get, whereas richer people (and rich joint stock companies) may hold large sums unspent, as was explained earlier. But the other objection—that unplanned economies are visited by recurrent depressions involving widespread unemployment—is much less easy to meet ; and the State, if it assumes responsibility for maintaining full employment, cannot avoid " planning " in order to achieve this purpose.

How Much Planning ? It remains an open question *how much* planning the maintenance of full employment calls for. Some " half-planners ", especially in America, argue that the State can do most of what is needed by monetary manipulations, *plus* guaranteed prices or subsidies to producers, *plus* social service payments and perhaps tax remissions in bad times, without directly planning production. But even if this were true for the United States, with its great resources and its small dependence on foreign trade, it would not at all follow that it could be true for countries less fortunately placed. Such countries must at least go some way towards planning their imports and exports if they are not to run into serious difficulties over their balance of payments ; and the planning of imports and exports involves a good deal of planning of home output—*e.g.* of food production in relation to food imports. Moreover, if private business men cannot be persuaded by other methods to maintain the level of investment in bad times—and it is by no means certain they can—the State may have to step in as an investor ; and, if it does, it will soon find itself promoting lop-sided investment in a narrow range of services unless there is a wide range of investments open to it—including investments in the basic capital-using industries.

Planning and Nationalization. The more " socialistic " advocates of economic planning stress this aspect of the matter, and urge that the State cannot be well equipped to steady the volume of investment unless it owns and controls a large section of the basic industries, so as to have open a balanced choice of investment programmes. This, of course, is not the only, or even the main, foundation of the socialist case for public ownership and operation of the main industries ; but it is a strong reinforcing argument, which can appeal to many who are not full Socialists. The main socialist contention is that private ownership of means of large-scale production is wrong because it leads to exploitation of workers and consumers in the interests of private profit, and often to restrictive monopoly and under-use of the factors of production. It is only a palliative, say the Socialists, to use taxation to achieve re-distribution of incomes which have been unfairly distributed in the first instance : nor can such re-distribution undo the evil consequences of letting production depend on expectations of profit rather than on considerations of the people's needs.

Consumers' Choice and Public Provision. To this the " free enterprisers " retort with assertions that nationalization involves " bureaucracy " and the " servile state " and is inconsistent with real freedom of choice for the consumers because the " bureaucrats " will always be substituting their notions of what people *ought to want* for what people *do actually want*. It has, however, to be borne in mind that in quite a number of cases modern States do already substitute collective for individual judgment of what is to be produced and supplied to the citizens. No one would now suggest that armaments should be left for individuals to buy as much of as they please, without the State making itself responsible for defence. The same collective principle has been almost everywhere applied to education, and in many countries to some parts at least of the health services. It has also been extensively applied to housing and to the supply of water.

These are all cases in which it is thought desirable to provide many people with more of a particular thing than they would buy if they were left entirely to their own choice in responding to offers of private suppliers aiming at profit. In some of these cases the entire cost is met out of taxation : in others a large part is met by compulsory insurance contributions : in yet others, part of the cost is collected from the individual consumers, but public subsidies are provided in order to keep the total charge down. As against such encouragements to consume there are other cases—notably intoxicants—in which the State levies taxes for the purpose of raising prices and thus discouraging consumption, or penalizes consumers of what are regarded as luxuries by imposing high taxes, the product of which can then be used for subsidizing more necessary forms of consumption—*e.g.* when taxes on tobacco go in part to pay for subsidies on food.

Consumers' Choice in Relation to Nationalization. When the State steps outside these fields, in which it wishes to get people to consume either more or less of a thing than they would buy if they were left to their own devices, it is usually laid down that industries or services which are nationalized shall be so conducted as to pay their own way over a period of years—that is, shall collect from the actual consumers enough money to meet the full cost. This involves that the nationalized industry or service must give the consumers what they are prepared to pay for ; for if it does not, it will be unable to make ends meet. The planners, wherever they depend on the market—on the consumers' willingness to pay—cannot substitute their judgment for the consumers' judgment, either in drawing up investment policies or in conducting their day-to-day operations, without incurring losses ; and it is surely fantastic to suppose that, where government is democratically controlled, they will deliberately set out to impose their will on the public by incurring losses which they will be unable to conceal. It may be conceded that where government is undemocratic, it is highly dangerous to give it too much economic power ; but to say this does not imply that economic planning under democratic government must lead either to the " servile state " or to substitution of the planners' choice for that of the individual consumers.

Planning and Bureaucracy. This, of course, does not meet the argument that planning involves " bureaucracy ". There is undoubtedly a danger of rigidity and over-centralization in State-run or State-controlled services, and active measures need to be taken to counteract such dangers by de-centralization and by calling both workers and consumers into effective consultation. It is a question of weighing the dangers of bureaucracy against those of anti-social monopoly and inability to maintain full employment, which beset the system of private enterprise, and of choosing in accordance with one's estimate of the relative merits and demerits of the two systems—or indeed of choosing neither as a whole, but of deciding how best to share the field between them. Planning does not mean that *everything* has to be planned ; nor do " private enterprisers " in practice stand for planning *nothing*. It is a question of deciding where, in any situation, to draw the line.

Why Economists Differ. It is no part of the purpose of this outline to tell students what view they ought to take on such controversial issues. They must make up their own minds, in the light of study and experience. On such matters they must not expect to find economists, any more than other people, in agreement. For in the last resort what people think about planning and nationalization and the like is settled not by considerations on which the economist is in a position to offer conclusive expert guidance, but rather by the social values by which each individual sets greatest store. No one can really pronounce a scientific general judgment on the relative efficiencies of " planning " and " no planning " ; of public and private enterprise, over the whole field of production and service : nor, even if anyone could, would such a judgment be conclusive. The basic socialist objection to uncontrolled private enterprise is that it sets too wide a gulf between rich and poor, and involves a system of class-antagonism, an unjust distribution of property as well as income, and an absence of democratic control over the vital economic sector of society. The real " private enterprise " objection to Socialism is that it involves an attempt to apply democratic control to economic as well as to political affairs, and that democratic control is inconsistent with the incentives of personal gain that are needed to get the world's work done. The writer's personal opinion on this problem will be known to many, but his purpose in writing this Introduction is not to put across his own view but to help his readers to form their own opinions in an intelligent way.

LEADING QUESTIONS

What are the main human wants, and how does the economist use them as the foundation of his studies ?

Refer to page 4.

How has man succeeded in increasing his productivity to such a vast extent ?   How was wealth first accumulated ?

Pages 10 and 18.

What decides how the wealth produced shall be divided ?   How are wages fixed ?

Pages 46 and 34.

How much money should be in circulation ?   Do banks create money ?

Pages 84 and 92.

Why are politics and economics so closely related to-day ?

Pages 73 and 156.

What are the causes, and the effects, of inflation ?   And of deflation ?

Page 119.

Why must inflation be avoided if exchange rates are to remain stable ?   How do exchange rates find their level under normal conditions ?

Pages 111 and 133.

What is the economist's ideal for International trade ?

Page 140.

What is the national income ?   Why is it equal to the social output of the community ?

Page 167.

What happens in slumps ?   What can be done to prevent them ?

Pages 194 to 217 and page 251.

On what principles are taxes levied ?   How are workers affected by taxation ?

Pages 218 and 230.

What are the main arguments for and against State Planning ?

Pages 238, 262 and 277.

If the State is to plan, what should it plan for ?   Security, Equality, or Efficiency ?   Can we have all three ?

Pages 285, 269 and 292.

BOOK I

PRODUCTION AND DISTRIBUTION

WHAT ECONOMICS IS ABOUT

ECONOMICS, as the Introduction has told us, is the study of the conditions which govern the production and distribution of wealth, " wealth " being anything that promotes the public or private " weal ", just as " health " is the state of being " heal " or " hale ". Some knowledge of Economics is therefore of interest and importance to us all, both in our private capacities and as citizens of a democratic state. Each one of us is a practical economist in the sense of being vitally interested in the distribution of wealth, and probably in its production too. Look on Economics as the study of how human needs find expression, and how human wants can best be satisfied, and the everyday importance of the subject will at once be evident.

It was a maxim of the late Lord Keynes, probably the greatest economist of modern times, that if only we delved beneath the surface of any subject we were bound to find it fascinating. We shall do this with our study of Economics, and our first task must be to gain a knowledge of the most important basic principles. Then we shall know where we stand when we come to consider modern problems.

What are the main human wants? This should clearly be the first question, and for an answer to it we turn to Alfred Marshall, one of the great line of British economists whose chief works on this subject have become classics. It was he who gave the name of " economics " to what had previously been called, or been included in, " political economy ". After some years of lecturing on the subject, mainly at Cambridge, he published his great work, the *Principles of Economics*. Possibly the labour of making his meaning clear to successive waves of undergraduates helped to give him that exceptional lucidity of thought and expression for which he is famous. Listen to what he has to say on human wants.

ALFRED MARSHALL

HUMAN WANTS

HUMAN wants and desires are countless in number and very various in kind: but they are generally limited and capable of being satisfied. The uncivilized man indeed has not many more than the brute animal; but every step in his progress upwards increases the variety of his needs together with the variety in his methods of satisfying them. He desires not merely larger quantities of the things he has been accustomed to consume, but better qualities of those things; he desires a greater choice of things, and things that will satisfy new wants growing up in him.

Thus though the brute and the savage alike have their preferences for choice morsels, neither of them cares much for variety for its own sake. As, however, man rises in civilization, as his mind becomes developed, and even his animal passions begin to associate themselves with mental activities, his wants become rapidly more subtle and more various; and in the minor details of life he begins to desire change for the sake of change, long before he has consciously escaped from the yoke of custom. The first great step in this direction comes with the art of making a fire: gradually he gets to accustom himself to many different kinds of food and drink cooked in many different ways; and before long monotony begins to become irksome to him, and he finds it a great hardship when accident compels him to live for a long time exclusively on one or two kinds of food.

As a man's riches increase, his food and drink become more various and costly; but his appetite is limited by nature, and when his expenditure on food is extravagant it is more often to gratify the desires of hospitality and display than to indulge his own senses.

That need for dress which is the result of natural causes varies with the climate and the season of year, and a little with the nature of a person's occupations. But in dress conventional wants overshadow those which are natural. Thus in many of the earlier stages of civilization the sumptuary mandates of Law and Custom have rigidly prescribed to the members of each caste or industrial grade, the style and the standard of expense up to which their dress must reach and beyond which they may not go; and part of the substance of these mandates remains now, though subject to rapid change. In Scotland, for instance, in Adam Smith's time many persons were allowed by custom to go abroad without shoes and stockings who may not do so now; and many may still do it in Scotland who might not in England.

But in the upper grades, though the dress of women is still various and costly, that of men is simple and inexpensive as compared with what it was in Europe not long ago, and is to-day in the East. For those men who are most truly distinguished on their own account, have a natural dislike to seem to claim attention by their dress; and they have set the fashion.

House room satisfies the imperative need for shelter from the weather; but that need plays very little part in the effective demand for house room. For though a small but well-built cabin gives excellent shelter, its stifling atmosphere, its necessary uncleanliness, and its want of the decencies and the quiet of life are great evils. It is not so much that they cause physical discomfort as that they tend to stunt the faculties, and limit people's higher activities. With every increase in these activities the demand for larger house room becomes more urgent.

And therefore relatively large and well-appointed house room is, even in the lowest social ranks, at once a " necessary for efficiency ", and the most convenient and obvious way of advancing a material claim to social distinction. And even in those grades in which everyone has house room sufficient for the higher activities of himself and his family, a yet further and almost unlimited increase is desired as a requisite for the exercise of many of the higher social activities.

It is, again, the desire for the exercise and development of activities, spreading through every rank of society, which leads not only to the pursuit of science, literature and art for for their own sake, but to the rapidly increasing demand for the work of those who pursue them as professions. Leisure is used less and less as an opportunity for mere stagnation; and there is a growing desire for those amusements, such as athletic games and travelling, which develop activities rather than indulge any sensuous craving.

Speaking broadly therefore, although it is man's wants in the earliest stages of his development that give rise to his activities, yet afterwards each new step upwards is to be regarded as the development of new activities giving rise to new wants, rather than of new wants giving rise to new activities.

There is an endless variety of wants, but there is a limit to each separate want. This familiar and fundamental tendency of human nature may be stated in the *law of satiable wants* or of *diminishing utility* thus: The *total utility* of a thing to anyone (that is, the total pleasure or other benefit it yields him) increases with every increase in his stock of it, but not as fast as his stock increases. If his stock of it increases at a uniform rate, the benefit derived from it increases at a diminishing rate. In other words, the additional benefit which a person derives from a given increase of his stock of a thing, diminishes with every increase in the stock that he already has.

That part of the thing which he is only induced just to purchase may be called his marginal purchase, because he is on the margin of doubt whether it is worth his while to incur the outlay required to obtain it. And the utility of his marginal purchase may be called the marginal utility of the thing to him. Or, if instead of buying it, he makes the thing himself, then its marginal utility is the utility of that part which he thinks it only just worth his while to make. And thus the law just given may be worded:—

The marginal utility of a thing to anyone diminishes with every increase in the amount of it he already has.

Now let us translate this law of diminishing utility into terms of price. Let us take an illustration from the case of a commodity such as tea, which is in constant demand and which can be purchased in small quantities. Suppose, for instance, that tea of a certain quality is to be had at 2s. per lb. A person might be willing to give 10s. for a single pound once a year rather than go without it altogether; while if he could have any amount of it for nothing he would perhaps not care to use more than 30 lb. in the year. But as it is, he buys perhaps 10 lb. in the year; that is to say, the difference between the satisfaction he gets from buying 9 lb. and 10 lb. is enough for him to be willing to pay 2s. for it: while the fact that he does not buy an eleventh pound, shows that he does not think that it would be worth an extra 2s. to him. That is, 2s. a pound measures the utility to him of the tea which lies at the margin or terminus end of his purchases; it measures the marginal utility to him. If the price which he is just willing to pay for any pound be called his *demand price*, then 2s. is his *marginal demand price*. And our law may be worded:—

The larger the amount of a thing that a person has the less, other things being equal (*i.e.* the purchasing power of money, and the amount of money at his command being equal), will be the price which he will pay for a little more of it; or in other words his marginal demand price for it diminishes.

His demand becomes *efficient*, only when the price which he is willing to offer reaches that at which others are willing to sell.

To obtain complete knowledge of demand for anything, we should have to ascertain how much of it he would be willing to purchase at each of the prices at which it is likely to be offered; and the circumstance of his demand for, say, tea can be best expressed by a list of the prices which he is willing to pay; that is, by his several demand prices for different amounts of it. (This list may be called his demand schedule.)

Thus for instance we may find that he would buy

6 lb. at 50d. per lb.	10 lb. at 24d. per lb
7 „ 40d. „	11 „ 21d. „
8 „ 33d. „	12 „ 19d. „
9 „ 28d. „	13 „ 17d. „

If corresponding prices were filled in for all intermediate amounts we should have an exact statement of his demand. We cannot express a person's demand for a thing by the " amount he is willing to buy ", or by the " intensity of his eagerness to buy a certain amount ", without reference to the prices at which he would buy that amount and other amounts. We can represent it exactly only by lists of the prices at which he is willing to buy different amounts.

When we say that a person's demand for anything increases, we mean that he will buy more of it than he would before at the same price, and that he will buy as much of it as before at a higher price. A general increase in his demand is an increase throughout the whole list of prices at which he is willing to purchase different amounts of it, and not merely that he is willing to buy more of it at the current prices.

So far we have looked at the demand of a single individual. And in the particular case of such a thing as tea the demand of a single person is fairly representative of the general demand of a whole market: for the demand for tea is a constant one; and, since it can be purchased in small quantities, every variation in its price is likely to affect the amount which he will buy. But even among those things which are in constant use, there are many for which the demand on the part of any single individual cannot vary continuously with every small change in price, but can move only by great leaps. For instance, a small fall in the price of hats or watches will not affect the action of every one; but it will induce a few persons, who were in doubt whether or not to get a new hat or a new watch, to decide in favour of doing so.

There are many classes of things the need for which on the part of any individual is inconstant, fitful, and irregular. There can be no list of individual demand prices for wedding-cakes, or the services of an expert surgeon. But the economist has little concern with particular incidents in the lives of individuals. He studies rather " the course of action that may be expected under certain conditions from the members of an industrial group " in so far as the motives of that action are measurable by a money price; and in these broad results the variety and the fickleness of individual action are merged in the comparatively regular aggregate of the action of many.

There is then one general law of demand: *The greater the amount to be sold, the smaller must be the price at which it is offered in order that it may find purchasers*; or, in other words, *the amount demanded increases with a fall in price, and diminishes with a rise in price.*

In this extract from his *Principles* Marshall has introduced to us the notion of Marginal Utility. This is one of the most important fundamental ideas for economic analysis. It has been applied to exchange, to production, to distribution, and indeed to almost every branch of economic study.

Now every step forward in civilization means the easier satisfaction of some human wants, and the creation of a great number of new wants. " Every step in man's upward progress increases the variety of his needs." That is a comforting thought for all the more advanced and highly industrialized nations, as we shall see more clearly later on. Our next question, however, is concerned more with the manner in which man has been able to satisfy these ever-increasing wants. *How has man managed to increase his productivity to such a vast extent, both in quantity and in range of products?*

For the answer we turn to Adam Smith, the first of the great writers on Economics. From 1752 to 1763 Smith was Professor of Moral Philosophy at Glasgow University, a period which he afterwards declared to have been " by far the most useful, and therefore by far the happiest and most honourable " in his life. His course of lectures, besides dealing with natural philosophy, ethics, and justice, included an examination of "those political regulations which are founded, not upon the principle of justice, but of expediency, and which are calculated to increase the riches, the power, and the prosperity of a State ". It was these lectures on political expediency which were later revised and published as the famous *Wealth of Nations*, from which the following extracts are taken.

ADAM SMITH

THE DIVISION OF LABOUR

THE greatest improvement in the productive powers of labour, and the greater part of the skill, dexterity, and judgment with which it is anywhere directed, or applied, seem to have been the effects of the division of labour.

The effects of the division of labour, in the general business of society, will be more easily understood by considering in what manner it operates in some particular manufactures.

To take an example, therefore, from a very trifling manufacture, but one in which the division of labour has been very often taken notice of, the trade of the pin-maker; a workman not educated to this business (which the division of labour has rendered a distinct trade), nor acquainted with the use of the machinery employed in it (to the invention of which the same division of labour has probably given occasion), could scarce, perhaps, with his utmost industry, make one pin in a day, and certainly could not make twenty. But in the way in which this business is now carried on, not only the whole work is a peculiar trade, but it is divided into a number of branches, of which the greater part are likewise peculiar trades.

One man draws out the wire, another straights it, a third cuts it, a fourth points it, a fifth grinds it at the top for receiving the head; to make the head requires two or three distinct operations; to put it on is a peculiar business, to whiten the pins is another; it is even a trade by itself to put them into the paper; and the important business of making a pin is, in this manner, divided into about eighteen distinct operations, which in some manufactories, are all performed by distinct hands, though in others the same man will sometimes perform two or three of them.

I have seen a small manufactory of this kind where ten men were employed, and where some of them consequently performed two or three distinct operations. But though they were very poor, and therefore but indifferently accommodated with the necessary machinery, they could, when they exerted themselves, make among them about twelve pounds of pins in a day. There are in a pound upwards of 4000 pins of middling size. Those ten persons, therefore, could make among them upwards of 48,000 pins in a day. Each person, therefore, making a tenth part of 48,000 pins, might be considered as making 4800 pins in a day. But if they had all wrought separately and independently, and without any of them having been educated to this peculiar business, they certainly could not each of them have made twenty, perhaps not one pin in a day.

In every other art and manufacture, the effects of the division of labour are similar to what they are in this very trifling one; though, in many of them, the labour can neither be so much subdivided, nor reduced to so great a simplicity of operation. The division of labour, however, so far as it can be introduced, occasions, in every art, a proportionate increase of the productive powers of labour. The separation of different trades and employments from one another seems to have taken place in consequence of this advantage. This separation, too, is generally carried furthest in those countries which enjoy the highest degree of industry and improvement; what is the work of one man in a rude state of society being generally that of several in an improved one. In every improved society, the farmer is generally nothing but a farmer; the manufacturer, nothing but a manufacturer. The labour, too, which is necessary to produce any one complete manufacture is almost always divided among a great number of hands. How many different trades are employed in each branch of the linen and woollen manufactures from the growers of the flax and the wool, to the bleachers and smoothers of the linen, or to the dyers and dressers of the cloth!

The nature of agriculture, indeed, does not admit of so many subdivisions of labour, nor so complete a separation of one business from another, as manufactures. It is impossible to separate so entirely the business of the grazier from that of the corn-farmer as the trade of the carpenter is commonly separated from that of the smith. The spinner is almost always a distinct person from the weaver; but the ploughman, the harrower, the sower of the seed, and the reaper of the corn, are often the same. The occasions for those different sorts of labour returning with the different seasons of the year, it is almost impossible that one man should be constantly employed in any one of them. This impossibility of making so complete and entire a separation of all the different branches of labour employed in agriculture is perhaps the reason why the improvement of the productive powers of labour in this art does not always keep pace with their improvement in manufactures.

This great increase of the quantity of work, which in consequence of the division of labour, the same number of people are capable of performing, is owing to three different circumstances:—

I. To the increase of dexterity in every particular workman.

II. To the saving of the time which is commonly lost in passing from one species of work to another.

III. To the invention of a great number of machines which facilitate and abridge labour, and enable one man to do the work of many.

I. The improvement of the dexterity of the workman necessarily increases the quantity of the work he can perform, and the division of labour, by reducing every man's business to some one simple operation, and by making this operation the sole employment of his life, necessarily increases very much the dexterity of the workman. A common smith, who, though accustomed to handle the hammer, has never been used to make nails, if upon some particular occasion he is obliged to attempt it, will scarce, I am assured, be able to make above two or three hundred nails in a day, and those, too, very bad ones. A smith who has been accustomed to make nails, but whose sole or principal business has not been that of a nailer, can seldom with his utmost diligence make more than 800 or 1000 nails in a day. I have seen several boys under twenty years of age who had never exercised any other trade but that of making nails, and who, when they exerted themselves, could make, each of them, upwards of 2300 nails in a day. The making of a nail, however, is by no means one of the simplest operations. The same person blows the bellows, stirs or mends the fire as there is occasion, heats the iron, and forges every part of the nail. In forging the head, too, he is obliged to change his tools. The different operations into which the making of a pin, or of a metal button, is subdivided, are all of them much more simple, and the dexterity of the person, of whose life it has been the sole business to perform them, is usually much greater. The rapidity with which some of the operations of those manufactures are performed, exceeds what the human hand could, by those who had never seen them, be supposed capable of acquiring.

II. The advantage which is gained by saving the time commonly lost in passing from one sort of work to another, is much greater than we should at first view be apt to imagine it. It is impossible to pass very quickly from one kind of work to another that is carried on in a different place and with quite different tools. A country weaver, who cultivates a small farm, must lose a good deal of time in passing from his loom to the field, and from the field to his loom. When the two trades can be carried on in the same workhouse, the loss of time is no doubt much less. It is even in this case, however, very considerable. A man commonly saunters a little in turning his hand from one sort of employment to another. When he first begins the new work he is seldom very keen and hearty;

his mind, as they say, does not go it, and for some time he
rather trifles than applies to good purpose. The habit of
sauntering and of indolent and careless application, which is
naturally, or rather necessarily, acquired by every country
workman who is obliged to change his work and his tools every
half-hour, and to apply his hand in twenty different ways
almost every day of his life, renders him almost always slothful
and lazy, and incapable of any vigorous application even on
the most pressing occasions. Independent, therefore, of his
deficiency in point of dexterity, this cause alone must always
reduce considerably the quantity of work which he is capable
of performing.

III. Everybody must be sensible how much labour is
facilitated and abridged by the application of proper machinery.
It is unnecessary to give any example. I shall only observe,
therefore, that the invention of all those machines by which
labour is so much facilitated and abridged, seems to have been
originally owing to the division of labour. Men are much more
likely to discover easier and readier methods of attaining any
object, when the whole attention of their minds is directed
towards that single object, than when it is dissipated among a
great variety of things. But in consequence of the division of
labour, the whole of every man's attention cames naturally to
be directed towards some one very simple object. It is naturally to be expected, therefore, that some one or other of those
who are employed in each particular branch of labour should
soon find out easier and readier methods of performing their
own particular work, wherever the nature of it admits of such
improvement.

A great part of the machines made use of in those manufactures in which labour is most subdivided were originally
the inventions of common workmen, who being each of them
employed in some very simple operation, naturally turned their
thoughts towards finding out easier and readier methods of performing it. Whoever has been much accustomed to visit such
manufactures must frequently have been shown very pretty

machines which were the inventions of such workmen, in order to facilitate and quicken their own particular part of the work. In the first steam-engines, a boy was constantly employed to open and shut alternately the communication between the boiler and the cylinder, according as the piston either ascended or descended. One of those boys, who loved to play with his companions, observed that, by tying a string from the handle of the valve which opened this communication, to another part of the machine, the valve would open and shut without his assistance, and leave him at liberty to divert himself with his playfellows. One of the greatest improvements that has been made upon this machine, since it was first invented, was in this manner the discovery of a boy who wanted to save his own labour.

It is the great multiplication of the productions of all the different arts, in consequence of the division of labour, which occasions, in a well-governed society, that universal opulence which extends itself to the lowest ranks of the people. Every workman has a great quantity of his own work to dispose of beyond what he himself has occasion for; and every other workman being exactly in the same situation, he is enabled to exchange a great quantity of his own goods for a great quantity, or, what comes to the same thing, for the price of a great quantity of theirs. He supplies them abundantly with what they have occasion for, and a general plenty diffuses itself through all the different ranks of the society.

Observe the accommodation of the most common artificer or day-labourer in a civilized and thriving country, and you will perceive that the number of people of whose industry a part, though but a small part, has been employed in procuring him this accommodation, exceeds all computation. The woollen coat, for example, which covers the day-labourer, as coarse and rough as it may appear, is the produce of the joint labour of a great multitude of workmen. The shepherd, the sorter of the wool, the wool-comber or carder, the dyer, the scribbler, the spinner, the weaver, the fuller, the dresser, with many others, must all join their different arts in order to complete even this homely production. How many merchants and carriers, besides, must have been employed in transporting the materials from some of those workmen to others who often live in a very distant part of the country! How much commerce and navigation in particular, how many ship-builders, sailors, sail-makers, rope-makers, must have been employed in order to bring together the different drugs made use of by the dyer, which often come from the remotest corners of the world!

What a variety of labour, too, is necessary in order to produce the tools of the meanest of those workmen! To say nothing of such complicated machines as the ship of the sailor, the mill of the fuller, or even the loom of the weaver, let us consider only what a variety of labour is requisite in order to form that very simple machine, the shears with which the shepherd clips the wool. The miner, the builder of the furnace for smelting the ore, the seller of the timber, the burner of the charcoal to be made use of in the smelting-house, the brick-maker, the brick-layer, the workmen who attend the furnace, the mill-wright, the forger, the smith, must all of them join their different arts in order to produce them.

Were we to examine, in the same manner, all the different parts of his dress and household furniture, the coarse linen shirt which he wears next his skin, the shoes which cover his feet, the bed which he lies on, and all the different parts which compose it, the kitchen-grate at which he prepares his victuals, the coals which he makes use of for that purpose, dug from the bowels of the earth, and brought to him perhaps by a long sea and a long land carriage, all the other utensils of his kitchen, all the furniture of his table, the knives and forks, the earthen or pewter plates upon which he serves up and divides his victuals, the different hands employed in preparing his bread and his beer, the glass window which lets in the heat and the light, and keeps out the wind and the rain, with all the knowledge and art requisite for preparing that beautiful and happy invention, without which these northern parts of the world could scarce have afforded a very comfortable habitation, together with the tools of all the different workmen employed in producing those different conveniences; if we examine, I say, all these things, and consider what a variety of labour is employed about each of them, we shall be sensible that, without the assistance and co-operation of many thousands, the very meanest person in a civilized country could not be provided for, even according to what we very falsely imagine the easy and simple manner in which he is commonly accommodated. Compared, indeed, with the more extravagant luxury of the great, his accommodation must no doubt appear extremely simple and easy; and yet it may be true, perhaps, that the accommodation of a European prince does not always so much exceed that of an industrious and frugal peasant as the accommodation of the latter exceeds that of many an African king, the absolute master of the lives and liberties of ten thousand naked savages.

Yes, we have travelled far since the era of the naked savage, and our next step must be to see what else besides the division of labour has played a part in the progress. *How was wealth first built up?*

Adam Smith is again our guide, and we shall see, as you probably anticipated, that the saving of part of man's resources to satisfy future needs played a vital rôle. Our Victorian forefathers thought that thrift was the greatest of all virtues, and it certainly paid handsome dividends in the nineteenth century. What would they have thought if they had been told that in the twentieth century some people would have blamed excessive saving as the main cause of slumps?

ADAM SMITH

SAVING AND SPENDING

IN that rude state of society in which there is no division of labour, in which exchanges are seldom made, and in which every man provides everything for himself, it is not necessary that any stock should be accumulated or stored up beforehand in order to carry on the business of the society. Every man endeavours to supply by his own industry his own occasional wants as they occur. When he is hungry, he goes to the forest to hunt; when his coat is worn out, he clothes himself with the skin of the first large animal he kills; and when his hut begins to go to ruin, he repairs it, as well as he can, with the trees and the turf that are nearest it.

But when the division of labour has once been thoroughly introduced, the produce of a man's own labour can supply but a very small part of his occasional wants. The far greater part of them are supplied by the produce of other men's labour, which he purchases with the produce, or, what is the same thing, with the price of the produce of his own. But this purchase cannot be made till such time as the produce of his own labour has not only been completed, but sold. A stock of goods of different kinds, therefore, must be stored up somewhere sufficient to maintain him, and to supply him with the materials and tools of his work till such time, at least, as both these events can be brought about. A weaver cannot apply himself entirely to his peculiar business, unless there is beforehand stored up somewhere, either in his own possession or in that of some other person, a stock sufficient to maintain him, and to supply him with the materials and tools of his work, till he has not only completed, but sold his web. This accumulation must, evidently, be previous to his applying his industry for so long a time to such a peculiar business.

As the accumulation of stock must, in the nature of things, be previous to the division of labour, so labour can be more and more subdivided in proportion only as stock is previously more and more accumulated. The quantity of materials which the same number of people can work up, increases in a great proportion as labour comes to be more and more subdivided; and as the operations of each workman are gradually reduced to a greater degree of simplicity, a variety of new machines come to be invented for facilitating and abridging those operations. As the division of labour advances, therefore, in order to give constant employment to an equal number of workmen, an equal stock of provisions, and a greater stock of materials and tools than what would have been necessary in a ruder state of things, must be accumulated beforehand. But the number of workmen in every branch of business generally increases with the division of labour in that branch, or rather it is the increase of their number which enables them to class and subdivide themselves in this manner.

As the accumulation of stock is previously necessary for carrying on this great improvement in the productive powers of labour, so that accumulation naturally leads to this improvement. The person who employs his stock in maintaining labour, necessarily wishes to employ it in such a manner as to produce as great a quantity of work as possible. He endeavours, therefore, both to make among his workmen the most proper distribution of employment, and to furnish them with the best machines which he can either invent or afford to purchase. His abilities in both these respects are generally in proportion to the extent of his stock, or to the number of people whom it can employ. The quantity of industry, therefore, not only increases in every country with the increase of the stock which employs it, but, in consequence of that increase, the same quantity of industry produces a much greater quantity of work.

Such are in general the effects of the increase of stock upon industry and its productive powers.

That brief lecture will have given us a good idea of what Adam Smith means by " stock ", and this meaning should be borne in mind during the reading of the next extract. We are gradually building up our conception of how wealth is produced—not only in the earliest times but in any age. And our next question must be, *What is capital?*

ADAM SMITH

CAPITAL

WHEN the stock which a man possesses is no more than sufficient to maintain him for a few days or a few weeks, he seldom thinks of deriving any revenue from it. He consumes it as sparingly as he can, and endeavours by his labour to acquire something which may supply its place before it be consumed altogether. His revenue is, in this case, derived from his labour only. This is the state of the greater part of the labouring poor in all countries.

But when he possesses stock sufficient to maintain him for months or years, he naturally endeavours to derive a revenue from the greater part of it; reserving only so much for his immediate consumption as may maintain him till this revenue begins to come in. His whole stock, therefore, is distinguished in two parts. That part which, he expects, is to afford him this revenue, is called his capital. The other is that which supplies his immediate consumption; and which consists either, first, in that portion of his whole stock which was originally reserved for this purpose; or, secondly, in his revenue, from whatever source derived, as it gradually comes in; or, thirdly, in such things as had been purchased by either of these in former years, and which are not yet entirely consumed; such as a stock of clothes, household furniture, and the like. In one, or other, or all of these three articles, consists the stock which men commonly reserve for their own immediate consumption.

There are two different ways in which a capital may be employed so as to yield a revenue or profit to its employer.

First, it may be employed in raising, manufacturing or purchasing goods, and selling them again with a profit. The capital employed in this manner yields no revenue or profit to its employer, while it either remains in his possession, or continues in the same shape. The goods of the merchant yield him no revenue or profit till he sells them for money, and the money yields him as little till it is again exchanged for goods. His capital is continually going from him in one shape, and returning to him in another, and it is only by means of such circulation or successive exchanges, that it can yield him any profit. Such capitals, therefore, may very properly be called circulating capitals.

Secondly, it may be employed in the improvement of land, in the purchase of useful machines and instruments of trade, or in such-like things as yield a revenue or profit without changing masters, or circulating any further. Such capitals, therefore, may very properly be called fixed capitals.

Different occupations require very different proportions between the fixed and circulating capitals employed in them.

The capital of a merchant, for example, is altogether a circulating capital. He has occasion for no machines or instruments of trade, unless his shop, or warehouse, be considered as such.

Some part of the capital of every master artificer or manufacturer must be fixed in the instruments of his trade. This part, however, is very small in some, and very great in others. A master tailor requires no other instruments of trade but a parcel of needles. Those of the master shoemaker are a little, though but a very little, more expensive. Those of the weaver rise a good deal above those of the shoemaker. The far greater part of the capital of all such master artificers, however, is circulated, in the wages of their workmen, or in the price of their materials, and repaid with a profit by the price of the work.

In other works a much greater fixed capital is required. In a great iron-work, for example, the furnace for melting the ore, the forge, the slitt-mill, are instruments of trade which cannot be erected without a very great expense. In coal-works and mines of every kind, the machinery necessary both for drawing out the water and for other purposes is frequently still more expensive.

That part of the capital of the farmer which is employed in the instruments of agriculture is a fixed, that which is employed in the wages and maintenance of his labouring servants, is a circulating capital. He makes a profit of the one by keeping it in his own possession, and of the other by parting with it.

The general stock of any country or society is the same with that of all its inhabitants or members, and therefore naturally divides itself into the same three portions, each of which has a distinct function or office.

The first is that portion which is reserved for immediate consumption, and of which the characteristic is, that it affords no revenue or profit. It consists in the stock of food, clothes, household furniture, etc., which have been purchased by their proper consumers, but which are not yet entirely consumed. The whole stock of mere dwelling-houses too, subsisting at any one time in the country, make a part of this first portion. The stock that is laid out in a house, if it is to be the dwelling-house of the proprietor, ceases from that moment to serve in the function of a capital, or to afford any revenue to its owner. A dwelling-house, as such, contributes nothing to the revenue of its inhabitant; and though it is, no doubt, extremely useful to him, it is as his clothes and household furniture are useful to him, which, however, make a part of his expense, and not of his revenue. If it is to be let to a tenant for rent, as the house itself can produce nothing, the tenant must always pay the rent out of some other revenue which he derives either from labour, or stock, or land. Though a house, therefore, may yield a revenue to its proprietor, and thereby serve in the function of a capital to him, it cannot yield any to the public, nor serve in the function of a capital to it, and the revenue of the whole body of the people can never be in the smallest degree increased by it. Clothes, household furniture, in the same manner, sometimes yield a revenue, and thereby serve in the function of a capital to particular persons. In countries where masquerades are common, it is a trade to let out masquerade dresses for a night. Upholsterers frequently let furniture by the month or by the year. Undertakers let the furniture of funerals by the day and by the week. Many people let furnished houses, and get a rent, not only for the use of the house, but for that of the furniture. The revenue, however, which is derived from such things must always be ultimately drawn from some other source of revenue. Of all parts of the stock, either of an individual, or of a society, reserved for immediate consumption, what is laid out in houses is most slowly consumed. A stock of clothes may last several years: a stock of furniture half a century: but a stock of houses, well built and properly taken care of, may last many centuries. Though the period of their total consumption, however, is more distant, they are still as really a stock reserved for immediate consumption as either clothes or household furniture.

The second of the three portions into which the general stock of the society divides itself, is the fixed capital, of which the characteristic is, that it affords a revenue or profit without circulating or changing masters. It consists chiefly of the four following articles:—

First, of all useful machines and instruments of trade which facilitate and abridge labour:

Secondly, of all those profitable buildings which are the means of procuring a revenue, not only to their proprietor who lets them for a rent, but to the person who possesses them and pays that rent for them; such as shops, warehouses, workhouses, farmhouses, with all their necessary buildings; stables, granaries, etc. These are very different from mere dwellinghouses. They are a sort of instruments of trade, and may be considered in the same light:

Thirdly, of the improvements of land, of what has been profitably laid out in clearing, draining, enclosing, manuring, and reducing it into the condition most proper for tillage and culture. An improved farm may very justly be regarded in the same light as those useful machines which facilitate and abridge labour, and by means of which an equal circulating capital can afford a much greater revenue to its employer. An improved farm is equally advantageous and more durable than any of those machines, frequently requiring no other repairs than the most profitable application of the farmer's capital employed in cultivating it:

Fourthly, of the acquired and useful abilities of all the inhabitants or members of the society. The acquisition of such talents, by the maintenance of the acquirer during his education, study, or apprenticeship, always costs a real expense, which is a capital fixed and realized, as it were, in his person. Those talents, as they make a part of his fortune, so do they likewise of that of the society to which he belongs. The improved dexterity of a workman may be considered in the same light as a machine or instrument of trade which facilitates and abridges labour, and which, though it costs a certain expense, repays that expense with a profit.

The third and last of the three portions into which the general stock of the society naturally divides itself, is the circulating capital; of which the characteristic is, that it affords a revenue only by circulating or changing masters. It is composed likewise of four parts:—

First, of the money by means of which all the other three are circulated and distributed to their proper consumers:

Secondly, of the stock of provisions which are in the possession of the butcher, the grazier, the farmer, the corn-merchant, the brewer, etc., and from the sale of which they expect to derive a profit:

Thirdly, of the materials, whether altogether rude, or more or less manufactured, of clothes, furniture, and building, which are not yet made up into any of those three shapes, but which remain in the hands of the growers, the manufacturers, the mercers and drapers, the timber merchants, the carpenters and joiners, the brickmakers, etc.

Fourthly, and lastly, of the work which is made up and completed, but which is still in the hands of the merchant or manufacturer, and not yet disposed of or distributed to the proper consumers; such as the finished work which we frequently find ready-made in the shops of the smith, the cabinet-maker, the goldsmith, the jeweller, the china-merchant, etc. The circulating capital consists in this manner, of the provisions, materials, and finished work of all kinds that are in the hands of their respective dealers, and of the money that is necessary for circulating and distributing them to those who are finally to use or to consume them.

Of these four parts, three—provisions, material, and finished work—are, either annually, or in a longer or shorter period, regularly withdrawn from it, and placed either in the fixed capital or in the stock reserved for immediate consumption.

Every fixed capital is both originally derived from, and requires to be continually supported by a circulating capital. All useful machines and instruments of trade are originally derived from a circulating capital, which furnishes the materials of which they are made, and the maintenance of the workmen who make them. They require, too, a capital of the same kind to keep them in constant repair.

No fixed capital can yield any revenue but by means of a circulating capital. The most useful machines and instruments of trade will produce nothing without the circulating capital which affords the materials they are employed upon, and the maintenance of the workmen who employ them. Land, however improved, will yield no revenue without a circulating capital, which maintains the labourers who cultivate and collect its produce.

To maintain and augment the stock which may be reserved for immediate consumption is the sole end and purpose both of the fixed and circulating capitals. It is this stock which feeds, clothes, and lodges the people. Their riches or poverty depends upon the abundant or sparing supplies which those two capitals can afford to the stock reserved for immediate consumption.

So great a part of the circulating capital being continually withdrawn from it, in order to be placed in the other two branches of the general stock of the society; it must in its turn require continual supplies, without which it would soon cease to exist. These supplies are principally drawn from three sources, the produce of land, of mines, and of fisheries. These afford continual supplies of provisions and materials, of which part is afterwards wrought up into finished work, and by which are replaced the provisions, materials, and finished work continually withdrawn from the circulating capital.

Land, mines, and fisheries, require all both a fixed and a circulating capital to cultivate them; and their produce replaces with a profit, not only those capitals, but all the others in the society. Thus the farmer annually replaces to the manufacturer the provisions which he had consumed and the materials which he had wrought up the year before; and the manufacturer replaces to the farmer the finished work which he had wasted and worn out in the same time. This is the real exchange that is annually made between those two orders of people, though it seldom happens that the rude produce of the one and the manufactured produce of the other, are directly bartered for one another; because it seldom happens that the farmer sells his corn and his cattle, his flax and his wool, to the very same person of whom he chooses to purchase the clothes, furniture, and instruments of trade which he wants. He sells, therefore, his rude produce for money, with which he can purchase, wherever it is to be had, the manufactured produce he has occasion for. Land even replaces, in part at least, the capitals with which fisheries and mines are cultivated. It is the produce of land which draws the fish from the waters; and it is the produce of the surface of the earth which extracts the minerals from its bowels.

The produce of land, mines, and fisheries, when their natural fertility is equal, is in proportion to the extent and proper application of the capitals employed about them. When the capitals are equal and equally well applied, it is in proportion to their natural fertility.

In all countries where there is tolerable security, every man of common understanding will endeavour to employ whatever stock he can command in procuring either present enjoyment or future profit. If it is employed in procuring present enjoyment, it is a stock reserved for immediate consumption. If it is employed in procuring future profit, it must procure this profit either by staying with him, or by going from him. In the one case it is a fixed, in the other it is a circulating capital. A man must be perfectly crazy who, where there is tolerable security, does not employ all the stock which he commands, whether it be his own or borrowed of other people, in some one or other of those three ways.

In those unfortunate countries, indeed, where men are continually afraid of the violence of their superiors, they frequently bury and conceal a great part of their stock, in order to have it always at hand to carry with them to some place of safety, in case of their being threatened with any of those disasters to which they consider themselves as at all times exposed. This is said to be a common practice in Turkey, in Indostan, and, I believe, in most other governments of Asia. It seems to have been a common practice among our ancestors during the violence of the feudal government. Treasure-trove was in those times considered as no contemptible part of the revenue of the greater sovereigns in Europe. It consisted in such treasure as was found concealed in the earth, and to which no particular person could prove any right. This was regarded in those times as so important an object, that it was always considered as belonging to the sovereign, and neither to the finder nor to the proprietor of

the land, unless the right to it had been conveyed to the latter
by an express clause in his charter. It was put upon the same
footing with gold and silver mines, which, without a special
clause in the charter, were never supposed to be com-
prehended in the general grant of the lands, though mines
of lead, copper, tin, and coal were, as things of smaller
consequence.

Adam Smith was the first interpreter of the Capitalist system, and
the ideas which he propounded soon came to be accepted as the gospel
of the Whig party, and to be freely quoted in Parliament and in general
conversation. The starting-points for his study of the ways in which a
nation can increase its wealth were two complementary ideas: first, that
man, in the business world, is ruled by self-interest; and secondly, that
he has a natural freedom to pursue that self-interest, and should be
allowed full scope to do so by the government. Then the working of
economic laws would ensure that in the long run everything would be
for the best, if not in the best of all possible worlds, at least in the world
as it existed in his day. This doctrine of natural liberty was a reaction
against the excesses of the mercantile system, which at that time was
strangling European trade in the red tape of official restrictions and
heavy customs duties.

The three agents of production, as we have seen, are land, labour
(including management), and capital. Our next step is to find out how
the wealth which is produced is divided among these three agents. For
land we pay " rent ", so let us ask another famous economist, *What is
rent?*

DAVID RICARDO

RENT

R ENT is that portion of the produce of the earth, which
is paid to the landlord for the use of the original and
indestructible powers of the soil.

It is often, however, confounded with the interest and
profit of capital, and, in popular language, the term is
applied to whatever is annually paid by a farmer to his landlord. If, of two adjoining farms of the same extent, and of
the same natural fertility, one had all the conveniences of
farming buildings, and, besides, were properly drained and
manured, and advantageously divided by hedges, fences, and
walls, while the other had none of these advantages, more
remuneration would naturally be paid for the use of one, than
for the use of the other; yet in both cases this remuneration
would be called rent. But it is evident, that a portion only of
the money annually to be paid for the improved farm, would
be given for the original and indestructible powers of the soil;
the other portion would be paid for the use of the capital which
had been employed in ameliorating the quality of the land,
and in erecting such buildings as were necessary to secure
and preserve the produce.

Adam Smith sometimes speaks of rent, in the strict sense
to which I am desirous of confining it, but more often in the
popular sense, in which the term is usually employed. He
tells us, that the demand for timber, and its consequent high
price, in the more southern countries of Europe, caused a rent
to be paid for forests in Norway, which could before afford
no rent. Is it not, however, evident, that the person who paid
what he thus calls rent, paid it in consideration of the valuable
commodity which was then standing on the land, and that he
actually repaid himself with a profit, by the sale of the timber?
If, indeed, after the timber was removed, any compensation
were paid to the landlord for the use of the land, for the
purpose of growing timber or any other produce, with a view

to future demand, such compensation might justly be called rent, because it would be paid for the productive powers of the land; but in the case stated by Adam Smith, the compensation was paid for the liberty of removing and selling the timber, and not for the liberty of growing it.

He speaks also of the rent of coal mines, and of stone quarries, to which the same observation applies—that the compensation given for the mine or quarry, is paid for the value of the coal or stone which can be removed from them, and has no connection with the original and indestructible powers of the land. This is a distinction of great importance, in an inquiry concerning rent and profits; for it is found, that the laws which regulate the progress of rent, are widely different from those which regulate the progress of profits, and seldom operate in the same direction. In all improved countries, that which is annually paid to the landlord, partaking of both characters, rent and profit, is sometimes kept stationary by the effects of opposing causes; at other times advances or recedes, as one or the other of these causes preponderates. In the future pages of this work, then, whenever I speak of the rent of land, I wish to be understood as speaking of that compensation, which is paid to the owner of land for the use of its original and indestructible powers.

On the first settling of a country, in which there is an abundance of rich and fertile land, a very small proportion of which is required to be cultivated for the support of the actual population, or indeed can be cultivated with the capital which the population can command, there will be no rent; for no one would pay for the use of land, when there was an abundant quantity not yet appropriated, and, therefore, at the disposal of whosoever might choose to cultivate it.

On the common principles of supply and demand, no rent could be paid for such land, for the reason stated why nothing is given for the use of air and water, or for any other of the gifts of nature which exist in boundless quantity. With a given quantity of materials, and with the assistance of the pressure of the atmosphere, and the elasticity of steam, engines may perform work, and abridge human labour to a very great extent; but no charge is made for the use of these natural aids, because they are inexhaustible, and at every man's disposal. In the same manner the brewer, the distiller, the dyer, make incessant use of the air and water for the production of their commodities; but as the supply is boundless, they bear no price. If all land had the same properties, if it were unlimited in quantity, and uniform in quality, no charge could be made for its use, unless where it possessed peculiar advantages of situation. It is only, then, because land is not unlimited in quantity and uniform in quality, and because in the progress of population, land of an inferior quality, or less advantageously situated, is called into cultivation that rent is ever paid for the use of it. When in the progress of society, land of the second degree of fertility is taken into cultivation, rent immediately commences on that of the first quality, and the amount of that rent will depend on the difference in the quality of these two portions of land.

When land of the third quality is taken into cultivation, rent immediately commences on the second, and it is regulated as before, by the difference in their productive powers. At the same time, the rent of the first quality will rise, for that must always be above the rent of the second, by the difference between the produce which they yield with a given quantity of capital and labour. With every step in the progress of population, which shall oblige a country to have recourse to land of a worse quality, to enable it to raise its supply of food, rent, on all the more fertile land, will rise.

Thus suppose land—No. 1, 2, 3—to yield, with an equal employment of capital and labour, a net produce of 100, 90, and 80 quarters of corn. In a new country, where there is an abundance of fertile land compared with the population, and where therefore it is only necessary to cultivate No. 1, the whole net produce will belong to the cultivator, and will be the profits of the stock which he advances. As soon as population had so far increased as to make it necessary to cultivate No. 2, from which ninety quarters only can be obtained after supporting the labourers, rent would commence on No. 1; for either there must be two rates of profit on agricultural capital, or ten quarters, or the value of ten quarters must be withdrawn from the produce of No. 1, for some other purpose. Whether the proprietor of the land, or any other person cultivated No. 1, these ten quarters would equally constitute rent; for the cultivator of No. 2, would get the same result with his capital, whether he cultivated No. 1, paying ten quarters for rent, or continued to cultivate No. 2, paying no rent. In the same manner it might be shown that when No. 3 is brought into cultivation, the rent of No. 2 must be ten quarters, or the value of ten quarters, whilst the rent of No. 1 would rise to twenty quarters; for the cultivator of No. 3 would have the same profits whether he paid twenty quarters for the rent of No. 1, ten quarters for the rent of No. 2, or cultivated No. 3 free of all rent.

It often, and, indeed, commonly happens, that before No. 2, 3, 4, or 5, or the inferior lands are cultivated, capital can be employed more productively on those lands which are already in cultivation. It may perhaps be found, that by doubling the original capital employed on No. 1, though the produce will not be doubled, will not be increased by 100 quarters, it may be increased by eighty-five quarters, and that this quantity exceeds what could be obtained by employing the same capital, on land No. 3.

In such case, capital will be preferably employed on the old land, and will equally create a rent; for rent is always the difference between the produce obtained by the employment of two equal quantities of labour and capital. If with a capital of £1000, a tenant obtain 100 quarters of wheat from his land, and by the employment of a second capital of £1000, he obtain a further return of eighty-five, his landlord would have the power at the expiration of his lease, of obliging him to pay fifteen quarters, or an equivalent value for additional rent;

for there cannot be two rates of profit. If he is satisfied with a diminution of fifteen quarters in the return for his second £1000, it is because no employment more profitable can be found for it. The common rate of profit would be in that proportion, and if the original tenant refused, some other person would be found willing to give all which exceeded that rate of profit to the owner of the land from which he derived it.

In this case, as well as in the other, the capital last employed pays no rent. For the greater productive powers of the first £1000, fifteen quarters is paid for the rent, for the employment of the second £1000 no rent whatever is paid. If a third £1000 be employed on the same land, with a return of seventy-five quarters, rent will then be paid for the second £1000, and will be equal to the difference between the produce of these two, or ten quarters; and at the same time the rent of the first £1000 will rise from fifteen to twenty-five quarters; while the last £1000 will pay no rent whatever.

If, then, good land existed in a quantity much more abundant than the production of food for an increasing population required, or if capital could be indefinitely employed without a diminished return on the old land, there could be no rise of rent; for rent invariably proceeds from the employment of an additional quantity of labour with a proportionally less return.

The most fertile, and most favourably situated, land will be first cultivated, and the exchangeable value of its produce will be adjusted in the same manner as the exchangeable value of all other commodities, by the total quantity of labour necessary in various forms from first to last, to produce it, and bring it to market. When land of an inferior quality is taken into cultivation, the exchangeable value of raw produce will rise, because more labour is required to produce it.

The exchangeable value of all commodities, whether they be manufactured, or the produce of the mines, or the produce of land, is always regulated, not by the less quantity of labour that will suffice for their production under circumstances highly favourable, and exclusively enjoyed by those who have peculiar facilities of production; but by the greater quantity of labour necessarily bestowed on their production by those who have no such facilities; by those who continue to produce them under the most unfavourable circumstances; meaning— by the most unfavourable circumstances—the most unfavourable under which the quantity of produce required renders it necessary to carry on the production.

Ricardo had a remarkable gift for intelligent discussion, and, according to Miss Edgeworth, no one argued more fairly, "or less for victory and more for truth". His main concern was the welfare of the community, and he believed that this depended mainly on the way in which the wealth produced by the nation was divided between wages and profits. He devoted the greater part of his *Principles of Political Economy* to an attempt to set forth, as accurately as possible, the laws which regulated this distribution of wealth.

Now, the rent having been settled and paid, how is labour rewarded for its toil? *How are wages fixed?*

For the answer we return to Adam Smith. He deals, naturally enough, with a " free " society, but his simple explanation will help us to understand wage movements, even if the complicated industrial society of to-day, as we shall see later on, demands some slight modification of his theory now.

ADAM SMITH

WAGES

THE produce of labour constitutes the natural recompense or wages of labour.

In that original state of things, which precedes both the appropriation of land and the accumulation of stock, the whole produce of labour belongs to the labourer. He has neither landlord nor master to share with him.

Had this state continued, the wages of labour would have augmented with all those improvements in its productive powers to which the division of labour gives occasion. All things would gradually have become cheaper. They would have been produced by a smaller quantity of labour; and as the commodities produced by equal quantities of labour would naturally in this state of things be exchanged for one another, they would have been purchased likewise with the produce of a smaller quantity.

But this original state of things, in which the labourer enjoyed the whole produce of his own labour, could not last beyond the first introduction of the appropriation of land and the accumulation of stock. It was at an end, therefore, long before the most considerable improvements were made in the productive powers of labour, and it would be to no purpose to trace further what might have been its effects upon the recompense or wages of labour.

As soon as land becomes private property, the landlord demands a share of almost all the produce which the labourer can either raise, or collect from it. His rent makes the first deduction from the produce of the labour which is employed upon land.

It seldom happens that the person who tills the ground has wherewithal to maintain himself till he reaps the harvest. His maintenance is generally advanced to him from the stock of a master, the farmer who employs him, and who would have no interest to employ him, unless he was to share in the produce of his labour, or unless his stock was to be replaced to him with a profit. This profit makes a second deduction from the produce of the labour which is employed upon land.

The produce of almost all other labour is liable to the like deduction of profit. In all arts and manufactures the greater part of the workmen stand in need of a master to advance them the materials of their work, and their wages and maintenance till it be completed. He shares in the produce of their labour, or in the value which it adds to the materials upon which it is bestowed; and in this share consists his profit.

It sometimes happens, indeed, that a single independent workman has stock sufficient both to purchase the material of his work, and to maintain himself till it be completed. He is both master and workman, and enjoys the whole produce of his own labour, or the whole value which it adds to the materials upon which it is bestowed. It includes what are usually two distinct revenues, belonging to two distinct persons the profits of stock, and the wages of labour.

Such cases, however, are not very frequent, and in every part of Europe, twenty workmen serve under a master for one that is independent; and the wages of labour are everywhere understood to be, what they usually are, when the labourer is one person, and the owner of the stock which employs him another.

What are the common wages of labour depends everywhere upon the contract usually made between those two parties, whose interests are by no means the same. The workmen desire to get as much, the masters to give as little as possible. The former are disposed to combine in order to raise, the latter in order to lower the wages of labour.

Although in disputes with their workmen, masters must generally have the advantage, there is, however, a certain rate below which it seems impossible to reduce, for any considerable time, the ordinary wages even of the lowest species of labour.

A man must always live by his work, and his wages must at least be sufficient to maintain him. They must even upon most occasions be somewhat more; otherwise it would be impossible for him to bring up a family, and the race of such workmen could not last beyond the first generation. Mr. Cantillon seems, upon this account, to suppose that the lowest species of common labourers must everywhere earn at least double their own maintenance, in order that one with another they may be enabled to bring up two children; the labour of the wife, on account of her necessary attendance on the children being supposed no more than sufficient to provide for herself.

There are certain circumstances, however, which sometimes give the labourers an advantage, and enable them to raise their wages considerably above this rate; evidently the lowest which is consistent with common humanity.

When in any country the demand for those who live by wages, labourers, journeymen, servants of every kind, is continually increasing; when every year furnishes employment for a greater number than had been employed the year before, the workmen have no occasion to combine in order to raise their wages. The scarcity of hands occasions a competition among masters, who bid against one another in order to get workmen, and thus voluntarily break through the natural combination of masters not to raise wages.

The demand for those who live by wages, it is evident, cannot increase but in proportion to the increase of the funds which are destined for the payment of wages. These funds are of two kinds; first, the revenue which is over and above what is necessary for the maintenance; and, secondly, the stock which is over and above what is necessary for the employment of their masters.

When the landlord, annuitant, or monied man, has a greater revenue than what he judges sufficient to maintain his own family, he employs either the whole or a part of the surplus in maintaining one or more menial servants. Increase this surplus, and he will naturally increase the number of those servants.

When an independent workman, such as a weaver or shoemaker, has got more stock than what is sufficient to purchase the materials of his own work, and to maintain himself till he can dispose of it, he naturally employs one or more journeymen with the surplus, in order to make a profit by their work. Increase this surplus, and he will naturally increase the number of his journeymen.

The demand for those who live by wages, therefore, necessarily increases with the increase of the revenue and stock of every country, and cannot possibly increase without it. The increase of revenue and stock is the increase of national wealth. The demand for those who live by wages, therefore, naturally increases with the increase of national wealth, and cannot possibly increase without it.

It is not the actual greatness of national wealth, but its continual increase, which occasions a rise in the wages of labour. It is not, accordingly, in the richest countries, but in the most thriving, or in those which are growing rich the fastest, that the wages of labour are highest. England is certainly, in the present times [1773], a much richer country than any part of North America. The wages of labour, however, are much higher in North America than in any part of England.

Though North America is not yet so rich as England, it is much more thriving, and advancing with much greater rapidity to the further acquisition of riches. The most decisive mark of the prosperity of any country is the increase of the number of its inhabitants. In Great Britain, and most other European countries, they are not supposed to double in less than five hundred years. In the British colonies in North America, it has been found that they double in twenty or five-and-twenty years. Nor in the present times is this increase principally owing to the continual importation of new inhabitants, but to the great multiplication of the species. Those who live to old age, it is said, frequently see there from fifty to a hundred, and sometimes many more, descendants from their own body.

Though the wealth of a country should be very great, yet if it has been long stationary, we must not expect to find the wages of labour very high in it. The funds destined for the payment of wages, the revenue and stock of its inhabitants, may be of the greatest extent; but if they have continued for several centuries of the same, or very nearly of the same extent, the number of labourers employed every year could easily supply, and even more than supply, the number wanted the following year. There could seldom be any scarcity of hands, nor could the masters be obliged to bid against one another in order to get them. The hands, on the contrary, would, in this case, naturally multiply beyond their employment. There would be a constant scarcity of employment, and the labourers would be obliged to bid against one another in order to get it. If in such a country the wages of labour had ever been more than sufficient to maintain the labourer, and to enable him to bring up a family, the competition of the labourers and the interest of the masters would soon reduce them to this lowest rate which is consistent with common humanity.

China has been long one of the richest, that is, one of the most fertile, best cultivated, most industrious, and most populous countries in the world. It seems, however, to have been long stationary. Marco Polo, who visited it more than five hundred years ago, describes its cultivation, industry, and populousness, almost in the same terms in which they are described by travellers in the present times. It had perhaps, even long before his time, acquired that full complement of riches which the nature of its laws and institutions permits it to acquire. The accounts of all travellers, inconsistent in many other respects, agree in the low wages of labour, and in the difficulty which a labourer finds in bringing up a family in China.

China, however, though it may perhaps stand still, does not seem to go backwards. Its towns are nowhere deserted by their inhabitants. The lands which had once been cultivated are nowhere neglected. The same or very nearly the same annual labour must therefore continue to be performed, and the funds destined for maintaining it must not, consequently, be sensibly diminished. The lowest class of labourers, therefore, notwithstanding their scanty subsistence, must some way or another make shift to continue their race so far as to keep up their usual numbers.

But it would be otherwise in a country where the funds destined for the maintenance of labour were sensibly decaying. Every year the demand for servants and labourers would, in all the different classes of employments, be less than it had been the year before. Many who had been bred in the superior classes, not being able to find employment in their own business, would be glad to seek it in the lowest. The lowest class being not only overstocked with its own workmen, but with the overflowings of all the other classes, the competition for employment would be so great in it, as to reduce the wages of labour to the most miserable and scanty subsistence of the labourer. Many would not be able to find employment even upon these hard terms, but would either starve, or be driven to seek a subsistence either by begging, or by the perpetration perhaps of the greatest enormities. Want, famine, and mortality would immediately prevail in that class, and from thence extend themselves to all the superior classes, till the number of inhabitants in the country was reduced to what could easily be maintained by the revenue and stock which remained in it, and which had escaped either the tyranny or calamity which had destroyed the rest.

The liberal reward of labour, therefore, as it is the necessary effect, so it is the natural symptom of increasing national wealth. The scanty maintenance of the labouring poor, on the other hand, is the natural symptom that things are at a stand, and their starving condition that they are going fast backwards.

It is in the progressive state, while the society is advancing to the further acquisition, rather than when it has acquired its full complement of riches, that the condition of the labouring poor, of the great body of the people, seems to be the happiest and the most comfortable. It is hard in the stationary, and miserable in the declining state. The progressive state is in reality the cheerful and the hearty state to all the different orders of the society. The stationary is dull; the declining, melancholy.

It was Ricardo's opinion, as we said a short while ago, that the welfare of the state depended mainly on the way in which wealth was

divided between profits and wages. This is indeed a subject of prime
importance, and just as much a major problem to-day as it was in his
time. The solution is made more difficult by the fact that every factor
or quantity in the equation is a variable. In the complicated business
world of to-day there is nothing fixed, nothing constant. Some things,
like public demand, may be beyond the control of the producer; they
vary in spite of all he can do. But other things, such as the amount of
labour or of capital which he uses, are under his control, and he may,
and often will, substitute to some extent the one for the other. Before
we can ask for a summing up of how wealth is distributed we must
glance briefly at the consequences of this freedom of the entrepreneur
to improve the efficiency of his undertaking. *What is the principle of
Substitution?*

ALFRED MARSHALL

THE PRINCIPLE OF SUBSTITUTION

AT the beginning of his undertaking, and at every successive stage, the alert business man strives so to modify
his arrangements as to obtain better results with a given expenditure, or equal results with a less expenditure. In other
words, he ceaselessly applies the principle of substitution,
with the purpose of increasing his profits; and, in so doing,
he seldom fails to increase the total efficiency of work, the
total power over nature which man derives from organization
and knowledge.

Every locality has incidents of its own which affect in
various ways the methods of arrangement of every class of
business that is carried on in it: and even in the same place
and the same trade no two persons pursuing the same aims will
adopt exactly the same routes. The tendency to variation is a
chief cause of progress; and the abler are the undertakers in
any trade the greater will this tendency be. In some trades,
as for instance cotton-spinning, the possible variations are
confined within narrow limits; no one can hold his own at all

who does not use machinery, and very nearly the latest machinery, for every part of the work. But in others, as for instance in some branches of the wood and metal trades, in farming, and in shopkeeping, there can be great variations. For instance, of two manufacturers in the same trade, one will perhaps have a larger wages bill and the other heavier charges on account of machinery; of two retail dealers one will have a larger capital locked up in stock and the other will spend more on advertisements and other means of building up the immaterial capital of a profitable trade connexion. And in minor details the variations are numberless.

Each man's actions are influenced by his special opportunities and resources, as well as by his temperament and his associations: but each, taking account of his own means, will push the investment of capital in his business in each several direction until what appears in his judgment to be the outer limit, or margin, of profitableness is reached; that is, until there seems to him no good reason for thinking that the gains resulting from any further investment in that particular direction would compensate him for his outlay. The margin of profitableness, even in regard to one and the same branch or sub-branch of industry, is not to be regarded as a mere point on any one fixed line of possible investment; but as a boundary line of irregular shape cutting one after another every possible line of investment.

This principle of substitution is closely connected with, and is indeed partly based on, that tendency to a diminishing rate of return from any excessive application of resources or of energies in any given direction, which is in accordance with general experience. It is thus linked up with the broad tendency of a diminishing return to increased applications of capital and labour to land in old countries which plays a prominent part in classical economics. And it is so closely akin to the principle of the diminution of marginal utility that results in general from increased expenditure, that some applications of the two principles are almost identical. It has already been observed that new methods of production bring into existence new commodities so as to bring them within the reach of increased numbers of consumers: that on the other hand changes in the methods and volume of consumption cause new developments of production, and new distribution of the resources of production: and that though some methods of consumption which contribute most to man's higher life, do little if anything towards furthering the production of material wealth, yet production and consumption are intimately correlated. But now we are to consider more in detail how the distribution of the resources of production between different industrial undertakings is the counterpart and reflex of the distribution of the consumers' purchases between different classes of commodities.

Let us revert to the primitive housewife, who having " a limited number of hanks of yarn from the year's shearing, considers all the domestic wants for clothing and tries to distribute the yarn between them in such a way as to contribute as much as possible to the family wellbeing. She will think she has failed if, when it is done, she has reason to regret that she did not apply more to making, say, socks, and less to vests. But if, on the other hand, she hit on the right points to stop at, then she made just so many socks and vests that she got an equal amount of good out of the last bundle of yarn that she applied to socks, and the last she applied to vests." If it happened that two ways of making a vest were open to her, which were equally satisfactory as regards results, but of which one, while using up a little more yarn, involved a little less trouble than the other; then her problems would be typical of those of the larger business world. They would include first decisions as to the relative urgency of various ends; secondly, decisions as to the relative advantages of various means of attaining each end; thirdly, decisions, based on these two sets of decisions, as to the margin up to which she could most profitably carry the application of each means towards each end.

These three classes of decisions have to be taken on a larger scale by the business man, who has more complex balancings and adjustments to make before reaching each decision. Let us take an illustration from the building trade. Let us watch the operations of a " speculative builder " in the honourable sense of the term: that is, a man who sets out to erect honest buildings in anticipation of general demand; who bears the penalty of any error in his judgment; and who, if his judgment is approved by events, benefits the community as well as himself. Let him be considering whether to erect dwelling-houses, or warehouses, or factories or shops. He is trained to form at once a fairly good opinion as to the method of working most suitable for each class of building, and to make a rough estimate of its cost. He estimates the cost of various sites adapted for each class of building: and he reckons in the price that he would have to pay for any site as a part of his capital expenditure, just as he does the expense to which he would be put for laying foundations in it, and so on. He brings this estimate of cost into relation with his estimate of the price he is likely to get for any given building, together with its site. If he can find no case in which the price exceeds his outlays by enough to yield him a good profit, with some margin against risks, he may remain idle. Or he may possibly build at some risk in order to keep his most trusty workmen together, and to find some occupation for his plant and his salaried assistance: but more on this later on.

Suppose him now to have decided that (say) villa residences of a certain type, erected on a plot of ground which he can buy, are likely to yield him a good profit. The main end to be sought being thus settled, he sets himself to study more carefully the means by which it is to be obtained, and, in connexion with that study, to consider possible modifications in the details of his plans.

Given the general character of the houses to be built, he will have to consider in what proportions to use various materials—brick, stone, steel, cement, plaster, wood, etc., with a view to obtaining the result which will contribute most, in proportion to its cost, to the efficiency of the house in gratifying the artistic taste of purchasers and in ministering to their comfort. In thus deciding what is the best distribution of his resources between various commodities, he is dealing with substantially the same problem as the primitive house-wife, who has to consider the most economic distribution of her yarn between the various needs of her household.

Like her, he has to reflect that the yield of benefit which any particular use gave would be relatively large up to a certain point, and would then gradually diminish. Like her, he has so to distribute his resources that they have the same marginal utility in each use: he has to weigh the loss that would result from taking away a little expenditure here, with the gain that would result from adding a little there. In effect both of them work on lines similar to those which guide the farmer in so adjusting the application of his capital and labour to land, that no field is stinted of extra cultivation to which it would have given a generous return, and none receives so great an expenditure as to call into strong activity the tendency to diminishing return in agriculture.

Thus it is that the alert business man, as has just been said, " pushes the investment of capital in his business in each several direction until what appears in his judgment to be the outer limit, or margin, of profitableness is reached; that is, until there seems to him no good reason for thinking that the gains resulting from any further investment in that particular direction would compensate him for his outlay". He never assumes that roundabout methods will be remunerative in the long run. But he is always on the look out for roundabout methods that promise to be more effective in proportion to their cost than direct methods: and he adopts the best of them, if it lies within his means.

We have seen that the main agents of production are land, labour, and capital, and that these can usually be employed, and are employed, in varying proportions. We have also seen how each agent takes part of the product as its reward, and we can now turn to the rather difficult, but very important question of, *What decides how the wealth produced shall be divided between the producers?* Our guide is Alfred Marshall again, with some more extracts from his *Principles of Economics*. They make a long lecture, but if this involves any " labour " the reader may be sure that in this case at least it will be amply rewarded. Marshall first considers the problem of distribution in a very simple society and then introduces, one by one, the complicating factors—varying demand, new inventions, changes in population and rents, differences in labour-value, determined by different demand for different products, and finally the competition between labour and capital. The principle of substitution at which we glanced a short while ago is now seen to be constantly at work and to be the guiding principle of the entrepreneur under private enterprise.

ALFRED MARSHALL

THE DISTRIBUTION OF WEALTH

THE keynote of this book is in the fact that free human beings are not brought up to their work on the same principles as a machine, a horse, or a slave. If they were, there would be very little difference between the distribution and the exchange side of value; for every agent of production would reap a return adequate to cover its own expenses of production with wear-and-tear, etc.; at all events after allow-ance had been made for casual failures to adjust supply to demand. But as it is, our growing power over nature makes her yield an ever larger surplus above necessaries; and this is not absorbed by an unlimited increase in the population. There remain therefore the questions:— What are the general causes which govern the distribution of this surplus among the people? What part is played by conventional necessaries, *i.e.* the Standard of Comfort? What by the influence which methods of consumption and of living generally exert on efficiency; by wants and activities, *i.e.* by the Standard of Life? What by the many-sided action of the principle of substitution, and by the struggle for survival between hand-workers and brain-workers of different classes and grades? What by the power which the use of capital gives to those in whose hands it is? What share of the general flow is turned to remunerate those who work (including here the undertaking of ventures) and " wait " as contrasted with those who work and consume at once the fruits of their endeavours? An attempt is made to give a broad answer to those and some similar questions. . . .

It has now become certain that the problem of distribution is much more difficult than it was thought to be by earlier economists, and that no solution of it which claims to be simple can be true. Most of the old attempts to give an easy answer to it were really answers to imaginary questions that might have arisen in other worlds than ours, in which the conditions of life were very simple. The work done in answering these questions was not wasted. For a very difficult problem can best be solved by being broken up into pieces; and each of these simple questions contained a part of the great and difficult problem which we have to solve. Let us profit by this experience and work our way by successive steps in the remainder of this chapter towards understanding the general causes which govern the demand for labour and capital in real life.

Let us begin by studying the influence of demand on the earnings of labour, drawn from an imaginary world in which everyone owns the capital that aids him in his labour; so that the problem of the relations of capital and labour do not arise in it. That is, let us suppose but little capital to be used; while everyone owns whatever capital he does use, and the gifts of nature are so abundant that they are free and un-appropriated. Let us suppose, further, that everyone is not only of equal willingness to work, and does in fact work equally hard: also that all work is unskilled,—or rather unspecialized in this sense, that if any two people were to change occupations, each would do as much and as good work as the other had done. Lastly, let us suppose that everyone produces things ready for sale without the aid of others, and that he himself disposes of them to their ultimate consumers: so that the demand for everything is direct.

In this case the problem of value is very simple. Things exchange for one another in proportion to the labour spent in producing them. If the supply of any one thing runs short, it may for a little time sell for more than its normal price: it may exchange for things the production of which had required more labour than it had: but, if so, people will at once leave other work to produce it, and in a very short time its value will fall to a normal level. There may be slight temporary disturbances, but as a rule anyone's earnings will be equal to those of anyone else. In other words, each will have an equal share in the net sum total of things and services produced; or, as we may say, the *national income* or *dividend*; which will constitute the demand for labour.

If now a new invention doubles the efficiency of work in any trade, so that a man can make twice as many things of a certain kind in a year without requiring additional appliances, then those things will fall to half their old exchange value. The effective demand for everyone's labour will be a little increased, and the share which each can draw from the common earnings-stream will be a little larger than before. He may if he chooses take twice as many things of this particular kind, together with his old allowance of other things: or he may take somewhat more than before of everything. If there be an increase in the efficiency of production in many trades the common earnings-stream or dividend will be considerably larger; the commodities produced by those trades will constitute a considerably larger demand for those produced by others, and increase the purchasing power of everyone's earnings.

Next, let us still neglect the influence which the liberality of the expenditure on rearing and training workers exerts on their efficiency and let us look at the influence that changes in the numbers of the population exert on the incomes which nature will yield. We suppose then that the growth of population proceeds at a rate, which is either fixed, or at all events not affected by the rate of wages: it may be influenced by changes in custom, in moral opinion and in medical knowledge. And we still suppose all labour to be of the same grade, and the national dividend to be divided out equally to each family, save for some slight passing inequalities. In this case every improvement in the arts of production or transport, every new discovery, every new victory over nature will increase equally the comforts and luxuries at the command of each family.

But this case differs from the last; because in this case the increase of population, if maintained long enough, must ultimately outgrow the improvements in the arts of production, and cause the law of diminishing return to assert itself in agriculture. That is to say, those who work on the land will get less wheat and other produce in return for their labour and capital. An hour's labour will represent a less quantity of wheat than before throughout the agricultural trades, and therefore throughout all other trades; since all labour is supposed to be of the same grade, and earnings are therefore as a rule equal in all trades.

Further we must note that the surplus or rental value of land will tend to rise. For the value of any kind of produce must equal that of the labour, aided on our supposition by a uniform quantity of capital throughout, which is required to produce it, whether on good land or bad, under barely remunerative, or marginal conditions. More labour and capital than before will be needed to raise a quarter of wheat, etc., on the margin; and therefore the wheat, etc., which is returned by nature to the labour applied under advantageous circumstances, will have a higher value relatively to that labour and capital than before: or, in other words, it will yield a larger surplus value over that of the labour and capital used in raising it.

Let us now drop the supposition that labour is so mobile as to ensure equal remuneration for equal efforts throughout the whole of society, and let us approach much nearer to the actual condition of life by supposing that labour is not all of one industrial grade, but of several. Let us suppose that parents always bring up their children to an occupation in their own grade; that they have a free choice in that grade, but not outside it. Lastly, let us suppose that the increase of numbers in each grade is governed by other than economic causes: as before it may be fixed, or it may be influenced by changes in custom, in moral opinion, etc. In this case also the aggregate national dividend will be governed by the abundance of nature's return to man's work in the existing state of the arts of production; but the distribution of that dividend between the different grades will be unequal. It will be governed by the demand of the people themselves. The share of those in any industrial compartment will be the higher, the more extensive and urgent the needs which they are able to satisfy on the part of those who are themselves drawing large shares of the national income.

Suppose, for instance, artists to form a grade or caste or industrial compartment by themselves; then, their number being fixed, or at least controlled by causes independent of their earnings, their earnings will be governed by the resources and the eagerness of those classes of the population who care for such gratifications as artists can furnish.

We may now leave the imaginary world, in which everyone owns the capital that aids him in his work; and return to our own, where the relations of labour and capital play a great part in the problem of distribution. But let us still confine our attention to the distribution of the national dividend among the various agents of production, in accordance with the quantity of each agent, and the services which it renders; and leave the reflex influence which the remuneration of each agent exerts on the supply of that agent, to be considered later.

We have seen how the alert business man is ever seeking

for the most profitable application of his resources, and endeavouring to make use of each several agent of production up to that margin, or limit, at which he would gain by transferring a small part of his expenditure to some other agent; and how he is thus, so far as his influence goes, the medium through which the principle of substitution so adjusts the employment of each agent that, in its marginal application, its cost is proportionate to the additional net product resulting from its use. We have to apply this general reasoning to the case of the hire of labour.

A question constantly in the mind of the careful business man is whether he has the right number of men for his work. In some cases that is settled for him by his plant: there must be one and only one engine driver on each express locomotive. But some express trains have only one guard; and when the traffic is heavy they may lose a few minutes which could be saved by a second guard: therefore an alert manager is constantly weighing the net product in saving of time and of annoyance to passengers, that will accrue from the aid of a second guard on an important train, and considering whether it will be worth its cost. This question is similar in kind to, but simpler in form than, the question whether "it would pay" to put an additional train on the time-table, which would call for more expenditure on plant as well as on labour.

Again one sometimes hears it said that a certain farmer starves his land for labour. Perhaps he has enough horses and plant; but "if he took on another man, he would get his money back, and a good deal more": that is, the net product of an additional man would more than cover his wages. Let us suppose that a farmer is raising such a question as to the number of his shepherds. For simplicity, we may suppose that an additional man would not require any further expenditure on plant or stock: that he would save the farmer himself just as much trouble in some ways as he gives in others; so that nothing has to be allowed for earnings of management (even when these are interpreted broadly so as to include insurance against risk, etc.): and lastly that the farmer reckons that he would do just so much in preventing the wastage of lambs, and in other ways as will increase by twenty his annual output of sheep in good condition. That is to say, he reckons that the net product of an additional man will be twenty sheep. If he can be got for much less than the equivalent of their price, the alert farmer will certainly hire him; but, if only for about that price, the farmer will be on the margin of doubt; and the man may then be called a *marginal* shepherd, because his employment is marginal.

The additional product to be got by this shepherd's labour is largely influenced by the number of shepherds whom the farmer already employs. And this again is governed by general conditions of demand and supply, and especially by the number of those from whom the ranks of shepherds could have been recruited during the current generation; by the demand for mutton and wool and by the area from which supplies of them can be obtained; by the effectiveness of the shepherds on all other farms; and so on. And the amount of the marginal product is further largely influenced by the competition of other uses for land: the space available for sheep-farming is curtailed by the demand for land for growing timber or oats, preserving deer, etc.

This illustration has been chosen from a simple industry; but, though the form may be different, the substance of the problem is the same in every industry. Subject to conditions which are not important in our main purpose, the wages of every class of labour tend to be equal to the net product due to the additional labour of the marginal labourer of that class.

This doctrine has sometimes been put forward as a theory of wages. But there is no valid ground for any such pretension. The doctrine that the earnings of a worker tend to be equal to the net product of his work, has by itself no meaning; since in order to estimate net product, we have to take for granted all the expenses of production of the commodity on which he works, other than his own wages.

But though this objection is valid against a claim that it contains a theory of wages; it is not valid against a claim that the doctrine throws into clear light the action of one of the causes that govern wages.

Again, the earnings of a machine can sometimes be estimated by the addition to the output of a factory which it might effect in certain cases without involving any incidental extra expense.

Generalizing from the work of a particular machine to that of machinery of a given aggregate value, we may suppose that in a certain factory an extra £100 worth of machinery can be applied so as not to involve any other extra expense, and so as to add annually £4 worth to the net output of the factory, after allowing for its own wear-and-tear. If the investors of capital push it into every occupation in which it seems likely to gain a high reward; and if, after this has been done and equilibrium has been found, it still pays and only just pays to employ this machinery, we can infer from this fact that the yearly rate of interest is 4 per cent. But illustrations of this kind merely indicate part of the action of the great causes which govern value. They cannot be made into a theory of interest, any more than into a theory of wages, without reasoning in a circle.

It may, however, be well to carry a little further our illustration of the nature of the demand for capital for any use; and to observe the way in which the aggregate demand for it is made up of the demands for many different uses.

To fix the ideas, let us take some particular trade, say that of hat-making, and inquire what determines the amount of capital which it absorbs. Suppose that the rate of interest is 4 per cent. per annum on perfectly good security; and that the hat-making trade absorbs a capital of one million pounds. This implies that the hat-making trade can turn the whole million pounds' worth of capital to so good account that they would pay 4 per cent. per annum *net* for the use of it rather than go without any of it.

Some things are necessary to them; they must have not only some food, clothing, and house room, but also some circulating capital, such as raw material, and some fixed capital, such as tools and perhaps a little machinery. And though competition prevents anything more than the ordinary trade profit being got by the use of this necessary capital; yet the loss of it would be so injurious that those in the trade would have been willing to pay 50 per cent. on it, if they could not have got the use of it on easier terms. There may be other machinery which the trade would have refused to dispense with if the rate of interest had been 20 per cent. per annum, but not if it had been higher. If the rate had been 10 per cent., still more would have been used; if it had been 6 per cent., still more; if 5 per cent., still more; and finally the rate being 4 per cent. they use more still. When they have this amount, the marginal utility of the machinery, *i.e.* the utility of that machinery which it is only just worth their while to employ is measured by 4 per cent.

A rise in the rate of interest would diminish their use of machinery; for they would avoid the use of all that did not give a net annual surplus of more than 4 per cent. on its value. And a fall in the rate of interest would lead them to demand the aid of more capital, and to introduce machinery which gave a net annual surplus of something less than 4 per cent. on its value. Again, the lower the rate of interest, the more substantial will be the style of building used for the hat-making factories and the homes of the hat-makers; and a fall in the rate of interest will lead to the employment of more capital in the hat-making trade in the form of larger stocks of raw material, and of the finished commodity in the hands of retail dealers.

The methods in which capital will be applied may vary much even within the same trade. Each undertaker having regard to his own means, will push the investment of capital in his business in each several direction until what appears in his judgment to be the margin of profitableness is reached;

and that margin is, as we have said, a boundary line cutting one after another every possible line of investment, and moving irregularly outwards in all directions whenever there is a fall in the rate of interest at which extra capital can be obtained. Thus the demand for the loan of capital is the aggregate of the demands of all individuals in all trades; and it obeys a law similar to that which holds for the sale of commodities: just as there is a certain amount of a commodity which can find purchasers at any given price. When the price rises the amount that can be sold diminishes, and so it is with regard to the use of capital.

And as with borrowings for productive purposes, so with those of spendthrifts or governments who mortgage their future resources in order to obtain the means of immediate expenditure. It is true that their actions are often but little governed by cool calculation, and that they frequently decide how much they want to borrow with but little reference to the price they will have to pay for the loan; but still the rate of interest exercises a perceptible influence on borrowings even of this kind.

To sum up the whole in a comprehensive, if difficult statement:—Every agent of production, land, machinery, skilled labour, unskilled labour, etc., tends to be applied in production as far as it profitably can be. If employers, and other business men, think that they can get a better result by using a little more of any one agent they will do so. They estimate the net product (that is the net increase of the money value of their total output after allowing for incidental expenses) that will be got by a little more outlay in this direction, or a little more outlay in that; and if they can gain by shifting a little of their outlay from one direction to another, they will do so.

Thus then the uses of each agent of production are governed by the general conditions of demand in relation to supply: that is, on the one hand, by the urgency of all the uses to which the agent can be put, taken together with the means at the command of those who need it; and, on the other hand, by the available stocks of it. And equality is maintained between its values for each use by the constant tendency to shift it from uses, in which its services are of less value to others in which they are of greater value, in accordance with the principle of substitution.

If less use is made of unskilled labour or any agent, the reason will be that at some point at which people were on the margin of doubt whether it was worth while to use that agent, they have decided that it is not worth their while. That is what is meant by saying that we must watch the *marginal* efficiency of each agent. We must do so, simply because it is only at the margin that any of those shiftings can occur by which changed relations of supply and demand manifest themselves.

We must not imagine, however, that this is the only way in which the wealth which is produced by labour and capital can be shared out. Marshall's principles are seen to be at work over the greater part of the world, but in Communist countries they do not apply. Hitherto we have given lectures on fundamental principles, and they have been couched in cool and objective language. Now that the foundations have been built on a rock we can allow the hot winds of political controversy to blow from time to time, first from one quarter and then from another. They will add point and interest to the statement of economic doctrines Before we do this, however, let us ask a former Professor of Political Economy at London University to give us a brief review of the earliest economic systems and their application to trade and industry in Western Europe. His lecture will also serve to sum up the knowledge we have so far gained.

JOHN RAMSAY M'CULLOCH

THE OBJECT OF POLITICAL ECONOMY

POLITICAL Economy *is the science of the laws which regulate the production, distribution, and consumption of those articles or products which have exchangeable value, and are either necessary, useful or agreeable to man.*

Political Economy has been frequently defined to be " the science which treats of the production, distribution, and consumption of *woalth* "; and if by wealth, be meant those articles or products which possess exchangeable value, and are either necessary, useful, or agreeable, the definition is quite unexceptionable.

Capacity of appropriation is indispensably necessary to constitute an article of wealth. And I shall invariably employ this term to distinguish those products only which are obtained by the intervention of human labour, and which, consequently, can be appropriated by one individual, and consumed exclusively by him. A man is not said to be wealthy because he has an indefinite command over atmospheric air, for this is a privilege which he enjoys in common with every other man, and which can form no ground of distinction; but he is said to be wealthy, according to the degree in which he can afford to command those necessaries, conveniences, and luxuries which are not the gifts of Nature, but the products of human industry.

The object of Political Economy is to point out the means by which the industry of man may be rendered most productive of those necessaries, comforts, and enjoyments which constitute *wealth*; to ascertain the proportions in which this wealth is divided among the different classes of the community; and the mode in which it may be most advantageously consumed. The intimate connexion of such a science with all the best interests of society is abundantly obvious. There is no other, indeed, which comes so directly home to the everyday occupations and business of mankind. The consumption of wealth is indispensable to existence; but the eternal law of Providence has decreed that wealth can only be procured by industry—that man must earn his bread in the sweat of his brow. This twofold necessity renders the production of wealth a constant and principal object of the exertions of the vast majority of the human race; has subdued the natural aversion of man from labour; given activity to indolence; and armed the patient hand of industry with zeal to undertake, and patience to overcome, the most irksome and disagreeable tasks.

But when wealth is thus necessary, when the desire to acquire it is sufficient to induce us to submit to the greatest privations, the science which teaches the means by which its acquisition may be most effectually promoted—by which we may be enabled to obtain the greatest possible amount of wealth with the least possible difficulty—must certainly deserve to be carefully studied and meditated. There is no class of persons to whom this knowledge can be considered as either extrinsic or superfluous. There are some, doubtless, to whom it may be of more advantage than to others; but it is of the utmost consequence to all. The prices of all sorts of commodities—the profits of the manufacturer and merchant, the rent of the landlord, the wages of the day labourer, and the incidence and effect of taxes and regulations—all depend on principles which Political Economy can alone ascertain and elucidate.

The one prevalent opinion, that wealth consists exclusively of Gold and Silver, naturally grew out of the circumstance of the money of all civilized countries being almost entirely formed of these metals. Having been used both as standards whereby to measure the relative value of different commodities, and as the equivalent for which they were most frequently exchanged, gold and silver, or money, acquired a factitious importance, not in the estimation of the vulgar only, but in that of persons of the greatest discernment. The simple and decisive consideration, that all buying and selling is really

nothing more than the bartering of one *commodity* for another
—of a certain quantity of corn or cloth, for example, for a
certain amount of gold or silver, and *vice versa*—was entirely
overlooked. The attention was gradually transferred from
the *money's worth* to the money itself; and the wealth of
individuals and of States was measured, not by the abundance
of their disposable products—by the quantity and value of the
commodities with which they could afford to purchase the
precious metals—but by the quantity of these metals actually
in their pooocooion.

And hence the policy, as obvious as it was universal, of
attempting to increase the amount of national wealth by for-
bidding the exportation of gold and silver, and encouraging
their importation.

The extraordinary extension of commerce during the
fifteenth and sixteenth centuries occasioned the substitution
of a more refined and complex system for increasing the supply
of the precious metals, in place of the coarse and vulgar one
that had previously obtained. The establishment of a direct
intercourse with India by the Cape of Good Hope seems to
have had the greatest influence in effecting this change. The
precious metals have always been among the most advantageous articles of export to the East: and notwithstanding
the old and deeply rooted prejudices against their exportation,
the East India Company obtained, when first instituted, in
1600, leave annually to export foreign coins, or bullion, of
the value of £30,000; on condition, however, that they should
import, within six months after the termination of every
voyage, except the first, as much gold and silver as should
together be equal to the value of the silver exported by them.

But the enemies of the Company contended that this condition was not complied with; and that it was *contrary to all
principle*, and highly injurious to the public interests, to permit
gold and silver to be sent out of the kingdom. The merchants,
and others interested in the support of the Company, could
not controvert the reasonings of their opponents, without

openly impugning the ancient policy of absolutely preventing the exportation of the precious metals. They did not, however, venture to contend, nor is there indeed any good reason for thinking that it really occurred to them, that the exportation of bullion to the East was advantageous, on the ground that the commodities purchased by it were of greater value in England. But they contended that the exportation of bullion to India was advantageous, because the commodities imported from thence were chiefly re-exported to other countries, from which a much greater quantity of bullion was obtained than had been required to pay for them in India. Mr. T. Mun, the ablest of the Company's advocates, ingeniously compares the operations of the merchant in conducting a trade carried on by the exportation of gold and silver, to the seed-time and harvest of agriculture.

"If we only behold" says he "the actions of the husbandman in the seed-time, when he casteth away much good corn into the ground, we shall account him rather a madman than a husbandman. But when we consider his labours in the harvest, which is the end of his endeavours, we shall find the worth and plentiful increase of his actions."

Such was the origin of what had been called the *Mercantile System*. And, when compared with the previous prejudice—for it hardly deserves the name of system—which wholly interdicted the exportation of gold and silver, it must be allowed that its adoption was a considerable step in the progress to sounder opinions. The supporters of the mercantile system, like their predecessors, held that gold and silver alone constituted wealth; but they thought that sound policy dictated the propriety of allowing their exportation to foreigners, provided the commodities imported in their stead, or a portion of them, were afterwards sold to other foreigners for a greater amount of bullion than had been originally laid out on their purchase; or, provided the importation of the foreign commodities caused the exportation of so much more native produce than would otherwise have been exported, as would more than equal their cost.

These opinions necessarily led to the celebrated doctrine of the *Balance of Trade*. It was obvious that the precious metals could not be imported into countries destitute of mines, except in return for exported commodities; and the grand object of the supporters of the mercantile system was to monopolize the largest possible supply of the precious metals, by the adoption of various complex schemes for encouraging exportation, and restraining the importation of almost all products, except gold and silver, that were not intended for future exportation. In consequence, the *excess of the value of the Exports over that of the Imports* came to be considered as being at once the sole cause and measure of the progress of a country in the career of wealth. This excess, it was taken for granted, could not be balanced otherwise than by the importation of an equal value of gold and silver, or of the only real wealth it was then supposed a country could possess.

The gain on our foreign commerce is here supposed to consist exclusively of the gold and silver which, it is taken for granted, must necessarily be brought home in payment of the excess of the exported commodities. Mr. Mun lays no stress whatever on the circumstance of foreign commerce enabling us to obtain an infinite variety of useful and agreeable products, which it would either have been impossible for us to produce at all, or to produce so cheaply at home. We are desired to consider all this accession of wealth—all the vast addition made by commerce to the motives which stimulate, and to the comforts and enjoyments which reward the labour of the industrious—as *nothing*, and to fix our attention exclusively on the balance of £200,000 of gold and silver! This is much the same as if we were desired to estimate the comfort and advantage derived from a suit of clothes, by the number and glare of the metal buttons by which they are fastened. And yet the rule for estimating the advantageousness of foreign commerce, which Mr. Mun has here given, was long regarded by the generality of merchants and practical statesmen as infallible; and such is the inveteracy of ancient prejudices, that we are still annually congratulated on the excess of our exports over our imports!

It is to the celebrated M. Quesnay, a physician, attached to the court of Louis XV, that the merit unquestionably belongs of having first attempted to investigate and analyse the sources of wealth, *with the intention of ascertaining the fundamental principles of Political Economy*; and who thus gave it a systematic form, and raised it to the rank of a science. Quesnay's father was a small proprietor, and having been educated in the country, he was naturally inclined to regard agriculture with more than ordinary partiality. At an early period of his life he had been struck with its depressed state in France, and had set himself to discover the causes which prevented its making that progress, which the industry of the inhabitants, the fertility of the soil, and the excellence of the climate seemed to ensure. In the course of this inquiry he speedily discovered that the prevention of the exportation of corn to foreign countries, and the preference given by the regulations of Colbert to the manufacturing and commercial classes over the agriculturists, formed the most powerful obstacles to the progress and improvement of agriculture.

But Quesnay was not satisfied with exposing the injustice of this preference, and its pernicious consequences. His zeal for the interests of agriculture led him, not merely to place it on the same level with manufactures and commerce, but to raise it above them—by endeavouring to show that it was the only species of industry which contributed to increase the riches of a nation. Founding on the indisputable fact, that everything that either ministers to our wants or gratifies our desires, must be orginally derived from the earth, Quesnay assumed as a self-evident truth, and as the basis of his system, that the *earth is the only source of wealth*; and held that industry was altogether incapable of producing any new value, except when employed in agriculture, including under that term fisheries and mines. His observation of the striking effects of the *vegetative* powers of nature, and his inability to explain the real origin and causes of *rents*, confirmed him in this opinion.

The circumstance, that of those who are engaged in industrious undertakings, none but the cultivators of the soil paid rent for the use of *natural agents*, appeared to him an incontrovertible proof that agriculture was the only species of industry which yielded a net surplus (*produit net*) over and above the expences of production. Quesnay allowed that manufacturers and merchants were highly useful; but, as they realized no net surplus in the shape of rent, he contended they did not add any greater value to the raw material of the commodities they manufactured or carried from place to place, than was just equivalent to the value of the capital or stock consumed by them during the time they were necessarily engaged in these operations. These principles once established, Quesnay proceeded to divide society into three classes: the *first*, or *productive* class, by whose agency all wealth is produced, consists of the farmers and labourers engaged in agriculture, who subsist on a portion of the produce of the land reserved to themselves as the wages of their labour, and as a reasonable profit on their capital; the *second*, or *proprietary* class, consists of those who live on the rent of the land, or on the *net surplus produce* raised by the cultivators after their necessary expenses have been deducted; and the *third*, or *unproductive* class, consists of manufacturers, merchants, menial servants, etc., whose labour, though exceedingly useful, adds nothing to the national wealth, and who subsist entirely on the wages paid them by the other two classes.

In assuming agriculture to be the only source of wealth, because the matter of which all commodities are composed must be originally derived from the earth, M. Quesnay and his followers mistook altogether the nature of production, and really supposed wealth to consist of matter; whereas, in its natural state, matter is very rarely possessed of immediate and direct utility, and *is always destitute of value.* It is only by means of the *labour* which must be laid out in appropriating matter, and in fitting and preparing it for our use, that it acquires exchangeable value, and becomes wealth. Human industry does not produce wealth by making any addition to the matter of our globe; this being a quantity susceptible neither of augmentation nor diminution. Its real and only effect is to produce wealth *by giving utility to matter already in existence*; and it has been repeatedly demonstrated that the labour employed in manufactures and commerce is just as productive of utility, and consequently of wealth, as the labour employed in agriculture. It is to be regretted that the friends and disciples of Quesnay, among whom we have to reckon Mirabeau, Mercier de la Rivière, Dupont de Nemours, Saint-Peravy, Turgot, and other distinguished individuals, in France, Italy, and Germany, should, in their zeal for his peculiar doctrines, which they enthusiastically exerted themselves to defend and propagate, have exhibited more of the character of partisans than of (what there is the best reason to think they really were) sincere and honest inquirers after truth. Hence it is that they have always been regarded as a sect, known by the name of *Economists* or *Physiocrats*;—and that their works are characterized by an unusual degree of sameness.

But, in despite of all these defects, there can be no question that the labours of the French Economists powerfully contributed to accelerate the progress of economical science. In reasoning on subjects connected with national wealth, it was now found to be necessary to subject its sources, and the laws which regulate its production and distribution, to a more accurate and searching analysis. In the course of this examination, it was speedily ascertained that both the mercantile and economical theories were erroneous and defective; and that, to establish the science of Political Economy on a firm foundation, it was necessary to take a much more extensive survey, and to seek for its principles, not in a few partial and distorted facts, or in metaphysical abstractions, but in the connexion and relation subsisting among the various phenomena manifested in the progress of civilization.

At length, in 1776, our illustrious countryman Adam Smith published the *Wealth of Nations*—a work which has done for Political Economy what the Essay of Locke did for the philosophy of mind. In this work the science was, for the first time, treated in its fullest extent; and the fundamental principles on which the *production* of wealth depend, placed beyond the reach of cavil and dispute. In opposition to the French Economists, Dr. Smith has shown that *labour* is the only source of wealth, and that the wish to augment our fortunes and to rise in the world—a wish that comes with us from the womb, and never leaves us till we go into the grave—is the cause of wealth being saved and accumulated: he has shown that labour is productive of wealth when employed in manufactures and commerce, as well as when it is employed in the cultivation of the land: he has traced the various means by which labour may be rendered most effective; and has given a most admirable analysis and exposition of the prodigious addition made to its powers by its *division* among different individuals, and by the employment of accumulated wealth, or *capital*, in industrious undertakings.

Dr. Smith has also shown, in opposition to the commonly received opinions of the merchants, politicians, and statesmen of his time, that wealth does not consist in the abundance of gold and silver, but in the abundance of the various necessaries, conveniences, and enjoyments of human life; he has shown that it is in every case sound policy to leave individuals to pursue their own interest in their own way; that, in prosecuting branches of industry advantageous to themselves, they necessarily prosecute such as are, at the same time, advantageous to the public; and that every regulation intended to force industry into particular channels, or to determine the species of commercial intercourse to be carried on between different parts of the same country, or between distant and independent countries, is impolitic and pernicious—injurious to the rights of individuals—and adverse to the progress of *real* opulence and lasting prosperity.

That last paragraph gives us the doctrine of *laissez-faire* in a nutshell. Britain's lead in the industrial world in the nineteenth century was built up on this principle, but long before the century had reached its half-way stage the doctrine was vigorously challenged, both at home and abroad. Robert Owen, in his New Lanark mills, showed that a business could be run on humanitarian lines and still be a commercial success. And about the middle of the century two formidable opponents of orthodox economic doctrine began to make their voices heard.

Does the left-wing worker recognize the Principle of Substitution? No, he sees it as a conflict between labour and capital, and he calls it the Class Struggle. *How does the class struggle arise?*

The answer is given in the following brief extracts from the Communist Manifesto of 1848. This was the work of Marx and Engels, and it contained the germ of Marx's famous study of political economy, *Das Kapital*. In this book Marx tried to establish the laws governing the development of capitalism, and from them he argued that the spread of capitalist methods all over the world would eventually produce an " inner contradiction " in the system of private production for profit. This " contradiction ", which might be identified with the pre-war dilemma of " poverty in the midst of plenty ", would result in slumps, imperialist wars, and class conflict of increasing intensity. The crisis, he said, could only be resolved by establishing a socialist economy. It quite upset a large number of believers in this theory when the first practical expression of the doctrine, instead of being established, as one would expect, in a fully developed capitalist country, took place in Russia, the least " capitalized " of all the Great Powers.

KARL MARX and FRIEDRICH ENGELS

THE CLASS STRUGGLE

THE history of all hitherto existing society is the history of class struggles.

Freeman and slave, patrician and plebeian, lord and serf, guild-master and journeyman, in a word, oppressor and oppressed, stood in constant opposition to one another, carried on an uninterrupted, now hidden, now open fight, a fight that each time ended either in a revolutionary reconstitution of society at large, or in the common ruin of the contending classes.

The modern bourgeois society that has sprouted from the ruins of feudal society has not done away with class antagonisms. It has but established new classes, new conditions of oppression, new forms of struggle in place of the old ones.

Our epoch, the epoch of the bourgeoisie, possesses, however, this distinctive feature: it has simplified the class antagonisms. Society as a whole is more and more splitting up into two great hostile camps, into two great classes directly facing each other—bourgeoisie and proletariat.

[The Manifesto then traces the growth of the " bourgeoisie " or capitalist class, from the guild-masters or master craftsmen of the Middle Ages to the nineteenth-century industrial magnate.]

The bourgeoisie cannot exist without constantly revolutionizing the instruments of production, and thereby the relations of production, and with them the whole relations of society. Conservation of the old modes of production in unaltered form was, on the contrary, the first condition of existence for all earlier industrial classes. Constant revolutionizing of production, uninterrupted disturbance of all social conditions, everlasting uncertainty and agitation distinguish the bourgeois epoch from all earlier ones. All fixed, fast-frozen relations, with their train of ancient and venerable prejudices and opinions, are swept away, all new-formed ones become antiquated before they can ossify. All that is solid melts into air, all that is holy is profaned, and man is at last compelled to face with sober senses his real conditions of life and his relations with his kind.

[Capitalist modes of production extend throughout the world. This disintegrates the separate national cultures.]

The bourgeoisie keeps more and more doing away with the scattered state of the population, of the means of production, and of property. It has agglomerated population, centralized means of production, and has concentrated property in a few hands. The necessary consequence of this was political centralization. Independent, or but loosely connected provinces, with separate interests, laws, governments, and systems of taxation, became lumped together into one nation, with one government, one code of laws, one national class interest, one frontier and one customs tariff.

The bourgeoisie, during its rule of scarce one hundred years, has created more massive and more colossal productive forces than have all preceding generations together. Subjection of Nature's forces to man, machinery, application of chemistry to industry and agriculture, steam-navigation, railways, electric telegraphs, clearing of whole continents for cultivation, canalization of rivers, whole populations conjured out of the ground—what earlier century had even a presentiment that such productive forces slumbered in the lap of social labour?

We see then: the means of production and of exchange, on whose foundation the bourgeoisie built itself up, were generated in feudal society. At a certain stage in the development of these means of production and of exchange, the conditions under which feudal society produced and exchanged, the feudal organization of agriculture and manufacturing industry, in one word, the feudal relations of property became no longer compatible with the already developed productive forces; they became so many fetters. They had to be burst asunder; they were burst asunder.

Into their place stepped free competition, accompanied by a social and political constitution adapted to it, and by the economical and political sway of the bourgeois class.

A similar movement is going on before our own eyes. Modern bourgeois society with its relations of production, of exchange and of property, a society that has conjured up such gigantic means of production and of exchange, is like the sorcerer who is no longer able to control the powers of the nether world whom he has called up by his spells. For many a decade past the history of industry and commerce is but the history of the revolt of modern productive forces against modern conditions of production, against the property relations that are the conditions for the existence of the bourgeoisie and of its rule. It is enough to mention the commercial crises that by their periodical return put the existence of the entire bourgeois society on its trial, each time more threateningly. In these crises a great part not only of the existing products, but also of the previously created productive forces, are periodically destroyed. In these crises there breaks out an epidemic that, in all earlier epochs, would have seemed an absurdity—the epidemic of over-prduction. Society suddenly finds itself put back into a state of momentary barbarism; it appears as if a famine, a universal war of devastation had cut off the supply of every means of subsistence; industry and commerce seem to be destroyed. And why? Because there is too much civilization, too much means of subsistence, too much industry, too much commerce. The productive forces at the disposal of society no longer tend to further the development of the conditions of bourgeois property; on the contrary, they have become too powerful for these conditions, by which they are fettered, and so soon as they overcome these fetters, they bring disorder into the whole of bourgeois society, endanger the existence of bourgeois property. The conditions of bourgeois society are too narrow to comprise the wealth created by them. And how does the bourgeoisie get over these crises? On the one hand by enforced destruction of a mass of productive forces; on the other, by the conquest of new markets, and by the more thorough exploitation of the old ones. That is to say, by paving the way for more extensive and more destructive crises, and by diminishing the means whereby crises are prevented.

The weapons with which the bourgeoisie felled feudalism to the ground are now turned against the bourgeoisie itself.

But not only has the bourgeoisie forged the weapons that bring death to itself; it has also called into existence the men who are to wield those weapons—the modern working class— the proletarians.

In proportion as the bourgeoisie, *i.e.* capital, is developed, in the same proportion is the proletariat, the modern working class, developed—a class of labourers, who live only so long as they find work, and who find work only so long as their labour increases capital. These labourers, who must sell themselves piecemeal, are a commodity, like every other article of commerce, and are consequently exposed to all the vicissitudes of competition, to all the fluctuations of the market.

Owing to the extensive use of machinery and to division of labour, the work of the proletarians has lost all individual character, and, consequently, all charm for the workman. He becomes an appendage of the machine, and it is only the most simple, most monotonous, and most easily acquired knack, that is required of him.

Modern industry has converted the little workshop of the patriarchal master into the great factory of the industrial capitalist. Masses of labourers, crowded into the factory, are organized like soldiers. As privates of the industrial army they are placed under the command of a perfect hierarchy of officers and sergeants.

The lower strata of the middle class—the small tradespeople, shopkeepers, and retired tradesmen generally, the handicraftsmen and peasants—all these sink gradually into the proletariat, partly because their diminutive capital does not suffice for the scale on which modern industry is carried on, and is swamped in the competition with the large capitalists, partly because their specialized skill is rendered worthless by new methods of production. Thus the proletariat is recruited from all classes of the population.

The proletariat goes through various stages of development. With its birth begins its struggle with the bourgeoisie. At first the contest is carried on by individual labourers, then by the workpeople of a factory, then by the operatives of one trade, in one locality, against the individual bourgeois who directly exploits them. They direct their attacks not against the bourgeois conditions of production, but against the instruments of production themselves; they destroy imported wares that compete with their labour, they smash to pieces machinery, they set factories ablaze, they seek to restore by force the vanished status of the workmen of the Middle Ages.

But with the development of industry the proletariat not only increases in number; it becomes concentrated in greater masses, its strength grows, and it feels that strength more. The collisions between individual workmen and individual bourgeois take more and more the character of collisions between two classes. Thereupon the workers begin to form combinations (trades unions against the bourgeois; they club together in order to keep up the rate of wages; they found permanent associations in order to make provision beforehand for these occasional revolts. Here and there the contest breaks out into riots.

Now and then the workers are victorious, but only for a time. The real fruit of their battles lies, not in the immediate result, but in the ever-expanding union of the workers. This union is helped on by the improved means of communication that are created by modern industry, and that place the workers of different localities in contact with one another. It was just this contact that was needed to centralize the numerous local struggles, all of the same character, into one national struggle between classes. But every class struggle is a political struggle. And that union, to attain which the burghers of the Middle Ages, with their miserable highways, required centuries, the modern proletarians, thanks to railways, achieve in a few years. . . .

The essential condition for the existence and for the sway of the bourgeois class is the formation and augmentation of capital; the condition for capital is wage-labour. Wage-labour rests exclusively on competition between the labourers. The advance of industry, whose involuntary promoter is the bourgeoisie, replaces the isolation of the labourers, due to competition, by their revolutionary combination, due to association. The development of modern industry, therefore, cuts from under its feet the very foundation on which the bourgeoisie produces and appropriates products. What the bourgeoisie therefore produces, above all, are its own gravediggers. Its fall and the victory of the proletariat are equally inevitable.

With that last sentence we shall probably not agree, and in any case a process of evolution is much more likely to work out some new synthesis to replace the catastrophic climax which seemed so inevitable to Karl Marx.

The undisguised hatred which Marx felt for the capitalists calls to mind a forceful passage from P. H. Wicksteed's book, *The Scope and Method of Political Economy*:—

" Social reformers and legislators will never be economists, and they will always work on economic theory of one kind or another. They will quote and apply such dicta as they can assimilate, and such acknowledged principles as seem to serve their turn. Let us suppose there were a recognized body of economic doctrine, the truth and relevancy of which perpetually revealed itself to all who looked below the surface; which taught men what to expect and how to analyse their experience; which insisted at every turn on the illuminating relation between our conduct in life and our conduct in business. . . . Economics might even then be no more than a feeble barrier against passion, and might afford but a feeble light to guide honest enthusiasm, but it would exert a steady and cumulative pressure, making for the truth . . . and the roughly understood dicta bandied about in the name of Political Economy would at any rate stand in some relation to truth and to experience, instead of being, as they too often are at present, a mere armoury of consecrated paradoxes which cannot be understood because they are not true, that every one uses as weapons while no one grasps them as principles."

Nevertheless, what Marx had to say was important, and we therefore turn to G. D. H. Cole for a few comments on this subject. Let us ask him *How are politics and economics inter-related?* The answer is taken from his book, *What Marx Really Meant*, and that explains why the illustrations which he gives deal with the subject we have just been considering.

G. D. H. COLE

POLITICS AND ECONOMICS

ANY economic system, involving as it does a particular set of relationships between men and things and between men and men, needs the support of a corresponding system of political and social relationships. It cannot function successfully unless the individuals and classes who are its active agents are protected in, or compelled to, the rights and duties assigned to them under it. In other words, any economic system requires a legal system whose concepts and precepts correspond to the needs of the economic situation. The economic purpose of the legal system is to secure the appropriate conditions for the effective use of the resources of production, and to repress any claims or activities likely to interfere with these conditions. No economic system can develop its full potentialities except with the aid of a legal system in harmony with its needs. This is why economic revolutions always carry with them the necessity for corresponding political and legal revolutions.

For the form and content of the law, and the political structure of the Society which upholds it, are intimately connected with the underlying needs of the economic system. A Society of hunters or fishers is bound to organize itself, politically, after a different fashion from a Society of men who live by agriculture or by industrial production, or depend on international commerce for the means of life. It is easy to trace broad correspondences between the underlying economic structures of different Societies and their political organization, and to see how, in the past, political systems have been adapted to changes in the fundamental economic conditions. This can be seen most plainly of all in the different forms which the institution of property assumes in different civilizations, or phases in the growth of civilization, and in the changing status of the human beings who perform the ordinary labour required. Slavery corresponds to one phase, serfdom to another, and " free " wage-labour to a third; and slavery, serfdom, and wage-labour are all legal and political as well as economic concepts, expressed in different systems of law and in different political institutions.

In the Marxian view, political and legal systems, and the theories which men frame in explanation and justification of them, are derived from the necessities of the economic order. They embody in laws, political institutions, and theories of jurisprudence and politics, the precepts required to uphold particular economic systems which arise out of the development of the powers, or resources, of production; and they are subject to change, in face of whatever resistance, in response to changes in the economic conditions of Society. For economic changes, by forcing upon men new methods of exploiting the available resources of production, compel them to modify the relations of men to things and of men to men, and accordingly to readjust the political systems which uphold such relations. It is inconceivable that a modern Society, employing the resources of large-scale machine production, should continue for long to be organized politically after the fashion of a feudal monarchy, or that the localism of the mediaeval system of city government should survive the impact of the world market. At every stage of civilization, there must be a sufficient degree of correspondence between the conditions of production and the political and social system embodied in law and custom; for otherwise there will develop a conflict between the rising economic forces and the established political system, and the latter, so far from upholding the conditions required for further economic advance, will be found to stand perilously in the way of the effective use of the available productive resources.

According to Marxism, economic forces play throughout history the creative and dynamic part. The resources of production are in constant evolution as men's knowledge and command over Nature increase, and consequently there is a constant need for changes in the political structure of Society. But political systems do not change constantly and gradually in step with the development of the powers of production. For any system of government, once established, embodies the authority of a particular class; and this class, having seated itself in political power, is by no means willing to yield up its privileges without a struggle merely because the economic conditions have so changed as to make its supersession desirable. Its authority is the guardian of countless vested interests and claims, for the defence of which it exists. The entire system of law which has grown up within it is the expression of these claims in the form of rights and prohibitions; and the government itself is the political representative of the dominant class. Accordingly, while the political system does change gradually in response to changing economic needs, it changes slowly and against the will of those who control it; and its adaptation usually both lags behind the changes which occur in the economic sphere, and is limited to what can be done without departing from its essential class character, or admitting claims inconsistent with the vested rights of the dominant class.

The resistance to necessary changes causes major change, when it does come, to take a revolutionary form. The need for change accumulates, in face of increasing resistance, as the proposed modifications threaten more deeply the essential institutions of the dominant order, until at length the forces making for a change of system grow too powerful to be resisted, and the old political system is broken by revolution and superseded by a new system embodying a different set of class ideas and claims. The class struggle, which has been in progress within the dying system, enters on a revolutionary phase; and a new class, previously held in subjection, assumes in its turn the powers and responsibilities of making a new State.

We shall have to examine more fully later on this Marxian concept of revolution. Here the point is that the political institutions of Society are regarded as a superstructure raised upon economic foundations, and embodying the rule of the class which is predominant in the economic field.

This, however, does not mean that all political developments are capable of explanation in purely economic terms. For, even if the roots of political systems are in the economic order, any set of institutions which men create is bound to acquire a life and potency of its own. A system of government, when once it has been established, has therefore a secondary power of influencing the movement of history, and of reacting on the course of economic development. Human history does not proceed solely under the impulsion of economic forces, but is affected profoundly by the forms which the social and political life of Society assumes. What is itself mainly the outcome of economic forces is capable of becoming an independent, though still a secondary, cause.

What is true of political institutions is no less true of other forms of social organization. Any underlying economic condition of Society, embodied in a particular system of production, involves a corresponding set of values, not only in an economic but also in an ethical sense. Things and forms of conduct are regarded as good or bad at different stages of civilization according as they further or hamper the carrying on of production in accordance with the requirements of the predominant economic system. This involves, in ethics as well as law, a system of values which reflects the ideas and interests of the controlling economic class, that is, of the class upon which devolves the responsibility for the successful management of production.

These ethical ideas, appropriate to a particular phase of social evolution, acquire, like the political institutions of Society, a sanctity of their own, and become highly resistant to change. Equally with the law, they help to uphold and sanction conduct in harmony with the needs of the established economic order; and, equally with law, they become, when once established in men's minds, independent causes, capable of influencing the further development of Society. For men think within a social framework, and the shape of thought on political and economic matters is derived from, and corresponds to, the shape of the Society within which the thinking is done. The forces which arise within a given social system, as a challenge to its economic and political institutions, have perforce to challenge also those elements in the established morality which reflect the needs and notions of the system that is to be attacked. But it is often harder to get the attacking forces to attack ideas than institutions; for every dominant class teaches the absoluteness of moral precepts with even more fervour and assurance than the finality of the established type of State and of the existing class-relationships. Besides, morals are entangled with religion, and men are less accessible to reasonings about morality than about politics or economics.

It is nevertheless clear, and affirmed by all sociologists, that moral ideas about social relationships are not absolute, but relative to the needs and conditions of different types of Society. Even if there is an absolute moral law, it can have, in such matters, no absolute and timeless content. There is no positive individual human action that can be pronounced *a priori* to be absolutely right or wrong, wholly without regard to the circumstances in which it is performed. When once this is recognized, it is easy to accept the view that positive precepts of social morality must change with changes in the economic and political conditions of Society, and that current codes of conduct are profoundly influenced by the character of the contemporary economic and political system.

Nor does this apply only within the field of moral ideas and precepts. Men's entire way of thinking is obviously conditioned by the nature of the Society in which they live. This is not so much because social conditions affect the answers men make to the questions which they ask themselves—though of course this is the case—as because social conditions affect the framing of the questions. Each age has its own problem, dictated to it by the conditions in which it lives, and imperatively demanding a solution; and the philosophies and sciences of every age, while they are built upon the legacies of the past, are essentially attempts to find answers to contemporary problems.

Of course this does not mean that every individual is limited to thinking only in terms of the problems of his own age. No one, indeed, can help being influenced by his age, however much he may try to escape from it; but, subject to this, thought is free, and can range at will over all questions that men can frame. A man can live in a past age, and think in terms of its problems; or he can construct a dream-world of his own, and do his thinking in terms of the imaginary concepts appropriate to his dream. A scientific inquirer can pursue his researches, without caring a whit about their practical results, in a spirit of disinterested curiosity.

But, out of all the welter of contemporary thought, the age will select. More thinkers and inquirers will be attracted to those problems which peculiarly vex the age than to others; and thinkers, no matter how subtle or profound, who have no message for their age, will be passed over—to be rediscovered, perhaps, centuries later, when their thought has become appropriate to the problems of a different stage of social development. The Marxian contention is not that men can think only in terms dictated by current economic conditions, but that out of men's thoughts those alone will influence the course of social evolution which are relevant to contemporary problems.

BOOK II

MONEY AND TRADE

MONEY AND TRADE

To facilitate the exchange of goods, money was invented. A great variety of commodities have been used as " money " in different places and different times, cattle perhaps more widely than most others. Our word " pecuniary " comes from the Latin *pecus*, cattle. Metals, however, with the aid in some cases of paper tokens carrying a direct promise to give metals in exchange, eventually replaced all other forms of " money " in highly civilized countries, partly because of their durability, and partly because of the ease with which subdivisions could be made without loss of value.

At first the metals were paid by weight. Our pound used to be a pound of silver, and our pennyweight is the weight of an old silver penny. But the trouble of constant weighing, and also of having to assay the purity of the metals, led to pieces being stamped with some sign which guaranteed both the weight and the fineness of that piece. Thus coins arose.

For many long centuries coins had to be worth their face value if they were to circulate freely. The debasing of the coinage was a favourite trick of corrupt or hard-pressed rulers, while a coinage of recognized integrity was eagerly sought, and proved a great help to the trade of the issuing country. Gresham's law that bad money drives out good found many an illustration. On the other hand, coins like the British sovereign, which was worth its full face value in gold when new, were acceptable tender all over the world.

To-day it has been replaced by a piece of ephemeral paper, and even our " silver " coins are one-quarter nickel and three-quarters copper. Modern progress has discovered that this token money need not be of any intrinsic value at all; the main requisite is that it shall not easily be counterfeited.

The money we carry in our pockets, however, is not the only kind of money in use to-day. What does the economist understand by " money "? " The essence of money ", as G. D. H. Cole says in his book, *Money: Its Present and Future*, "is that it can be passed from hand to hand in one act of circulation after another." Thus a bill of exchange may be regarded as money if it is discounted several times before it is paid, and in some countries which have not yet developed the cheque system as we have done, and indeed in our own country in former days, bills did serve as money in this way to a very large extent. A cheque, however, as a rule only facilitates one transaction. It is made out by one man and it is paid in by another. A cheque, therefore, is not " money " to the economist. But the account at the bank which allows one to write a cheque *is* money. The sum of these accounts, indeed, is the largest and most important form of money in the present-day world. Let us put this question to our authority: *Do banks create money?* The answer will be found in the following extract from the book above-mentioned.

G. D. H. COLE

MONEY IN THE BANK

A PERSON who has a bank account keeps a certain amount of purchasing power about him, or locked up at home, in the form of cash. But the amount so kept is usually small. Most of the purchasing power that accrues to him he probably keeps in the form of a deposit at his bank, until he decides to spend it. He can write a cheque against any sum standing to his credit in the books of his bank whenever he wishes to do so. Such a credit is, for most purposes, fully as good as cash, provided only that he can reasonably rely on the bank's ability to pay; and it is much more convenient to keep large sums in the form of bank deposits than to hold them in coin or notes. Where fears arise about the solvency of banks, as they did in the United States in the crisis of 1932-1933, many men will withdraw money from the banks in cash, and keep it about them. But normally, in the modern world, banks are regarded as safe deposits for supplies of purchasing power; and the convenience of holding money in the form of bank deposits causes most of the bank-using classes to hold most of their supply of ready money in this form.

Bank deposits are of two kinds—*current* accounts and *deposit* accounts. Current accounts consist of sums which can be drawn upon at any time without notice. The banks hold such sums on behalf of the owners, but pay no interest upon them. Deposit accounts, in the narrower sense—sometimes called " time deposits "—consist of sums deposited on the condition that they will not be withdrawn without a certain number of days' notice. On such accounts the banks pay interest, usually at a low rate. In practice, deposit accounts can be drawn upon without notice because a banker will nearly always be ready to advance a sum at once to anyone who has it on time-deposit. In general, sums standing in current accounts are those which the owners think they may want to use almost at once, or at any moment; whereas time-deposits are sums which the owners expect to leave in the bank for an appreciable period. The difference, however, is by no means hard-and-fast; and some large concerns, which have big fluctuating deposits at the bank, are in a position to arrange with it to receive interest on their current accounts without the formality of converting them into time-deposits.

Bank deposits *are* money, though cheques are not. Bank deposits have exactly the same qualities as coin or notes, in that they can be transferred indefinitely from hand to hand, in payment for goods or services or in settlement of debts or obligations of any sort. A bank-note is a bank's promise to pay, embodied in a transferable bit of paper: a bank deposit is a similar promise to pay, inscribed in the bank's books, and drawn upon by cheque as required.

Bank deposits are, in the world of to-day, much the largest and most important element in the supply of money. They would become even more important if, as has sometimes been proposed, wages were paid by cheque instead of in coin and notes. The reason why this is not done is that it would involve too much trouble. Either the wage-earners would present their cheques at the bank, and change them for cash—in which event there would be no advantage over payment in cash at the works—or they would settle their own bills largely by cheque. As their transactions are mostly small, the handling of these cheques by the banks would involve much book-keeping for which the banks would have to make a charge in order to cover their costs. The wage-earners would thus suffer a deduction from their earnings which they can avoid by receiving and paying out their incomes in cash, and thus acting as their own book-keepers. This is not to say that no wage-earners keep bank accounts; but it explains why most working-class spending is done by cash payments, and not by cheque.

The banks of which I have been speaking so far are the ordinary deposit banks, sometimes called " commercial banks ". ... Savings banks differ from the commercial banks in that they deal mainly with small deposits and with money which is to be saved up rather than withdrawn speedily in order to meet ordinary current expenditure. Savings bank deposits are, of course, often drawn upon to meet charges for which persons with small incomes save up over a period of weeks or months; but they are not ordinarily used for meeting regular weekly payments. Usually, such accounts are drawn upon, not by cheque, but by the presentation of a bank-book, the payment being thereupon marked up in the book and paid out in cash. Thus, savings bank deposits do not circulate as a rule from owner to owner in the same way as commercial bank deposits, and can hardly be regarded as " money " in the same sense. They are convertible into money on demand; but they are not themselves " money " in the sense in which I am at present using the word.

So far, I have been speaking as if bank deposits consisted entirely of sums deposited in the banks by their owners. This is the case with deposits in savings banks, but not with deposits in the commercial banks. A considerable part of the total which figures as " deposits " in the accounts of the commercial banks consists, not of sums deposited by the owners, but of advances made by the banks to their customers. These advances take two forms—*loans* and *overdrafts*. When a bank makes a loan, the sum lent is credited directly to the borrower's account and becomes a deposit in his name, with a debt to the bank standing against it. When a bank grants facilities for an overdraft, the sum allowed is not credited at once to the borrower, but is added to, and at once subtracted from, his deposit as he writes cheques against it. The bank, of course, charges interest on both loans and overdrafts, at whatever are the prevailing rates. The normal period for which advances are made is six months; but they can often be renewed for a further period.

Bank advances can be made to individuals for their private spending; but the great bulk of them is made to businesses for financing the costs of production or trade over the period between the incurring of expenditure and the receipt of payment for goods or services supplied. Some businesses can usually finance their operations out of their own capital, without calling for loans or overdrafts from the banks. But many businesses, especially trading businesses, habitually carry overdrafts, which vary in size according as trade is busy or slack. Banks also advance money on special terms to financial specialists for the discounting of bills or for stock market transactions; but I wish to leave these particular types of loan out of consideration for the present.

When a bank grants a loan or overdraft, the borrower draws upon it by writing cheques, and the sums advanced thus pass into the hands of others, who for the most part pay them in to their own bank accounts. Thus, a loan granted by a bank reappears, in the same or in a different bank, as a sum deposited by the recipient. When a bank receives a deposit, there is no means of telling whether it arises out of money belonging to the person who drew the cheque, or out of an advance made to him by his bank.

This point is important, because it provides the answer to a question about which there has been much foolish and unprofitable disputation. Bankers sometimes indignantly deny that they create money, and maintain that they do nothing more than lend out to some people money which others have left idle in their hands. This is not true. Every time a bank makes a loan or overdraft, it creates purchasing power, that is, money, which would not otherwise exist; and the banker, when he does this, has no means of telling whether what he is lending out is based on a deposit which someone has made out of his own money or on a loan or overdraft made by some other bank or even by the same bank to some other borrower.

It is, however, quite true that the power of the commercial banks to create money is by no means without limit. As we shall see later, in countries which possess a developed system of central banking, it is narrowly restricted by the policy of the Central Bank. In such countries, this limit in the main replaces the limit which is set, in the absence of an effective Central Bank, by considerations of prudence. Where there is no Central Bank, the limitations on the power of commercial banks to create deposits by making advances are twofold. First, if one bank outruns others in granting advances, it will find the other banks making claims upon it which it will have to meet in cash or bullion; for the recipients of its advances will draw cheques in favour of persons who will pay most of them into other banks, and these other banks will accordingly make claims upon it. This means that the various commercial banks are to a large extent bound to follow a common policy in making advances, so that their claims on one another tend to cancel out. Secondly, some part though not the whole of what the banks advance will be called for in the form of cash, and not of a mere transfer of bank deposits; and the banks must therefore avoid creating claims for cash against themselves beyond what they are in a position to meet. This second limitation is important in countries in which the banking system is relatively undeveloped. It does not count for much in countries with advanced banking techniques; for in such countries the amount of cash available is usually regulated so as to meet all demands arising out of the amount of " bank money " that is allowed to exist, and the factor subject to control is the amount of bank deposits rather than that of cash. The first limitation, however, applies to advanced equally with more primitive banking systems; for even where there is a strong Central Bank it is necessary for the various commercial banks to keep in step one with another in order to avoid having to meet claims for the transfer of cash. In advanced countries there is almost always a Clearing House, to which most of the important banks belong; and cheques drawn upon one bank and payable to someone's account in another are cancelled out against similar cheques drawn the other way round, so as to leave only quite small balances to be settled between banks, as long as they are following a broadly common policy.

The bank deposits which are to be regarded as money thus include the loans and overdrafts made by the banks themselves, as well as the sums actually belonging to their depositors; and the two are indistinguishable, because the sums advanced are paid over to others, who pay them into their banks as their own property.

So far, then, the " money " we are discussing consists of coins, notes, and bank deposits. Some, however, of the coins and notes in existence are not circulating in the hands of the public, but are held by the banks as till-money, or as a reserve against claims for cash that may be made upon them by their depositors. The banks do not keep more money in this form than they think they need to meet probable claims; for money so kept earns no interest. But the total amount of cash lying at any moment in the banks, and therefore not in active circulation, is bound to be quite considerable. It would, indeed, be much larger than it is were it not for the fact that under the banking system which has grown up in this country —and has been to a great extent imitated elsewhere—the Central Bank, that is, the Bank of England, acts as a reserve repository of cash. The commercial banks can at any time draw from the Bank of England such supplies of " till-money " as they require; they can do this, because they keep at the Bank of England accounts which are always in credit, and can be drawn upon at will. This involves that the Bank of England itself keeps in its banking department a reserve of coin and notes which is available for meeting these demands; but the total supply of cash thus held in reserve, and not in circulation, is very much smaller than it would need to be if each bank had to keep a reserve of its own adequate to deal with any contingency. That this was necessary was an outstanding weakness of the American banking system before the reforms of 1913, which set up the Federal Reserve Banks; and a similar diffusion of reserves among a large number of separate banks existed in Great Britain in the early days of commercial banking. There must always be, under any banking arrangements, some reserve of notes and coin kept out of active circulation in order that it may be available in case of need. But the size of the reserve required can be greatly reduced by linking the banks together in a co-ordinated system, and using the Central Bank as a bank of reserve.

If cash consists of token money, of little or no intrinsic value, the real cost of holding a reserve supply of it is negligible. It costs the Bank of England nearly nothing to print the paper notes which form the main part of its reserve. Cost considerations arise only if a reserve of something more valuable has to be kept against the notes themselves. Before 1914, when the reserve consisted partly of gold sovereigns, it cost an appreciable sum to maintain it; for the Bank of England had to pay the Mint for the gold of which these sovereigns were made and no interest could be earned on them as long as they remained locked up in the vaults. To the extent to which the notes held in reserve are backed by gold bullion lying in the Bank's vaults, a similar cost is incurred. Under the arrangements made for governing the issue of bank-notes at the time when the Treasury Notes were transferred to the Bank of England, there was to be a fixed " fiduciary " issue—that is to say, an issue of notes not backed by gold—and all notes issued in excess of this fixed issue were to be covered up to their full face value by gold held by the Bank. The fiduciary issue was not, however, fixed absolutely. Normally it was to amount to £260 millions—a sum settled on because it seemed to approximate to what would be needed to replace the Treasury Notes that were to be withdrawn; but power was given to the Bank of England to apply to Parliament to vary the amount of the permitted fiduciary issue, and it has been from time to time both raised and lowered since the act of 1928 came into force. [It was £1300 millions in 1950.]

Under these conditions, the holding of a reserve in notes by the Central Bank does involve cost; for the need to hold a reserve in notes means that the total supply of notes must be higher than it would otherwise need to be, and, as the total note issue exceeds the fiduciary limit, it follows that the additional notes needed to constitute the reserve must be backed by gold, and must therefore cost whatever it costs to hold so much gold idle. The position is somewhat different in most other countries; for most Central Banks are not tied down to a fixed fiduciary issue, but only to the keeping of a supply of gold representing a certain proportion of the notes issued. This means that the cost of maintaining a reserve of notes is lower—only half as great if the proportion required is 50 per cent., and so on. The cost, however, exists, wherever there is any requirement that an increase in the manufacture of paper money shall be accompanied by an increased holding of gold.

In war, of course, such requirements go by the board, and notes are issued in the quantities needed to finance cash expenditure irrespective of gold holdings. Under such conditions, the very notion of a reserve in precious metals loses its significance; for the printing press can always be resorted to, and the quantity of notes kept as till-money by the Central Bank becomes a mere matter of administrative convenience.

The supply of cash consists, then, of the notes and coins in the hands of the public—which, less any hoarding, constitute the active cash circulation—*plus* the till-money held in notes and coin by the commercial banks, *plus* the reserve of secondary till-money held in notes and coin by the Central Bank. Only the first of these makes up the active circulation. Of course, cash is continually flowing into and out of the commercial banks; but we must understand their " till-money " as meaning the amount held by them in excess of their normal outgoings. This is not, in practice, a fixed amount, for the active circulation varies at different times in the week, as wages are paid and thereafter returned via tradesmen and others to the banks, and also at different times of the year, especially round about Christams and at times of holiday, when the public spends more in cash and therefore makes larger demands for it upon the banks. At the rush seasons, the commercial banks will make calls for additional cash on the Central Bank, which will have to keep a reserve adequate to supply them, or to be empowered to issue additional paper money to meet the emergency need.

This brings us to the next question. *How much money should be available?* What level of supplies will best suit the best interests of— not the " best people ", but of a majority of the people? The answer is given in a further extract from Professor Cole's book on *Money*.

G. D. H. COLE

THE SUPPLY OF MONEY

I T used at one time to be supposed that the key to a right monetary and banking policy lay in taking the right measures to regulate the supply of cash. This view lay behind the Bank Charter Act of 1844, which furnished the foundations for the modern system of central banking. That Act laid down careful regulations under which a limit was set to the fiduciary issue of paper money, and the permitted issue was gradually concentrated in the hands of the Bank of England under the provision which caused the note-issuing rights of other banks to be progressively withdrawn. The draftsmen of that Act, very mindful of the unregulated issues of paper money which had occurred during and after the Napoleonic Wars and of the instability of the banking system which had been manifested in numerous bank failures, believed that if they could but put the issue of notes on a sound and conservative foundation the rest of the financial system could safely be left to look after itself without interference from the State. In this belief, they set up a régime under which increased supplies of cash could be made available only as a result of increased supplies of the precious metals acquired by the Bank; and they did this at a time when the world supply of gold was increasing but slowly. If their legitimate expectations had been fulfilled, it would have been impossible for the supply of cash to be increased at all rapidly, and any large increase in the quantity of goods and services needing to be exchanged would have had to be dealt with without a parallel increase in the cash available for effecting the exchanges.

In fact, all the expectations of 1844 speedily proved to be wrong. Within a few years the great gold discoveries in California and Australia brought with them a vast increase in the annual addition to the supply of monetary gold; and this enabled the Bank of England to issue an increasing supply of paper money, and the Mint of sovereigns, far beyond what had seemed possible in 1844. But this was not all. During the years which followed the Bank Charter Act banking methods were revolutionized by the rapid spread of the cheque system, with the result that many transactions which would previously have been settled in cash were dealt with by cheque so as to make no call on the supply of cash. There was more gold to serve as a basis for the issue of cash; and each unit issued went further, because it became possible, through the extended use of cheques, to raise upon it a larger superstructure of credit. Consequently, in the eighteen-fifties, prices, instead of being driven downwards by shortage of gold-based money, rose in consequence of its plenty and of the economies made by the cheque system in the use of cash.

Under the new conditions, men continued to think of cash, and accordingly of the gold on which the amount of cash depended, as the ultimate regulator of the supply of means of payment, and to regard the credit supplied by the commercial banks as a superstructure raised upon the foundation of the available gold. So, in a sense, it was; for the supply of cash, which depended mainly on the Bank of England's holding of gold *plus* the number of gold sovereigns in circulation or in the possession of the commercial banks, set limits to the amount of purchasing power which could be created. There had to be enough cash to meet the demands made for it by the banks' customers; and the demand so made would be affected by the amounts of loaned purchasing power which the banks advanced in credits. The banks therefore could not create credits on such a scale as to lead to demands for cash which they would be unable to satisfy; but the more their customers, instead of paying one another in cash, took to doing so by transferring their bank deposits by cheque without demanding cash, the larger became the credit superstructure which the banks could afford to raise upon any given cash basis. The credit structure became more and more elastic, and would probably have become even more elastic than it did had not the increase in the supply of gold been enlarging the cash basis at the same time.

This is not the place to pursue the history of the later developments either of gold supply or of the elasticity of the credit structure. (I am not writing a history of monetary development, but only a commentary illustrated from history as need arises.) Gold supplies languished again in the 'eighties and 'nineties until the further gold discoveries in South Africa brought a vast accession to ease the strain. Meanwhile, the extension of advanced banking methods based on the gold standard to further countries increased the demand for gold; and as against this the continued spread of the cheque system added to the elasticity of the credit structure. Gradually, bankers settled down to a series of conventions about the volume of credit which they could venture to base on any given amount of cash; and gold seemed still to be the master, because the amount of cash appeared to be regulated by the available amount of gold.

There grew up, however, one convention which was in time to undermine the supremacy of gold as the regulator of credit. The commercial banks, as we have seen, keep deposit accounts at the Central Bank, and can always draw on the Central Bank for cash by cheques on these accounts. Consequently, the commercial banker comes to regard any amount standing to his credit in his account at the Central Bank as being as good as cash, because he can always get cash for it. Accordingly, the commercial banks count *as cash* the whole of the sums standing to their credit at the Bank of England, even if the Bank has not in fact nearly enough cash in hand to pay out in cash if all these sums were asked for at once. The effects of this convention are, first, to enlarge the " cash " basis on which the superstructure of credit is raised, and secondly, to transfer to the Bank of England the obligation of deciding how much credit there shall be—or, at all events, a maximum beyond which the creation of credit shall not go. For the Bank of England, if it is to be in a position to honour all demands for cash that are actually made upon it, must take steps to ensure that these demands do not go beyond what it can meet. It must therefore prevent the commercial banks from granting credits on such a scale as would lead to an excessive demand for cash.

But how is the Bank of England to do this? It has no control by law over the amounts which the commercial banks may choose to lend to their customers. It has, however, the power to affect the amount of the balances standing to the credit of the commercial banks in its own books, and thus of reducing or increasing the cash basis on which these banks regard themselves as entitled to erect a superstructure of credit. The method by which the Bank of England can affect these balances is known as the engaging in " open market operations ", by which is meant the purchase or sale of securities in the open market. Whenever the Bank of England sells a security, the purchaser has to make a payment to it, and will do this in most cases by means of a cheque drawn on his account in one of the commercial banks. The balance of the bank concerned will thereupon be diminished by the amount of the cheque, and this will involve a corresponding reduction in the " cash basis " on which that bank rests its creation of credit. Any considerable sale of securities by the Central Bank will result in a reduction of the balances of all the leading commercial banks, and will be effective in reducing the credit superstructure provided that these banks adhere to the conventional ratio between their holdings of " cash ", including their balances at the Central Bank, and the amount of credit they supply.

Purchases of securities by the Central Bank naturally engender opposite effects. The Central Bank pays by cheque the sellers of the securities; and the sellers pay the cheques into their accounts in the commercial banks. The commercial banks then present the cheques to the Bank of England, which credits their accounts with the sums involved, and thus increases the " cash basis " on which they feel entitled to erect credits. There is only this difference in the working of the two processes: the commercial banks, unless they are prepared to alter their conventional ratios, must restrict credit when the Central Bank deprives them of " cash "; but they need not expand their advances when their " cash basis " is enlarged. They have, doubtless, a strong inducement to do so; for they earn interest on their advances, and have therefore good reason for advancing as much as they dare. They will not, however, make advances except to borrowers whom they deem credit-worthy—that is, likely to be able to meet the interest charges and to repay the principal at the due time— nor can they make advances unless they can find persons who are ready to borrow. It may be the case that an enlargement of the " cash basis " by the Central Bank will fail to bring about an enlargement of the credit superstructure, either because there is a dearth of borrowers or because the borrowers who do present themselves are not deemed to be credit-worthy by the commercial banks. In other words, " open market operations " on the part of the Central Bank are much more assured of success when their object is to contract credit than when their object is to expand it.

Even within these limits, the success of the Central Bank's policy depends, not on any power placed in its hands by law, but on a pure convention. If the commercial banks choose to disregard the cash-credit ratio which is traditionally observed, there is no legal obstacle in their way. They do in fact to some extent disregard it, by allowing themselves a little elasticity when they feel so disposed. But, in the main, they observe the conventional limit; and no one bank can break away far from it unless the other banks are prepared to behave in the same way. This is because any bank which outran its fellows in expanding credit would at once find itself paying over to the other banks more than it was receiving from them; and, as the commercial banks settle their mutual indebtedness by transferring sums to one another's accounts out of their balances at the Bank of England, the bank which granted credit more freely than the rest would find its " cash basis " reduced by these transfers, and would thus have to face a still wider gap between its available " cash " and the credit raised upon it, with the prospect of finding its balance at the Central Bank exhausted if it persisted in its course.

No such condition would apply if all the commercial banks were to act together. They could, by doing so, expand their credits to any extent, by altering their notion of the appropriate ratio between " cash " and credit. But, if this happened, the Bank of England could, by continued open market operations, go on depleting their " cash " until their balances were exhausted, so that they would no longer be able to call on it for further supplies to replenish their " till-money ". In practice, such a situation would never arise. The Bank of England and the commercial banks work in together as parts of a single system. They may bicker, and have their differences, from time to time; but the commercial banks are much too well aware of the importance of keeping in with the Bank of England ever to engage with it in a trial of strength that might bring the entire system crashing down.

The general conclusion is that, under the prevailing conditions, the available supply of credit, though it is actually issued for the most part by the commercial banks, depends on the Bank of England, which can make credit scarce or plentiful practically at pleasure by means of open market operations. The commercial banks create credit, by making advances to their customers; but how much credit they can create depends on the policy followed by the Central Bank.

Thus the Central Bank, though legally it is the guardian only of the currency—that is, of the supply of bank-notes— is in practice no less the guardian of the supply of credit available to the business world. Moreover, whereas in earlier days the Central Bank did in fact regulate the supply of currency and leave the other banks to follow their own devices in the matter of credits, nowadays it tends more and more to think first of regulating the supply of credit, and to regard the supply of cash in the form of notes as quite a secondary matter. The amount of notes required is derived from the amount of credit created. If so much purchasing power is made available to borrowers in the form of bank advances, they will tend to draw out so much in the form of notes and coin in order to pay wages and meet such other expenses as require cash money. The Central Bank must therefore make available whatever amount of cash is called for as a result of the amount of credit which it allows to be created. Instead of the supply of cash in the form of notes and coin governing the supply of credit, the amount of credit that is made available comes to determine the need for cash.

This truth is concealed because of the double sense in which the term " cash " is currently employed. In the narrower sense, cash consists of coins and notes; in the wider, it includes besides these the balances standing in the Central Bank to the credit of the commercial banks, because these are treated as equivalent to cash in the narrower sense. These so-called " cash balances " have, however, in truth a key function of their own. They are not cash in the ordinary sense, but the instrument whereby the Central Bank regulates the supply of credit. . . .

We can now come back to our original point of departure. We have seen that, in the world of to-day, not only coins and notes, but also bank deposits, have all the essential qualities of " money ", in the sense of generalized purchasing power transferable from person to person. We have seen further that bank deposits constitute by far the largest element in the total supply of " money ", in this sense, and that the volume of bank deposits is under effective regulation by the Central Bank. Now that gold sovereigns no longer circulate in the hands of the public, coined money has lost all independent significance; it is merely the small change that is used in retail transactions and is made available in such quantities as are needed as a consequence of the major decisions which regulate the supply of money in a wider sense. Bank-notes are vastly more important than coins; but they too fulfil a subordinate function and are supplied in such quantities as are needed in consequence of the policy followed in regulating the volume of bank deposits. Bank deposits are, in effect, the predominant element in the supply of money; and the determination of their volume by the Central Bank is the essential factor in settling the plenty or scarcity of the means of payment.

One great service which money performs for the economist is that of allowing him to measure and compare different economic factors.

If one man's demand for a new hat means that he will spend fifty shillings on it, while another man is willing to spend only forty shillings, then, other things being equal, we have an exact comparison between their demands. And, even if other things never are equal, the ability to thus give a quantitative expression to their relative demands is very useful. To each of those "other things" we can also give a quantitative expression in the same terms of £ s. d. and by ingenious mathematical devices and much hard work we can arrive at a more exact idea of the inter-relations of the factors we are studying.

Money, however, is not only a measuring-rod of the value of other commodities; it is itself a commodity which can be the subject of market operations just like any other commodity. The demand for money varies with the business climate just as the demand for coal varies with the temperature. *How does this demand for the right to make use of money find expression?* For the answer we turn to another great British economist, P. H. Wicksteed, whose opinion on the value and use of Economics has already been quoted. The extract is from his book, *The Scope and Method of Political Economy.*

P. H. WICKSTEED

INTEREST

THE phenomenon of interest has engaged the attention of theologians and moralists, as well as economists. Calvin has the reputation of being the first great theologian who frankly defended the receipt of interest. Possibly (but not probably) Ruskin will be recorded as the last great moralist and social reformer who ever succeeded in catching the ear of a wide public for a denunciation of it. But be that as it may, in spite of all that has been written on the subject, the true nature of interest, its relation to other economic phenomena, and the play of forces of which it is the manifestation, still seem to be very imperfectly understood, and some attempt must now be made to elucidate them.

We have already seen that a man's expenditure must be

distributed between what may be called short-service and long-service commodities; that is to say, between commodities which are used up and perish and have to be renewed, and commodities that last for longer or shorter periods in continuous or intermittent use. It follows that the man who is to provide himself with a suit of clothes that will last him six or twelve months must, at the beginning of the period, be in possession of his whole provision for six months' wear; whereas at the beginning of the same six months he only needs to be in possession of bread that will last him a few hours, and will find it inconvenient to have provision for more than a few days. We see from this that if a man should start with little or nothing in hand—that is to say, with no provision of anything he requires that will last him more than a few hours—and during the next six months expects to come into command of a certain defined amount of things in the circle of exchange, it would not be a matter of indifference to him whether this command came in an even stream, day by day, or week by week, or in a stream of changing volume, broad at first, and narrower afterwards. It may be a matter of vital importance to him to bring the rate at which his command of commodities accrues into some kind of correspondence with the irregular way in which the necessity for providing for his wants asserts itself. If instead of £1 a week for twenty-six weeks a man could receive, say, £5: 1: 3 for the first week, and 16s. 9d. each of the other twenty-five weeks, he would only receive £26 altogether during the twenty-six weeks, but he would be far better off, for he could provide himself with a due proportion of long-service commodities, and yet keep his expenditure on short-service commodities even throughout the period. It follows, therefore, that he will be willing (if that is the only alternative) to accept something less than £26 distributed over the time in a way that will suit him, instead of £26 distributed evenly over the whole six months.

And if we take a longer period, and include articles of greater permanence than clothes, such as furniture, standard books, or even houses, the same principle applies still more obviously. These things must exist in the mass before they can be used continuously or in fragments. And unless a man has something in hand—that is to say, unless he has saved something, or has come into possession of what others have saved or otherwise command—he will be very willing, if he can, to make some kind of bargain in virtue of which he can get possession of things at the start, and pay for them gradually as he uses them and as his resources continuously accrue. That is, given the prices of several commodities, he will be willing to contract the whole range of his options if thereby he can get leave to anticipate the exercise of some of them. His future command of commodities will then suffer a double contraction, partly due to the anticipation he has been allowed to make, and partly owing to the price he has paid for this privilege.

But the opposite case is equally conceivable. We have taken the case of a man whose command of resources is expected to flow in at the rate of £1 a week, so that in twenty years he will have had roughly £1040. But suppose a man has not any prospect of earning, or otherwise receiving, any continuous command of things in the circle of exchange for the next ten or fifteen years, but has present command of £1000. If he were required there and then to exercise his privilege and call out of the circle of exchange the actual things that he will require for the next ten years, what would he do? He would ask, say, for a house, for furniture, for books, for clothes, and so forth. But moth and rust corrupt. He will require larger premises than he would have needed had he been able to get these things as he wanted them; and a constant deflection of energies from other channels will be needed to keep them from deteriorating. When it comes to providing many years' stock of food, the man will be at a terrible additional disadvantage, for he will be confined to kinds of food that will keep indefinitely; and finally, it will be absolutely impossible for him to lay in a stock of direct " services "—

that is to say, of the output of human effort to meet the recurrent requirements of his life.

Thus the man who is to receive his resources in a regular stream may find it difficult to provide himself with others, which his total resources could easily command if he could distribute them in time according to his taste, taking more now and less afterwards. And the man who should be required to exercise at once the whole power of calling things out of the circle of exchange which will accrue to him during a series of years, would be severely restricted as to some things and would have to go altogether without others which his resources would command if he were able to distribute over future years some of the options which he is required to exercise at once. The same difficulties would arise if he were expecting to receive a given income for a certain period, after which it was to decline or cease. He could not during one term of years gradually store all the things that he would need during a subsequent term. We shall soon arrive at a clearer conception of the process by which saving and accumulation are actually conducted, and shall understand why, as a matter of fact, no man is ever called upon thus to store up in times of prosperity the actual concrete things that he will want in future years. But the point that I am emphasizing at the moment is that if he were called upon to do this he would be placed at a terrible disadvantage.

We see, then, that two men situated as we have supposed would both of them wish to redistribute their resources in time, but would wish to do so in contrary senses. The one would prefer present to future command of a part of the wealth that is to accrue to him in a given period and the other would prefer future to present exercise of a portion of the options which have already accrued to him. Now since each of these men has relatively too much of that of which the other has relatively too little it is manifest that the conditions for a profitable exchange are present. The man who has present command of things in the circle of exchange, and would willingly forgo a part of it for the sake of future command, meets the one who anticipates a stream of future command and would gladly contract it if he might exercise a certain measure of present command as a compensation. Each of them therefore can give what he values less, and receives what he values more. And the preferences of each alike are subject to the law of declining marginal significance. For it is obvious that as each of the two men is better supplied with that of which he is in relative lack and worse supplied with that in which he relatively abounds, there is a gradual approach to equilibrium.

We have supposed that to one of the exchanging parties an extra £1 down would actually have more value than an extra £1 distributed over a stretch of the future, and that to the other an extra £1 distributed over the same period would actually have more value than £1 down; but the exchange might take place even though both preferred £1 down to £1 distributed evenly over a given period of the future, if the preference were greater in one case than in the other, and if the man whose preference was the lower possessed £1. For in this case the advantage of present over future command would stand relatively higher on one man's scale than on the other's, and it would be possible to fix on a premium so high that the one man would accept it, and yet so low that the other would pay it. This is exactly what lies at the basis of the ordinary law of the market. In order for an exchange to take place some commodity must stand relatively higher with respect to another commodity on one man's scale than it does on another's, though it may be valued by both; and the man on whose scale it stands relatively lower must possess a supply of it. In the case in hand the things exchanged and to which the parties attach different relative values are a defined command of things in the circle of exchange now, and the same command in the future; or, to put it another way, the thing for sale is the privilege (valued by both men, but not equally) of anticipating future resources.

The extreme suppositions with which we began this

investigation may now be modified. We need not necessarily assume that there are some who have little or nothing in hand but have prospects of incomings in the future, and others that have no prospect of incomings in the future (or after a certain period of the future) but have something in hand. All we need suppose is that there are certain persons whose wealth in hand and wealth in prospect are so proportioned as to give the present a higher relative place on their scales of preference than it occupies on that of certain other persons.

Here, as in any other market, the individual scales might be combined into a communal scale. The possessors of accumulations in relative excess would cede present command of things in the circle of exchange to those who anticipated a relative excess in the continuous stream of their future command of them. On the scales of these latter such future command would stand relatively low, until they had ceded so much of it that equilibrium was reached. If, when the equilibrium point was reached, there was a premium on present command of accumulated wealth, what would this mean? It would mean that those persons who had surrendered a portion of their present wealth, but had also retained a portion, valued the present more than the future, at the existing margins in a ratio at (or just above) that represented by the premium.

It is but natural that amongst those who offer present command in exchange for future command of commodities there should be some who, to begin with, have so large a relative excess of the power of present command that they would, if necessary, pay any one who would enable them to defer exercising it till some future date; and who at the same time so highly value some of this command, that if a certain part of their stock has already been transmuted they would decline to transmute more except on increasingly exacting terms. How much of it they will actually transmute depends on the market price they can realize. When one man transmutes present command of wealth-in-volume to future command of wealth-in-stream, his correspondent effects the reverse transmutation; and therefore the price he pays, which will be the market price of the commodity, is the equilibrating value, on the collective scale, of leave to transmute a stream of wealth that is about to accrue into a volume of wealth that has accrued. This price the seller receives for those portions of his own counter transmutation which he would have paid for being allowed to make, no less than for those portions of it which the premium he receives is only just enough to induce him to make.

And, in like manner, just as the consumer of tea or of any other commodity pays the same price for the increments which satisfy his keenest wants and those which satisfy a want only just keen enough to make the price worth paying, so the man who buys the privilege of transmuting the stream of wealth that will accrue to him in future into a present volume of wealth gets those portions of this privilege which are necessary to make any kind of civilized life possible to him, and those which merely provide him with some relatively slight convenience, at the same price. And that price corresponds to the significance of the least valued exercises of the privilege.

It will be well to note at once (inasmuch as no one can actually give to-day a command of commodities which will not accrue till to-morrow) that what is actually received in return for the exercise of present command can only be a promise; and as the value of the promise (that is to say, the assurance that it will be fulfilled) may vary indefinitely, the question of the price at which the exchange between present and future command of wealth is effected may be indefinitely complicated by questions of insurance or covering or risk; but we have seen that, if we were altogether to eliminate this element of uncertainty, the mere fact that some persons can make credible promises to give future command of wealth, and other persons have actual command of wealth at the moment, is enough to constitute a market. And under given conditions as to the quantity of wealth accumulated and the relative wants of members of the community as to short-time and long-time expenditure, it might happen that a man, by handing over to another his immediate power of calling £100 worth of goods out of the circle of exchange, might receive the right to call for £2 worth of goods every week throughout the course of a year. In that case, at the end he would have called altogether for £104 worth of commodities and services; and the extra £4 would be the price or premium he had received for enabling his correspondent to exchange a stream of wealth about to accrue into a volume of wealth that had accrued.

Now suppose that this man saves the £100 and only spends the £4. He may then be in a position to repeat the transaction and spend another £4 in the course of the next year, and still have his £100; and so on for an indefinite series of years. Moreover, the period of one week is clearly arbitrary. The arrangement might be that the instalments should be paid once a fortnight, once a month, or once a quarter. The person who receives the £100 worth of goods may not be sure exactly when he may find it most convenient to pay his instalments. He may expect to earn larger sums one week than another, and he may find it difficult to pay £2 every week, though he might be sure of being able to pay £26 in the thirteen weeks of the quarter, one week taken with another. He might even wish to be allowed the whole year over which to collect, according to his own circumstances or discretion, the total sum due. Or he might pay small sums quarterly, amounting to the premium and the lump sum at the end of the year. All such variations in the bargain would be matters of convenience and arrangement, and the terms for each might vary. But the general rule is obvious. By hypothesis the present possession of £1 stands marginally higher on the collective scale than the promise of £1 to be paid by instalments in the future and it follows that a promise to pay a sum by instalments, over a given period, stands marginally higher than a promise to pay the sum in a lump at the *end* of the period. But each instalment as it is received will, by hypothesis, be worth more than if the payment of it were to be spread over all that remains of the period. In the limit, therefore, instalments over any period, however short, will be worth more than the whole sum paid in a lump at the end of that period. The man who defers his instalments, and concentrates them at certain points, will therefore have to pay a further premium for being allowed to do so. Thus we could imagine that the man who could get £100 in return for a promise to pay £2 a week for a year (£104 in all, £4 premium and £100 returned) might find that if he wishes to pay his premium quarterly, and to return the lump sum at the end of the year, he would be required to pay 30s. a quarter premium instead of £1, or £6 in the course of the year, and £100 at the end of it. The lender, on his side, might spend his 30s. a quarter premium as he received it and when he got his £100 at the end of the year might repeat the arrangement. In that case he will no sooner receive his £100 back than he will exchange it for a promise of £106, to be paid in instalments of 30s. a quarter and £100 at the end of the year. Then why not accept this promise at once instead of the £100? Why insist on first having the £100 and then exchanging it for the promise instead of accepting the promise at once? If this arrangement is made it may go on indefinitely. The one man may always be liable at the end of every year for £100 to the other man, and may always offer him 30s. a quarter for accepting a promise to pay in a year instead of payment now. Or the terms might be such that the whole transaction may be closed at the end of any quarter if the borrower likes to pay up the whole sum of £101 : 10s., or if the lender chooses to require it.

Such a transaction as we have described, therefore, may be regarded in two lights, either as a hire or as a purchase. If I lend you £100 at 6 per cent., the interest to be paid quarterly, we may either consider that you are paying me 30s. a quarter for the control of £100 worth of goods as long as you retain it (in a word, that you are hiring £100 worth of goods from me), or we may say that at the beginning of the quarter you buy £100 worth of present goods by the promise to pay £101:10s. worth of goods three months hence, and that when the promise becomes due you pay the £1:10s., and substitute for the payment of the other £100 the promise to pay £101:10s. three months hence again; that is to say, the process of borrowing £100 at 6 per cent., the interest to be paid quarterly may be looked upon either in the light of hiring the command of commodities, or in the light of purchasing present commodities in terms of a promise of future commodities. Some writers have laid stress on the theoretical superiority of one or the other of these views, but on this matter we need not trouble ourselves. There may be special transactions which are more conveniently regarded in the one light than in the other; but, broadly speaking, borrowing at interest may be equally well thought of as a species of generalized hire, or as a constantly renewed exchange of present wealth for promises of future wealth. The essential point is that we should recognize the identity of the underlying principle in either case, and should understand that what is hired or bought is the anticipation of resources which the hirer or purchaser himself does not yet command.

We can now perfectly understand that any one who wishes to receive present command of resources in any form, in return for promises to pay a lump sum in the future, on going into the open market and trusting to economic forces to supply his wants, will find that he has to pay a premium in one form or another. He will have to promise more wealth in the future than he receives in the present; and this will be the case whatever the terms of the bargain may be, whether the borrower promises to pay back by instalments, or in a lump sum at the time the lender chooses or at the time he chooses himself.

There are persons, then, who actually control present wealth and desire to increase their control of future wealth, and there are persons who expect to control wealth in the future and desire to increase their control of wealth in the present; and these two sets of people will exchange, on terms, until all their relative estimates of present and future wealth coincide. At that point there will be subjective or vital equilibrium between the marginal value of the unit command of things in the circle of exchange to-day, and the unit command of them at any given period in the future, on each individual's scale; and there will be objective equilibrium between these units on the communal scale. The market in which men buy and sell power to anticipate the command of things in the circle of exchange appears to conform exactly to other markets.

Considerations of national prestige and security make it necessary that every nation should have its own currency, its own supply of money peculiar to itself alone. It would be rather nice if our own government could print and issue American dollars, but what should we say if some impoverished republic started printing pound notes?

Now just as the money circulating inside a country facilitates all the exchanges of goods and services which take place inside that country, so the country's " bank " money facilitates its foreign trade. Although we cannot spend pounds in American shops, and although dollars are not legal tender here, the possession of a supply of pounds does make it possible for a business-man here to buy American goods, just as an American with dollars can buy some of our goods.

Before such a transaction can take place the money must be exchanged for the money of the country supplying the goods. So there is a constant demand, in every busy country, for the currencies of other countries. The money-changer has been seen in the world's markets from very ancient times. In the nineteenth century he dealt in bills of exchange. To-day he makes use of telegraphic transfers of bank balances, and indeed he is a banker himself as often as not.

Sometimes the rate of exchange between two currencies or groups of currencies is altered suddenly and perhaps violently by government fiat, as in the case of the devaluation of sterling in 1949. Leaving aside such action for the time being, *how are exchange rates fixed or varied under normal conditions?* An answer is found in Sir Geoffrey Crowther's book, *An Outline of Money*.

SIR GEOFFREY CROWTHER

EXCHANGE RATES

WHAT causes the rate of exchange to be what it is?
What causes it to move from time to time? . . .

The price of a currency is determined, just as the price of
anything else, by the relative strength of the demand for and
the supply of that currency in the foreign exchange market.
The exact meaning of these terms may be a little hard to
grasp. People in the United Kingdom may want to make
remittances to the United States for any one of hundreds of
reasons. They may want to pay for goods bought, or for
services rendered. They may have a debt to pay in America,
or interest on it. They may wish to buy American securities;
or Americans who have owned British securities, having sold
them, may wish to remit the proceeds home. English people
may wish to send presents of money to their American relatives,
to acquire dollars for the purpose of travelling in the United
States or on American ships, or to pay royalties on American
films. Any one who, having pounds, wishes to exchange them
into dollars, for whatever reason, is " demanding " dollars in
exchange for pounds. Any one who, having dollars, wishes
to exchange them into pounds, for whatever reason, is " offering " or " supplying " dollars in exchange for pounds. The
" demand " for dollars is, of course, the " supply " of pounds,
and the " supply " of dollars is the " demand " for pounds.
When we talk about the relative strength of the demand for,
and supply of dollars in exchange for pounds, we mean the
relation of the number of pounds that are being " offered "
for exchange into dollars to the number of pounds that are
being " demanded " in exchange for dollars.

The reasons which may underlie a demand for or an offer
of a currency are so many and so variable, and the origins of
" demand " are so independent of the origins of " supply "
that it would seem, on the face of it, to be a mere coincidence
if the number of dollars which are offered for sale on any one

day were exactly equal to the number of dollars which were
wanted for purchase. In fact, it is highly probable that the
" demand " and " supply " sides of the market will not be
equal. Nevertheless it is axiomatic that at the end of every
day the number of dollars bought must equal the number of
dollars sold, since every sale of dollars is also a purchase of
dollars by someone else. But if demand and supply were
originally unequal, this eventual equality of bargains accomplished can only be brought about by a change of price, that
is, by a movement of the exchange rate. Let us suppose that
at the close of business on Monday night the dollar-pound
exchange rate was $4·50=£1. Now on Tuesday morning
more people wish to buy dollars for pounds than wish to buy
pounds for dollars at that rate. Since the demand for dollars
in exchange for pounds exceeds the supply, the price of dollars
in terms of pounds will increase and the exchange rate will
move to, say, $4·40=£1. Now some possessors of dollars
who were unwilling to give $4·50 for £1 will be willing to
buy pounds at the cheaper price of $4·40 each. Similarly,
some possessors of pounds who were willing to exchange them
for dollars if they could get $4·50 for each pound, will be
unwilling to do so if they can only get $4·40 for a pound. In
other words, the supply of dollars to be exchanged into pounds
will be increased and the demand for dollars in exchange for
pounds will be diminished. By a process of trial and error
the exchange rate will eventually settle down at the figure
which will make the demand for and supply of dollars equal.
So long as there are more persons anxious to buy dollars on
that day than to sell, the price of the dollar will rise, that is,
the exchange rate will " move in favour of the dollar ". So
long as sellers exceed buyers, the price will fall and the exchange rate will " move in favour of the pound sterling ".

But two currencies cannot be considered in this way in
isolation. At all times when business is being transacted both
in London and in New York, the exchange rate between the
dollar and the pound must be virtually the same in both

centres. If the rate were $4.50 in London and $4.40 in New York, any one would be able to exchange $440 for £100 in the New York market and then re-exchange the £100 into $450 in the London market, making a profit of $10 in ten minutes. The rush to do this would increase the demand for pounds in New York and for dollars in London. The exchange rate would rise in New York and fall in London until the divergence was wiped out. This sort of transaction is given the name of arbitrage, and as there is a large body of skilled arbitrageurs in every centre, keenly on the look-out for the small profits that can be made from temporary divergences, the divergences never last for more than a few minutes.

But arbitrage need not confine itself to two currencies. Let us suppose that the exchange rate between dollar and pound is $5=£1, both in London and New York, the exchange rate between pound and franc is 100 frs.=£1, both in London and Paris, while the exchange rate between franc and dollar is 5 cents=1 fr., both in Paris and in New York. These rates are all in equilibrium, there are no divergences out of which an arbitrageur can make a profit. Now let us suppose that there is suddenly a large payment to be made from London to New York, which increases the supply of pounds relatively to dollars, but does nothing to affect the flow of payments between London and Paris, or between Paris and New York. The increased demand for dollars in London will force the exchange rate down to, say, $4.95 and arbitrage transactions will see that the movement is the same both in London and in New York. But if neither of the rates in which Paris is concerned has moved there will be a profit on three-cornered arbitrage. A sum of £100 in London will still buy 10,000 frs., and 10,000 frs. will still buy $500. But $500, at the new London-New York rate, is now worth slightly over £101. It is therefore profitable to send money chasing round the circle and the arbitrageurs will promptly do so. The supply of pounds relatively to francs will increase, while the demand for dollars in exchange for francs will also increase. The

London-Paris rate will fall to, say, 4.965 cents=1 fr. In other words, the dollar will have risen both in London and in Paris, but more in London than in Paris, while the pound will have fallen more in New York than in Paris, and the franc will have fallen in New York and risen in London. In this way, changes in the conditions of demand and supply between any pair of currencies are communicated to the remainder. If the increased demand in London had been for dollars and francs equally, the pound would have fallen equally relatively to both franc and dollar while the franc-dollar " cross-rate " would not have been affected. We cannot thus accurately speak of the demand for or supply of a currency in exchange for any one other currency. We must think of the demand for or supply of a currency in exchange for all other currencies together.

The fluidity of the foreign exchange market and the incomparable ease with which transactions can be completed in a trice over thousands of miles make it almost impossible to disentangle the causes which are operating at any moment. The root cause of a minute fluctuation in the exchange rates may be the decision of an American magnate to remit $10,000,000 to London to purchase an English business. This is a demand for pounds in exchange for dollars, and even though there has been no change in the mutual relationships of any other pair of currencies, the transaction may leave New York in the shape of a demand for lire, pesos, or pesetas in exchange for dollars, and it may arrive in London in the shape of a demand for pounds in exchange for francs, guilders, or Swedish crowns. All we know is that, as the net result of many movements, the pound is a little higher all round and the dollar a little lower, that the improvement of the pound has been just enough to persuade the holders of, say, about £2,000,000 (assuming the rate of exchange to be in the neighbourhood of $5=£1) to part with it in exchange for a variety of foreign currencies, while the decline in the dollar has been just sufficient to persuade owners of another variety of foreign currencies to exchange them for $10,000,000.

We have now given a formal answer to the question: What determines the rate of exchange? But it is not a wholly satisfying answer to say that a variety of inscrutable decisions, working themselves out in ways which cannot be traced, cause the balance of Demand and Supply to alter and the exchange rates to move. For the small day-to-day movement of the exchanges, this answer must nevertheless suffice. Skilled observers can guess what it is that has made the dollar rise a point or the lira weaken a shade; nobody can *know*. But if we take a view over a longer period we can make some observations about the fundamental factors that lie behind the momentary Demand and Supply and sketch out some of the principles which ultimately determine the relative values of different currencies.

THE VALUE OF CURRENCIES

The reasons which impel people to exchange currencies are, as we have seen, manifold. But it is possible to classify them into three great categories. The first and most obvious category of international remittances is in respect of ordinary trade. " Trade " in this sense does not mean merely the purchase and sale of goods that can be seen and handled. It includes also the purchases and sale of services—the sale of steamer freight, of services to tourists, of insurance, of the right to use patents, and other services of the sort. In fact " trade " includes both " visible " and " invisible " trade.

The second great category relates to movements of capital and interest on capital. Englishmen in the past have invested vast sums of money in foreign countries, by the direct purchase of properties, by the purchase of shares in foreign companies, and by making loans to foreign countries and industrial companies. Whenever interest or dividends are paid on these investments or the original loans are repaid, a payment is made by foreign countries to Great Britain and the demand for pounds is increased. Similarly, whenever a foreigner wishes to make an investment in Great Britain, either by buying a house or factory or by purchasing British securities on the London Stock Exchange, he must first exchange his own money into pounds.

One form of international investment warrants special mention. It was explained [earlier] that bankers are constantly faced with the problem of investing their funds in ways which combine profitability and liquidity in the desired proportions. Part of their funds they customarily lend to the money market, either by direct loans to discount brokers and stockbrokers, or by purchasing bills of exchange and Treasury Bills. Now if, as frequently happens, a higher rate of interest with the same degree of liquidity can be earned in New York than in London, a certain part of the funds of the British banks will be moved to New York. When the rate of interest in New York falls below that in London, these funds will be moved back to London, and will be followed by part of the funds of the American banks. This will only be true, however, if the banks can make sure of getting their money back at the same exchange rate as that prevailing when they lend it, for otherwise they would run the risk of losing more through a movement of the exchange rate than they gained in interest. This is a point to which we shall recur later. In times of trade depression, when safe investments are scarce, or when the future value of individual currencies is doubtful, many private individuals will prefer to keep their capital on deposit in the currency which seems for the moment to be the safest. As such money is in search of security rather than a high rate of interest it will quickly flee from one currency to another. In recent years the amount of this " international short-term capital ", or " hot money ", has grown very large and its movement between the various financial centres has become increasingly rapid.

The third category is that of speculative transactions. People may wish to acquire dollars for no reason other than their belief that the dollar is about to rise in value relative to other currencies; owners of pounds may be anxious to exchange them for other currencies because they fear that the pound is going to fall in value. Nearly every foreign exchange transaction can be fitted into one of these three categories— either it is payment for goods received or services rendered; or else it is a movement of capital for investment or security, or of interest on capital previously invested; or else it is a speculative transaction designed to make a profit, or avoid a loss, out of the movements of the rates of exchange themselves. We may name these three categories " trade ", " capital ", and " speculation ".

Our first category, that of trade, is the only one of the three which is not self-reversing. When the Liverpool cotton broker buys dollars to pay for raw cotton he has bought, there is nothing in the transaction which will lead to a reverse transaction at a later date. It is finished, and whatever influence that exchange of pounds for dollars may have had on the exchange rates is permanent, in the sense that it will not give rise to an opposite effect at a later date. Now this distinction between the categories gives us a most important clue in our search for the principles that determine the relative values of different currencies. So far as day-to-day fluctuations in the rates of exchange are concerned we have to take account of every variety of payment passing. But since " capital " and " speculative " payments sooner or later reverse themselves, we can ignore them when we are considering the permanent or " long run " causes of a currency's value and confine our-selves to " trade " payments alone. If we can discover what determines the size of the payments which a country makes for goods and services bought relative to the size of the payments it receives for goods and services sold, we shall have discovered the origins of the value of that currency relative to others. . . .

Now, it is obvious that one of the very largest of these influences is *price*. People only buy foreign goods when they can get a better article for the same price, or the same article cheaper, than by buying at home. And if foreign goods get cheaper, more of them will be bought. If the general level of prices in Great Britain falls, more British goods will be exported, while fewer foreign goods will be imported into Great Britain, since they will have more difficulty in competing with the home-made goods which have fallen in price. Thus the demand for foreign currencies in payment of imports will decline, while the demand for pounds in payment for British exports increases; the demand for pounds will increase relatively to the supply and the pound will rise in value in relation to other currencies. This series of events applies to a fall of prices in Great Britain only *relatively to* prices in other countries. If foreign prices fall as rapidly as British prices, there is clearly no reason why British exports should increase or British imports decline. Conversely, if British prices remain steady while foreign prices rise, the effects will be the same as those of a fall of British prices. The effects of a relative *rise* of British prices are, of course, the opposite of those of a relative fall: British imports increase and British exports fall off.

This connexion between prices and exchange rates is really a very simple matter. The value of money is measured inversely by prices. When prices are high the value, or purchasing power, of money is low and *vice versa*. Value measured by prices we may call the *internal value* of a currency, while the *external value* of a currency can be taken as measured by the ratio at which it exchanges for other currencies. All, then, that we have been saying is that movements of the *external* value of a currency tend to follow movements of its *internal* value. More accurately, movements in the external value of a currency tend to follow movements in its internal value *relative to the internal value of other currencies*. Or put in still another way, the ratio of exchange between two currencies tends to be the same as the ratio between their respective purchasing powers. This whole theory has accordingly been given the name of the Purchasing Power Parity Theory.

This theory is open to criticism if we try to apply it with mathematical accuracy, but there is much to be said for it. Professor Gustav Cassel, the Swedish economist, made great play with it during the inflationary period which followed the first World War, and he was able to convince most of the European governments of that time that the first step towards a recovery, both in the value of their respective currencies and in international trade, was to balance their budgets. They had to take firm measures to stop the inflationary spiral. With apologies to geometricians, an inflationary spiral can be described as a vicious circle in which prices and profits and some wages go up and up. But we want to know more about this economic whirlwind, and our next question is, *What are the causes and effects of inflation and deflation?*

For the answer we turn to one of Maynard Keynes's *Essays in Persuasion.* In his Preface to this remarkable book the author says that " it might have been entitled ' Essays in Prophecy and Persuasion ' for the *Prophecy*, unfortunately, has been more successful than the *Persuasion.* But it was in a spirit of persuasion that most of the essays were written, in an attempt to influence public opinion." No one can deny Keynes's claim to a clear vision of the future, and indeed if our capitalist system is to survive it will have to take even greater heed of his words and his warnings than it already has done. His central thesis —to quote the Preface again—is " the profound conviction that the Economic Problem, as one may call it for short, the problem of want and poverty and the economic struggle between classes and nations, is nothing but a frightful muddle, a transitory and unnecessary muddle ".

J. M. KEYNES (LORD KEYNES)

INFLATION AND DEFLATION

LENIN is said to have declared that the best way to destroy the Capitalist System was to debauch the currency. By continuing a process of inflation, Governments can confiscate, secretly and unobserved, an important part of the wealth of their citizens. By this method they not only confiscate, but they confiscate *arbitrarily*; and, while the process impoverishes many, it actually enriches some. The sight of this arbitrary rearrangement of riches strikes not only at security, but at confidence in the equity of the existing distribution of wealth. Those to whom the system brings windfalls, beyond their deserts and even beyond their expectations or desires, become " profiteers ", who are the object of the hatred of the bourgeoisie, whom the inflationism has impoverished, not less than of the proletariat. As the inflation proceeds and the real value of the currency fluctuates wildly from month to month, all permanent relations between debtors and creditors, which form the ultimate foundation of capitalism become so utterly disordered as to be almost meaningless; and the process of wealth-getting degenerates into a gamble and a lottery.

Lenin was certainly right. There is no subtler, no surer means of overturning the existing basis of Society than to debauch the currency. The process engages all the hidden forces of economic law on the side of destruction, and does it in a manner which not one man in a million is able to diagnose. . . .

The fluctuations in the value of money since 1914 have been on a scale so great as to constitute, with all that they involve, one of the most significant events in the economic history of the modern world. The fluctuation of the standard, whether gold, silver, or paper, has not only been of unprecedented violence, but has been visited on a society of which the economic organization is more dependent than that of any earlier epoch on the assumption that the standard of value would be moderately stable.

During the Napoleonic Wars and the period immediately succeeding them the extreme fluctuation of English prices within a single year was 22 per cent.; and the highest price level reached during the first quarter of the nineteenth century, which we used to reckon the most disturbed period of our currency history, was less than double the lowest and with an interval of thirteen years. Compare with this the extraordinary movements of the past nine years.[1] From 1914 to 1920 all countries experienced an expansion in the supply of money to spend relatively to the supply of things to purchase, that is to say *Inflation*. Since 1920 those countries which have regained control of their financial situation, not content with bringing the Inflation to an end, have contracted their supply of money and have experienced the fruits of *Deflation*. Others have followed inflationary courses more riotously than before.

Each process, Inflation and Deflation alike, has inflicted great injuries. Each has an effect in altering the *distribution* of wealth between different classes, Inflation in this respect being the worse of the two. Each has also an effect in over-stimulating or retarding the *production* of wealth, though here Deflation is the more injurious. The division of our subject thus indicated is the most convenient for us to follow,— examining the effect of changes in the value of money on the distribution of wealth with most of our attention on Inflation, and next their effect on the production of wealth with most of our attention on Deflation.

(A) Changes in the Value of Money, as Affecting Distribution

(i) *The Investing Class*

Of the various purposes which money serves, some essentially depend upon the assumption that its real value is nearly constant over a period of time. The chief of these are those connected, in a wide sense, with contracts for the *investment of money*. Such contracts—namely, those which provide for the payment of fixed sums of money over a long period of time—are the characteristic of what it is convenient to call the *Investment System*, as distinct from the property system generally.

Under this phase of capitalism, as developed during the nineteenth century, many arrangements were devised for separating the management of property from its ownership.

---

[1] This was written in 1923.

These arrangements were of three leading types: (1) Those in which the proprietor, while parting with the management of his property, retained his ownership of it—*i.e.* of the actual land, buildings, and machinery, or of whatever else it consisted in, this mode of tenure being typified by a holding of ordinary shares in a joint-stock company; (2) those in which he parted with the property temporarily, receiving a fixed sum of *money* annually in the meantime, but regained his property eventually, as typified by a lease; and (3) those in which he parted with his real property permanently, in return either for a perpetual annuity fixed in terms of money, or for a terminable annuity and the repayment of the principal in money at the end of the term, as typified by mortgages, bonds, debentures, and preference shares. This third type represents the full development of *Investment*.

Contracts to receive fixed sums of money at future dates (made without provision for possible changes in the real value of money at those dates) must have existed as long as money has been lent and borrowed. In the form of leases and mortgages, and also of permanent loans to Governments and to a few private bodies, such as the East India Company, they were already frequent in the eighteenth century. But during the nineteenth century they developed a new and increased importance, and had, by the beginning of the twentieth, divided the propertied classes into two groups—the " business men " and the " investors "—with partly divergent interests. The division was not sharp as between individuals; for business men might be investors also, and investors might hold ordinary shares; but the division was nevertheless real, and not the less important because it was seldom noticed.

By this system the active business class could call to the aid of their enterprises not only their own wealth but the savings of the whole community; and the professional and propertied classes, on the other hand, could find an employment for their resources, which involved them in little trouble, no responsibility, and (it was believed) small risk.

For a hundred years the system worked, throughout Europe, with an extraordinary success and facilitated the growth of wealth on an unprecedented scale. To save and to invest became at once the duty and the delight of a large class. The savings were seldom drawn on, and, accumulating at compound interest, made possible the material triumphs which we now all take for granted. The morals, the politics, the literature, and the religion of the age joined in a grand conspiracy for the promotion of saving. . . . [Keynes goes on to show what a good investment consols proved to be.]

Thus there grew up during the nineteenth century a large, powerful, and greatly respected class of persons, well-to-do individually and very wealthy in the aggregate, who owned neither buildings, nor land, nor business, nor precious metals, but titles to an annual income in legal-tender money. In particular, that peculiar creation and pride of the nineteenth century, the savings of the middle class, had been mainly thus embarked. Custom and favourable experience had acquired for such investments an unimpeachable reputation for security.

Before the war these medium fortunes had already begun to suffer some loss (as compared with the summit of their prosperity in the middle 'nineties) from the rise in prices and also in the rate of interest. But the monetary events which have accompanied and have followed the war have taken from them about one-half of their real value in England, seven-eighths in France, eleven-twelfths in Italy, and virtually the whole in Germany and in the succession states of Austria-Hungary and Russia.

Thus the effect of the war, and of the monetary policy which has accompanied and followed it, has been to take away a large part of the real value of the possessions of the investing class. The loss has been so rapid and so intermixed in the time of its occurrence with other worse losses that its full measure is not yet separately apprehended. But it has effected, nevertheless, a far-reaching change in the relative position of different classes. Throughout the Continent the pre-war savings of the middle class, so far as they were invested in bonds, mortgages, or bank deposits, have been largely or entirely wiped out. Nor can it be doubted that this experience must modify social psychology towards the practice of saving and investment. What was deemed most secure has proved least so. He who neither spent nor " speculated ", who made " proper provision for his family ", who sang hymns to security and observed most straitly the morals of the edified and the respectable injunctions of the worldly-wise,—he, indeed, who gave fewest pledges to Fortune has yet suffered her heaviest visitations.

What moral for our present purpose should we draw from this ? Chiefly, I think, that it is not safe or fair to combine the social organization developed during the nineteenth century (and still retained) with a *laisser-faire* policy towards the value of money. It is not true that our former arrangements have worked well. If we are to continue to draw the voluntary savings of the community into " investments ", we must make it a prime object of deliberate State policy that the standard of value, in terms of which they are expressed, should be kept stable; adjusting in other ways (calculated to touch all forms of wealth equally and not concentrated on the relatively helpless " investors ") the redistribution of the national wealth, if, in course of time, the laws of inheritance and the rate of accumulation have drained too great a proportion of the income of the active classes into the spending control of the inactive.

(ii) *The Business Class*

It has long been recognized by the business world and by economists alike, that a period of rising prices acts as a stimulus to enterprise and is beneficial to business men.

In the first place there is the advantage which is the counterpart of the loss to the investing class which we have just examined. When the value of money falls, it is evident that those persons who have engaged to pay fixed sums of money yearly out of the profits of active business must benefit, since their fixed money outgoings will bear a smaller proportion than formerly to their money turnover. This benefit persists not only during the transitional period of change, but also, so far as old loans are concerned, when prices have settled down at their new and higher level. For example, the farmers throughout Europe, who had raised by mortgage the funds to purchase the land they farmed, now find themselves almost freed from the burden at the expense of the mortgagees.

But during the period of change, while prices are rising month by month, the business man has a further and greater source of windfall. Whether he is a merchant or a manufacturer, he will generally buy before he sells, and on at least a part of his stock he will run the risk of price changes. If, therefore, month after month his stock appreciates on his hands, he is always selling at a better price than he expected and securing a windfall profit upon which he had not calculated. In such a period the business of trade becomes unduly easy. Any one who can borrow money and is not exceptionally unlucky must make a profit, which he may have done little to deserve. Thus, when prices are rising, the business man who borrows money is able to repay the lender with what, in terms of real value, not only represents no interest, but is even less than the capital originally advanced.

But if the depreciation of money is a source of gain to the business man, it is also the occasion of opprobrium. To the consumer the business man's exceptional profits appear as the cause (instead of the consequence) of the hated rise of prices. Amidst the rapid fluctuations of his fortunes he himself loses his conservative instincts, and begins to think more of the large gains of the moment than of the lesser, but permanent, profits of normal business. The welfare of his enterprise in the relatively distant future weighs less with him than before, and thoughts are excited of a quick fortune and clearing out. His excessive gains have come to him unsought and without fault or design on his part, but once acquired he does not lightly surrender them, and will struggle to retain his booty. With such impulses and so placed, the business man is himself not free from a suppressed uneasiness. In his heart he loses his former self-confidence in his relation to Society, in his utility and necessity in the economic scheme. He fears the future of his business and his class, and the less secure he feels his fortune to be the tighter he clings to it. The business man, the prop of Society and the builder of the future, to whose activities and rewards there had been accorded, not long ago, an almost religious sanction, he of all men and classes most respectable, praiseworthy, and necessary, with whom interference was not only disastrous but almost impious, was now to suffer sidelong glances, to feel himself suspected and attacked, the victim of unjust and injurious laws,—to become, and know himself half guilty, a profiteer.

No man of spirit will consent to remain poor if he believes his betters to have gained their goods by lucky gambling. To convert the business man into the profiteer is to strike a blow at capitalism, because it destroys the psychological equilibrium which permits the perpetuance of unequal rewards. The economic doctrine of normal profits, vaguely apprehended by every one, is a necessary condition for the justification of capitalism. The business man is only tolerable so long as his gains can be held to bear some relation to what, roughly and in some sense, his activities have contributed to Society.

This, then is the second disturbance to the existing economic order for which the depreciation of money is responsible. If the fall in the value of money discourages investment, it also discredits enterprise.

Not that the business man was allowed, even during the period of boom, to retain the whole of his exceptional profits. A host of popular remedies vainly attempted to cure the evils of the day; which remedies themselves—subsidies, price and rent fixing, profiteer hunting, and excess profits duties— eventually became not the least part of the evils.

In due course came the depression, with falling prices,

which operate on those who hold stocks in a manner exactly opposite to rising prices. Excessive losses, bearing no relation to the efficiency of the business, took the place of windfall gains; and the effort of every one to hold as small stocks as possible brought industry to a standstill, just as previously their efforts to accumulate stocks had over-stimulated it. Unemployment succeeded Profiteering as the problem of the hour.

(iii) *The Earner*

It has been a commonplace of economic text-books that wages tend to lag behind prices, with the result that the real earnings of the wage-earner are diminished during a period of rising prices. This has often been true in the past, and may be true now of certain classes of labour which are ill-placed or ill-organized for improving their position. But in Great Britain, at any rate, and in the United States also, some important sections of labour were able to take advantage of the situation not only to obtain money wages equivalent in purchasing power to what they had before but to secure a real improvement, to combine this with a diminution in their hours of work (and, so far, of the work done), and to accomplish this (in the case of Great Britain) at a time when the total wealth of the community as a whole had suffered a decrease. This reversal of the usual course has not been due to an accident and is traceable to definite causes.

The organization of certain classes of labour—railwaymen, miners, dockers, and others—for the purpose of securing wage increases is better than it was. Life in the army, perhaps for the first time in the history of wars, raised in many respects the conventional standard of requirements,—the soldier was better clothed, better shod, and often better fed than the labourer, and his wife, adding in war time a separation allowance to new opportunities to earn, had also enlarged her ideas.

But these influences, while they would have supplied the

motive, might have lacked the means to the result if it had not been for another factor—the windfalls of the profiteer. The fact that the business man had been gaining, and gaining notoriously, considerable windfall profits in excess of the normal profits of trade, laid him open to pressure, not only from his employees but from public opinion generally; and enabled him to meet this pressure without financial difficulty. In fact, it was worth his while to pay ransom, and to share with his workmen the good fortune of the day.

Thus the working classes improved their *relative* position in the years following the war, as against all other classes except that of the " profiteers ". In some important cases they improved their absolute position—that is to say, account being taken of shorter hours, increased money wages, and higher prices, some sections of the working classes secured for themselves a higher real remuneration for each unit of effort or work done. But we cannot estimate the *stability* of this state of affairs, as contrasted with its desirability, unless we know the source from which the increased reward of the working classes was drawn. Was it due to a permanent modification of the economic factors which determine the distribution of the national product between different classes? Or was it due to some temporary and exhaustible influence connected with Inflation and with the resulting disturbance in the standard of value?

The period of depression has exacted its penalty from the working classes more in the form of unemployment than by a lowering of real wages, and State assistance to the unemployed has greatly moderated even this penalty. Money wages have followed prices downwards. But the depression of 1921-2 did not reverse or even greatly diminish the relative advantage gained by the working classes over the middle class during the previous years. In 1923 British wage rates stood at an appreciably higher level above the pre-war rates than did the cost of living, if allowance is made for the shorter hours worked.

(B) Changes in the Value of Money, as Affecting Production

If, for any reason right or wrong, the business world *expects* that prices will fall, the processes of production tend to be inhibited; and if it expects that prices will rise, they tend to be over-stimulated. A fluctuation in the measuring-rod of value does not alter in the least the wealth of the world, the needs of the world, or the productive capacity of the world. It ought not, therefore, to affect the character or the volume of what is produced. A movement of *relative* prices, that is to say of the comparative prices of different commodities, *ought* to influence the character of production, because it is an indication that various commodities are not being produced in the exactly right proportions. But this is not true of a change, as such, in the *general* price level.

The fact that the expectation of changes in the *general* price level affects the processes of production, is deeply rooted in the peculiarities of the existing economic organization of society. We have already seen that a change in the general level of prices, that is to say a change in the measuring-rod, which fixes the obligation of the borrowers of money (who make the decisions which set production in motion) to the lenders (who are inactive once they have lent their money), effects a redistribution of real wealth between the two groups. Furthermore, the active group can, if they foresee such a change, alter their action in advance in such a way as to minimize their losses to the other group or to increase their gains from it, if and when the expected change in the value of money occurs. If they expect a fall, it may pay them, as a group, to damp production down, although such enforced idleness impoverishes Society as a whole. If they expect a rise, it may pay them to increase their borrowings and to swell production beyond the point where the real return is just sufficient to recompense Society as a whole for the effort made. Sometimes, of course, a change in the measuring-rod, especially if it is unforeseen, may benefit one group at the expense of the other disproportionally to any influence it exerts on the volume of production; but the tendency, in so far as the active group anticipate a change, will be as I have described it. This is simply to say that the intensity of production is largely governed in existing conditions by the anticipated real profit of the entrepreneur. Yet this criterion is the right one for the community as a whole only when the delicate adjustments of interests is not upset by fluctuations in the standard of value.

There is also a considerable risk directly arising out of instability in the value of money. During the lengthy process of production the business world is incurring outgoings in terms of *money*—paying out in money for wages and other expenses of production—in the expectation of recouping this outlay by disposing of the product for *money* at a later date. That is to say, the business world as a whole must always be in a position where it stands to gain by a rise of price and to lose by a fall of price. Whether it likes it or not, the technique of production under a régime of money-contract forces the business world to carry a big speculative position; and if it is reluctant to carry this position, the productive process must be slackened. The argument is not affected by the fact that there is some degree of specialization of function within the business world, in so far as the professional speculator comes to the assistance of the producer proper by taking over from him a part of his risk.

Now it follows from this, not merely that the *actual* occurence of price changes profits some classes and injures others (which has been the theme of the first section of this chapter), but that a *general fear* of falling prices may inhibit the productive process altogether. For if prices are expected to fall, not enough risk-takers can be found who are willing to carry a speculative " bull " position, and this means that entrepreneurs will be reluctant to embark on lengthy productive processes involving a money outlay long in advance of money recoupment,—whence unemployment. The *fact* of falling prices injures entrepreneurs; consequently the *fear* of falling prices causes them to protect themselves by curtailing their operations; yet it is upon the aggregate of their individual estimations of the risk, and their willingness to run the risk, that the activity of production and of employment mainly depends.

There is a further aggravation of the case, in that an expectation about the course of prices tends, if it is widely held, to be cumulative in its results up to a certain point. If prices are expected to rise and the business world acts on this expectation, that very fact causes them to rise for a time and, by verifying the expectation, reinforces it; and similarly, if it expects them to fall. Thus a comparatively weak initial impetus may be adequate to produce a considerable fluctuation.

The best way to cure this mortal disease of individualism must be to provide that there shall never exist any confident expectation either that prices generally are going to fall or that they are going to rise; and also that there shall be no serious risk that a movement, if it does occur, will be a big one. If, unexpectedly and accidentally, a moderate movement were to occur, wealth, though it might be redistributed, would not be diminished thereby.

To procure this result by removing all possible influences towards an initial movement would seem to be a hopeless enterprise. The remedy would lie, rather, in so controlling the standard of value that whenever something occurred which, left to itself, would create an expectation of a change in the general level of prices, the controlling authority should take steps to counteract this expectation by setting in motion some factor of a contrary tendency. Even if such a policy were not wholly successful, either in counteracting expectations or in avoiding actual movements, it would be an improvement on the policy of sitting quietly by whilst a standard of value, governed by chance causes and deliberately removed from central control, produces expectations which paralyse or intoxicate the government of production.

We see, therefore, that rising prices and falling prices each have their characteristic disadvantage. The Inflation which causes the former means Injustice to individuals and to classes,—particularly to rentiers; and is therefore unfavourable to saving. The Deflation which causes falling prices means Impoverishment to labour and to enterprise by leading entrepreneurs to restrict production, in their endeavour to avoid loss to themselves; and is therefore disastrous to employment. The counterparts are, of course, also true,—namely that Deflation means Injustice to borrowers, and that Inflation leads to the over-stimulation of industrial activity. But these results are not so marked as those emphasized above, because borrowers are in a better position to protect themselves from the worst effects of Deflation than lenders are to protect themselves from those of Inflation, and because labour is in a better position to protect itself from over-exertion in good times than from under-employment in bad times.

Thus Inflation is unjust and Deflation is inexpedient. Of the two perhaps Deflation is, if we rule out exaggerated inflations such as that of Germany, the worse; because it is worse, in an impoverished world, to provoke unemployment than to disappoint the rentier. But it is not necessary that we should weigh one evil against the other. It is easier to agree that both are evils to be shunned. The Individualistic Capitalism of to-day, precisely because it entrusts saving to the individual investor and production to the individual employer, *presumes* a stable measuring-rod of value, and cannot be efficient—perhaps cannot survive—without one.

It will perhaps help our comprehension of these connected problems about the value of a currency in terms of goods at home, and in terms of other currencies abroad, if we glance briefly at a modern example of their relationship. Here are some extracts from Sir Stafford Cripps's speech at the Guildhall on October 4, 1949. His announcement of the devaluation of sterling had been made on September 18. The problem which he had to face can be stated quite simply. We were spending more than we were earning, and our capital reserves, being drawn on to meet the deficit, were fast disappearing. But there was practically no unemployment; so why were we not earning enough? Mainly because our goods were too dear to sell in the dollar countries. Our imports were too large by comparison with our exports. But our imports were mainly essential food and raw materials; we could not afford to reduce them. So the only solution was to increase our exports, and the devaluation of the pound, making British and Dominion goods (assuming the Dominion currencies remained linked with sterling) cheaper in the dollar countries, was a necessary step towards this goal.

But this solution would only work provided that the pound was not devalued at home as well. If the devaluation was followed by inflation; if prices and wages, and consequently the costs of our export goods were allowed to rise, there would be no benefit from the devaluation. We should soon be back where we were before devaluation. We have then, in our own case, an excellent example of the answer to the question, *Why must inflation be avoided if exchange rates are to remain stable?*

SIR STAFFORD CRIPPS

DEVALUATION AND THE BUDGET

IT is customary on these occasions for the holder of my office to give some interim account of the country's economic and financial position and to report about the progress of the Budget. In view, however, of the recent debate in the House of Commons and the long and detailed statement that I then made, it would not be appropriate for me to repeat that same theme here on this occasion. Nevertheless the events of September 18 are so recent and so important that I could not pass them over without some further reference.

No Finance Minister can contemplate or bring about a major adjustment in the external value of the currency for which he is responsible without a great deal of thought and of anxiety. Apart altogether from any question of prestige, the effect upon national and international economy is so great, yet so uncertain, that any change must call for the deepest consideration. This is especially so when the currency is, like sterling, a major factor in the trade of the whole world, and one a change in which must affect practically all other currencies.

As the result of two world wars and the tremendous economic changes brought about by them, the world has been living for over three decades now in a state of financial and economic dislocation and uncertainty. We have been aiming all the time at a greater stability upon a new basis, trying to adapt ourselves to the changes that have in fact taken place so as to get from them the maximum benefit for our people and for the world as a whole.

The very widespread readjustment of exchange rates which was set in motion by our action had been discussed, debated, and indeed, almost expected, throughout the world, so that the time had, I believe, arrived when—unless some action had been taken—the damaging state of uncertainty would have continued to the loss of every country of the world. Though the actual date and the degree of change in the sterling exchange rate may have taken people somewhat by surprise— and I am delighted that it did so far as the speculators and profiteers are concerned—no one can suggest that it was a matter suddenly sprung upon an unsuspecting world.

Obviously this decision, though taken by the British Government before the Washington talks, had some relation to those talks both in time and content. It certainly helped in the solution of those other many subject-matters relating to the dollar-sterling difficulties which were there discussed and some of which are still under discussion in the Continuing Committee. That meeting at Washington has already produced some most valuable immediate results by getting rid of difficulties which were preventing us from deriving full benefit from our E.R.P. aid and from proceeding with the liberalization of European trade, to mention only two significant items.

But what was more important, as I have already emphasized, was the spirit of complete understanding and co-operation that ruled throughout, with the result that we were able to tackle a number of long-term matters that had hitherto been but very rarely considered between the parties. For the first time, I think, a clear joint definition of the obligations of debtor and creditor countries was arrived at and made public, based upon a complete understanding of the function and the value of the sterling area in world trade.

Whereas we in this country have had over a period of years to adapt ourselves to a position in which we are overall debtors compared to an overall creditor position before the first world war, the United States has had to adapt itself in exactly the opposite direction. It is a question of converting an essentially protective economy, suitable perhaps for a debtor country, into one where the free import of goods and the free export of capital encourage the high level of trade between the dollar area and the rest of the world, which is an essential basis for the solution of world economic problems. These are great changes which cannot happen in weeks or even in a few months for they demand the creation of a climate of public opinion suitable to their enactment.

[Sir Stafford went on to give some figures of the gold and dollar deficit. For the first quarter of 1949 it had been £82 million; for the second quarter £157 million, and for the third quarter £133 million.]

On September 18, when the exchange rate was altered, our reserves stood at £330 million, so that you will observe that in the 12 days to the end of the quarter they went up by about £20 million, as a result of money reaching this country after the alteration of the exchange rate. That of course is a temporary reversal of the previous trend which we had expected.

These figures are perhaps not so bad as some people may have feared—at least judging by suggestions made during the debate in the House of Commons. But they are quite bad enough and they disclose a continuing state of affairs up to September 18 which could not have been tolerated longer. Even taking the quarter as a whole, the annual rate of deficit is £532 million a year—at the old rate of exchange. An impossible burden, and one which would very rapidly, of course, have exhausted our reserves.

I think the only deduction to be made from these figures is that there is as great and urgent a need as ever there has been to make rapid progress towards diminishing our dollar drain.

Let me now pass to a short review of our budgetary progress. The last Budget presented to Parliament was designed, as you will remember, to encourage a continuing degree of disinflation, not quite so great as in the preceding year, but still substantial in amount. The 1948 Budget had, I think, had considerable success in diminishing the inflationary pressure, but there are certainly signs that that pressure is tending to build up again.

Prices have remained fairly stable—with some decreases and some increases. Industrial production has gone up some 6 to 7 per cent. above that of 1948, but in spite of this the pressure of demand persists. With this rise in production and some fall in the volume of exports we might have expected prices as a whole to fall. They have not. Unemployment has been fractionally lower than it was last year; in August it was only 261,000 against 299,000 a year earlier. These factors certainly do not show any further disinflation in our economy.

There have been suggestions that the Budget expectations are being hopelessly falsified—I am glad to say that this is not the case.

For the first half year the ordinary revenue is running very close to estimate—indeed the current figures are slightly above the proportionate estimate.

On the side of consumption, though the tobacco yield has fallen somewhat, that for beer is steady. The purchase tax is yielding approximately its estimate, while entertainments duty is slighty down, as we should expect with a very dry and warm summer.

On the inland revenue side the yield to date is a little above the proportionate estimate. Profits in 1948 were obviously running at a high level for they have yielded a large sum, though we cannot yet say what the final out-turn will be. Generally speaking, therefore, so far as we can judge from present indications, the estimates of revenue ought not to be far out.

On the expenditure side the outlook is not so good. Below the line expenditure is not far off the proportionate estimate, but above the line it is likely to be exceeded. As a result of obligations under the Atlantic Pact and Western Union, the expenditure on defence is almost certain to exceed the original estimates by quite an appreciable amount. There will also be increased cash requirements by the trading departments for renewal of stocks which have in some cases been run down and may require replacement, and in respect of the higher sterling prices in others, but I hope that most of them will be recouped, though probably not till the next financial year.

The maintenance of the Health Service and the improved conditions of those employed in it, such as nurses and hospital staffs, may also entail some additional expenditure. So that if the balance of the Budget is vitiated, it is more likely to come from increases in expenditure rather than from a shortfall in revenue.

Any such increase in expenditure will have to be compensated for by economies elsewhere or increased revenue if the disinflationary character of the Budget is to be preserved, *as it must be*. To increase our dollar exports and to maintain our home standards of living as far as possible, including the social services which form so important a part of them, we must both produce more and, in one way or another, prevent inflationary pressure from rising and so counteracting all our efforts to improve our situation.

As I said in the House of Commons, with all the emphasis that I could, this demands restraint, in the matter of personal incomes, by everyone in the country. On piece rates or incentive rates, based on production, we want people to earn all they can—the more the better because there'll be more production; it is basic rates that we cannot afford to see increased.

Second, it means putting out our maximum effort both in production and productivity, removing all rules, regulations, or traditions that hamper output in any way.

Third, it means that we must do our utmost to keep down prices by keeping down costs. But when we have got all these things under way we shall still find that we are trying to consume—in various ways—more than we can produce, and that spells inflation.

We can and must therefore reduce consumption in the realm of Government expenditure wherever that is possible without interfering with the scope of any of our essential social services, and also in the field of capital investment. Our social services have been built up over many decades and have been gradually developed under successive Parliaments and they now constitute so real and vital a part of the people's standards that it is as serious a matter to cut them down in scope as it is to cut down wages or salaries. We can stop them developing too quickly and that we shall have to do, but it is quite a different matter to go backwards and reduce their present scope.

People differ widely in their views as to how much inflationary pressure is present in our economy. All I am prepared to say now is that there is undoubtedly some such pressure—and it will probably be increased as the result of recent events. Steps must, therefore, be taken as early as possible to renew the effectiveness of our disinflationary policy, and we must watch continually to judge from time to time how drastic those steps must be.

The major immediate steps to deal with it must, as I have said, be in the area of capital investment and Government expenditure. Reviews of those two fields are now being completed, and within a comparatively short period of time we shall have arrived at our conclusions as to the best way to make the necessary savings. There will, of course, be some decrease in consumption due to the fact that the cost of living will rise without, we hope, any rise in personal incomes. That will be a burden that will fall almost entirely upon the wage-earner and will be felt most heavily by those with the lowest incomes. In these circumstances I feel sure the profit-earner will be willing to make some special contribution to affirm his belief in the principle of equality of sacrifice, and it is for that reason that I am very moderately increasing the profits tax.

This very short review of a few of the more outstanding points of our present economic situation will I hope underline the gravity of that situation as well as the opportunities and possibilities that it presents to all of us to redouble our efforts.

A solution of our difficulties is well within our capacity provided that we are prepared to go all out with our efforts of muscle and of brain; that we are prepared to continue our policy of fair shares in good and bad times alike; that we recognize the need for restraint in the matter of personal incomes and spending, and that we exercise the ingenuity and inventiveness which we as a nation undoubtedly possess.

The climate of international economic opinion is more realistic and more helpful than ever before. We have the advantage of co-operation from North America, from the Commonwealth, and from western Europe. With that co-operation we must, between us—and we shall—solve the world problem of matching the dollar and non-dollar economies. For upon the ability of the democratic nations to solve their economic problems depends the whole future safety and sanity of the world.

We have seen how important international trade is in these days to the welfare of every progressive country, and we have had some glimpse of how complicated and difficult can become the task of trying to foster it. Now let us study it a little closer, not as a factor in monetary policy but just for its own sake. *What is the ideal state of affairs for International Trade?* For the answer we turn to an idyllic picture drawn in *The Science of Wealth* by J. A. Hobson, who used to be a popular University Extension lecturer on Economics, and who wrote a large number of penetrating and progressive books on the subject.

J. A. HOBSON

INTERNATIONAL TRADE

A CENTURY and a half ago a band of British immigrants landing in North America made their way into an extreme southern part of the province of Ontario, where they settled down in a fertile valley traversed by a river, along the banks of which they built the clusters of log-huts that presently grew into a populous and prosperous village. The north side of the river had most of the better grazing land, and a creek running down from the neighbouring hills made it easier to work lumber on that side. But the south side had land more fertile for wheat and better protection for fruit and vegetables. There were specially favourable plots of soil on either side under the shelter of the hills, which took the fancy of some settlers, and other advantages of climate, soil or position, led to special sorts of cultivation and industries connected with them. A few smiths, carpenters, weavers, tailors, shoemakers, settled, according to personal convenience or family connexions, on the north or south side of the stream. Remote from other settlements, this village, with its neighbourhood of farmers, lumbermen, etc., formed a virtually self-supporting industrial community. There was a bridge across the river so that persons and goods passed freely to and fro, and market arrangements enabled every special advantage of soil or position, or any special skill which some artisan or manufacturer might possess, to be most fully utilized for his personal gain and for that of the whole body of customers who were free to buy what he had to sell. Here was a simple example of the economy of division of labour on a basis of free exchange. It was evidently advantageous for the villagers living on either side of the stream that there should be the closest contact and the freest commercial intercourse over the bridge. Anyone suggesting that the bridge should be broken down, or that a toll should be set up for persons and goods passing across, with the object of enabling each side to supply its own needs whenever it seemed possible to do so, would have been dubbed a lunatic.

Now it came to pass, after the American revolution had led to the establishment of the Republic, that a delimitation of frontiers between Canada and the new United States took place, in which the river passing through our village was a boundary line. Politically the village was cut in two. The inhabitants of the northern part remained Canadian citizens, obeying the laws and paying the taxes of Ontario as heretofore, the inhabitants of the southern part became citizens of the United States. In process of time the political severance would possibly affect the feelings of the two sets of villagers towards one another and lead to a diminution of social intercourse. But could it make that division of labour and that freedom of exchange, which were advantageous formerly, less advantageous? Would it be any less damaging than before to break down that bridge, or to put a toll upon the produce which sought a market across the stream? It would indeed be feasible, as it was before, to break the economic community into two, following the line of the river. But it would be just as evident that every person who had anything to sell would have only half the market he had before, while for everything he wanted to buy he was similarly restricted in the supply available to him. It might be possible for all the villagers to supply themselves with all they needed by dealing with neighbours on their own side of the stream, but they evidently lose their share of the natural advantages or special skill belonging to some villagers upon the other side, and the new restrictions on the market for the things which they are in a superior position to make, rob them of part of the fruits of their own industry. Each village manifestly loses, both as buyer and as seller, by any impediment put upon that free intercourse which existed before.

The political division does not affect the true economy of industry. It was advantageous before that the young men and women who grew up on the north side should be perfectly free to take up land or a trade upon the south side if a better opportunity presented itself there than on their own side. Such liberty of movement evidently led to a better development of the whole district, an advantage in which all would share. Similarly, if any thrifty farmer on the south had laid by a sum of money and saw a better use for his savings by putting up a saw-mill on the north side, instead of starting some less likely business on his own side, it would evidently be detrimental to the interests of all the villagers on either side to stop him from this most profitable use of his capital. For they would all gain more by the cheaper timber his saw-mill would supply than by any other use to which he could put his savings through employing them upon his own side of the stream. Under such circumstances any interference with the free flow of labour or capital is seen to be as injurious as any interference with freedom of markets. For the inhabitants of either or both sides to adopt a law of settlement which kept the growing population to its own side of the frontiers, or restrictions upon the export of timber or machinery or other sorts of " capital ", or by a tariff to prohibit or impede the importation of commodities which could be produced better or more cheaply on the other side, would manifestly be a suicidal policy.

If the villagers upon the north out of some mistaken patriotism adopted such a policy of exclusion, they could damage the villagers of the south. But they would damage themselves to a somewhat greater extent, because the costs of collecting the tolls, keeping out smugglers and administering the whole protective policy, would fall on them. Supposing, however, that they were so foolish as to attempt this economic separation, would the villagers of the south be well-advised in their turn to meet the injury inflicted on them by copying the exclusion policy? Why should they stop northern capital which sought to come in and develop their resources from doing so, or stop skilled labour from crossing the stream to help northern capital in their advantageous work? Why should they prevent their villagers from getting the better or cheaper produce which the northerners still sought to supply? To follow the bad example of the north would be to double the injury for their citizens as well as for the others, and to saddle themselves with the same costs of administering the exclusive policy.

So long as the village was all inside Ontario, it was quite obvious that the fullest co-operation among all its members, by division of labour, freedom of markets and full liberty of movement for capital and labour, was conducive to the common welfare of the village as a whole and of each section of it. It might be true that the soil and other natural conditions were upon the whole much more favourable on the south than on the north, and that consequently the young labour and the new savings went chiefly to the development and settlement of that section. But it would be quite evident that the villagers who stayed on the northern side were not made worse off but better off, by reason of the fuller development of the better resources on the southern side, and that if any foolish sentiment had operated to keep their young labour and the savings from seeking more profitable employment across the river, they would have been heavy losers. Now this evident economy could not be reversed or even modified by the purely political event which split the little industrial community into two political communities. What was good business before would remain good now, and any political interference with the liberty of movement for men and goods would evidently injure business. For if either of the sections of the village could be advantaged by restrictions upon free movements of men or goods, it might equally be argued that further barriers between the two parts of the north divided by the creek which ran into the river would be serviceable, at any rate to one part of the north, and this policy of subdivision might be carried so far as to make each street and finally each family a self-contained individual community.

This illustration will suffice to set forth the simple and sound doctrine of industrial and commercial relations between nations. What these two sections of the frontier village are to one another, are also the two nations to which they relatively belong, Canada and the United States. If an unimpeded flow of capital and labour and products is advantageous for both sides of the divided village, so is it for the two nations. And what is true for Canada and the United States is true for any other nations, whether possessing a common frontier or not. The inhabitants of every country benefit by the freest possible intercourse with all other countries, for in that way they can get most wealth, utilizing most completely and effectively any special qualities of natural resources or acquired skill they may possess, and sharing by exchange the similar advantages which the inhabitants of other countries possess.

We have there the case for Free Trade and, as the schoolboy said, it is obviously "better than perfection". The great lead which Britain took in the industrial race of the nineteenth century made Free Trade the best policy for that country for a great number of years. But other countries, including the young Dominions, found excellent reasons for not being Free Traders. They wanted to build up their own industries, and they could only do so behind a protective tariff wall. The Dominions tried to persuade the government of Britain to impose a general tariff, and then to reduce this for goods coming in from the empire. Alfred Deakin, the great Australian Premier, came to

Britain in 1907 to press this case. He failed, but a quarter of a century later the wisdom of his arguments was confirmed by events, and the Imperial Preference for which he had worked so long and so vainly, became the accepted British policy. *What brought about Britain's departure from her traditional policy of Free Trade?* For the answer we quote the famous speech by Neville Chamberlain delivered in the House of Commons on February 4, 1932. His speech gives a very practical illustration of the importance and of the fundamental accuracy of the theories outlined by our economists.

NEVILLE CHAMBERLAIN

RESTORING THE BALANCE OF TRADE

A GREAT exporting country like ours is forced to look overseas for a great part of its trade. That catastrophic fall in the gold prices of commodities which has been taking place and which, as yet, shows no signs of having reached bottom, has brought world trade into a truly deplorable condition. One of the first signs of this distress in world trade is the extraordinary growth of trade restrictions.

There is hardly any device, ranging from sur-taxes to quotas, which has not been applied by one country or another, and there has sprung into existence in many places so-called systems of reasoned control, planned on high protection lines, which have raised almost impassable barriers to the normal trading relations. Then there is that great problem which keeps Europe, or a great part of Europe, in a constant state of doubt and anxiety, the problem of reparations and War debts, still unsettled. Recent events in the Far East have raised a new source of anxiety, and he would be a bold man who would prophesy to-day what may be the repercussions of those events in other countries far removed from their centre.

The figures of unemployment still remain of colossal dimensions, and we must naturally look forward to some increase in the figures in succession to the usual seasonal activities at

Christmas time. The main industries of the country are very slow to move. Iron and steel remain in a stagnant condition; shipping and agriculture are still in the depths of depression. The effect of the depreciation of the pound, which at first seemed to hold out hopes of increased facilities for trading abroad, is being gradually whittled away, as one country after another has been departing from the gold standard, and although, as I have already pointed out, the pound has remained wonderfully steady over a long period, we cannot feel that confidence can be fully re-established while the trade balance remains so heavily against us. While we may admire and praise the public spirit of our taxpayers, we must not suppose that they can indefinitely be called upon to make sacrifices of this extent, or that the State can go on extracting such vast sums from the pockets of the people without seriously crippling the resources from which industry must be fed if it is to maintain its vitality.

These are the sort of considerations which have been under the examination of the Government, and we have given them careful and anxious consideration. Some of our problems are international in character, and can only be dealt with by the willing co-operation of other nations, and the best that we can do is to use such influence as we may possess to induce those who share our views to help with us in trying to put them into operation.

But there are others which are within our own control, and in particular, in accordance with the undertaking of the gracious Speech from the Throne, we have devoted ourselves to the consideration of this problem of the balance of trade, which to a country like ours, dependent to a large extent upon overseas for its supplies of foodstuffs and raw materials, must always be one of the very first importance. I am sorry to say that our investigations into the balance of trade have confronted us with disquieting results. The Committee is no doubt familiar with the way in which this balance of trade, or perhaps I should more properly call it this balance of payments, is dealt with. There are three sets of figures in question. There are the figures of the imports of merchandise, the figures of the exports of merchandise, and then there are what are known as invisible exports, consisting of the income from shipping, the income from foreign investments, the receipts from short interest and commissions, and some other minor items. The calculation is made by deducting the value of the exports from the value of the imports, leaving a surplus, against which is set off the value of the invisible exports.

If I give figures to the Committee of two years, 1929 and 1931, they will see how rapid and how disastrous has been the change. I must say that the figures for 1931 are not yet absolutely final, but they may be taken as a very close approximation to the truth. In 1929 the value of imports less exports, that is, of the surplus of imports over exports, was £382 million. The value of the invisible exports was £482 million, leaving a favourable surplus of exactly £100 million. In 1931 the surplus of imports over exports was £409 million, but the invisible exports were only £296 million, leaving an adverse balance in the neighbourhood of £113 million. In two years, therefore, the balance of payments had gone against us to the extent of over £200 million. But that is not the whole story, because I must point out that the value in prices of imports fell off far more than the values of exports. In order, therefore, to make a proper comparison, one must value the figures of 1929 at the prices of 1931 to see what is the change of volume, which, after all, is the thing that matters for the employment of our people. If that correction is made, we find that while the imports remained practically stationary for the two years, the volume of exports decreased by nearly 38 per cent.

I submit to the Committee that those figures establish the vital necessity for any action which it is in the power of the Government to take which may restore the balance of payments once more to the right side. It will not have escaped the notice of hon. members that the shrinkage in the invisible exports amounted to no less than £186 million, nearly the whole amount of the difference. Unfortunately that is the one of the three sets of figures which it is least possible for the Government to influence, because the bulk of the invisible exports comes from the receipts from shipping and from foreign investments, and both of those things must depend upon world and not upon home trade. Therefore we are driven back to the two remaining items, the items which, as I have already shown, were dealt with by the Prime Minister in his election manifesto. We had to put to ourselves the problem: How are we at one and the same time to diminish our imports and to increase our exports?

It is a complicated problem, and one that has to be attacked from many angles, because it is hardly possible to find a proposal which will advance one of these two objects without its having some reaction and without its affecting the other. The effect of the too sudden closing of the market of this country for one class of goods from another country may easily produce such a reduction in the purchasing power of one of our customers in another class of goods as to have serious results upon our export trade. If we are to increase our exports, we must necessarily contemplate that at the same time there must be an increase in imports, because it is certainly the case that the raw materials required for increased exports would not be producible in our own country. A revenue derived from a tariff may assist industry by relieving it of some of the burdens which now press so directly and so harshly upon it, but if we are to try to increase our exports by lowering our tariff either to foreign countries or to the countries of our own Empire, by so much we must immediately lower the revenue which otherwise would have been obtained from those duties.

In fact, the actions, the interactions, and the reactions of all these things—home trade, export trade, revenue, direct taxation, tariff, cost of production—are simply endless, and the reflection that is forced upon one is that, in any scheme which we may put forward for dealing with the situation, there must always be a balancing of advantages and disadvantages. What we have to seek for is a plan which will be flexible and elastic, a plan which can readily be varied and adapted to suit changing conditions, a plan which will allow first one element and then another element to come forward according as the balance of advantage lies on this side or on that. It is for such a plan that, with unremitting labour and concentrated attention, the Government have been seeking during the recess. . . .

Before I come to the details of the Government's intended measures, I think perhaps it would be convenient if I were to try to give to the Committee a very brief summary of the objects at which we are aiming in order that they may perhaps get a better picture of the general scope and range of our intentions.

First of all, then, we desire to correct the balance of payments by diminishing our imports and stimulating our exports.

Then we desire to fortify the finances of the country by raising fresh revenue by methods which will put no undue burden upon any section of the community.

We wish to effect an insurance against a rise in the cost of living, which might easily follow upon the unchecked depreciation of our currency.

We propose, by a system of moderate protection, scientifically adjusted to the needs of industry and agriculture, to transfer to our own factories and our own fields work which is now done elsewhere, and thereby decrease unemployment in the only satisfactory way in which it can be diminished.

We hope by the judicious use of this system of protection to enable and to encourage our people to render their methods of production and distribution more efficient.

We mean also to use it for negotiations with foreign countries which have not hitherto paid very much attention to our suggestions, and at the same time we think it prudent to arm ourselves with an instrument which shall at least be as effective as those which may be used to discriminate against us in foreign markets.

Last, but not least, we are going to take the opportunity of offering advantages to the countries of the Empire in return for the advantages which they now give or in the near future may be disposed to give to us.

In that summary, under seven heads, we believe that we have framed a policy which will bring new hope and new heart to this country and will lay the foundations of a new spirit of unity and co-operation throughout the Empire. The basis of our proposals is what we call a general *ad valorem* duty of 10 per cent. upon all imports to this country, with certain exceptions to which I shall allude directly. The purposes of that general duty are twofold. We desire to raise by it a substantial contribution to the revenue, and we desire also to put a general brake upon the total value of the imports coming in here. Of course, if our sole object were the reduction of imports we might achieve that purpose by a different method. We could take certain particular items and exclude them altogether. That would be a method which would bring about the greatest possible disturbance of trade, and in introducing a fundamental change of this character we naturally desire to do it with as little dislocation of existing arrangements as may be found necessary.

There are, however, certain exceptions to that rate. Wherever there is an existing duty the article so dutiable will not be subject to the 10 per cent., and that applies equally to such duties as those on tobacco or sugar or coffee, to the so-called McKenna Duties, to the Safeguarding Duties, the key industry duties, and also to the duties under the two Acts which I mentioned before, the Abnormal Importations and the Horticultural Products Acts, until those Acts expire, when they will be replaced by the flat-rate duty unless some other arrangement is made, of which I shall make mention again directly. There is also a free list, of no great length, which will be included in a Schedule to the Bill. I do not propose this afternoon to go through the free list, but I may give some indication to the Committee and mention one or two of the most important items which are included in it.

In the free list will appear wheat in grain. The Committee is aware that it is the intention of the Government to deal with the importation of wheat by means of a quota system. There is also meat, which includes bacon—one of the staple foods of the people—and fresh fish of British taking, which I am advised includes also those members of the mollusca and crustacea which are such an ornamental addition to our dinner table.

There will also be found in the free list the raw materials of two great textile industries, raw cotton and raw wool; and then there is tea, and I think I ought to tell the Committee that tea is put into the free list of this Bill because it is considered that it would be more convenient to deal with tea in conjunction with other beverages, such as coffee and cocoa, in the ordinary course of the Budget. I must also warn the Committee that they must not assume that that means that tea is going to be or is not going to be taxed in the next Budget, because that is a subject upon which I must reserve a doctor's mandate until Budget Day comes.

I now pass to the superstructure which it is proposed to build upon the *ad valorem* duties. That superstructure takes the form of additional duties which may be imposed upon non-essential articles, and when I say non-essential articles I mean either articles of luxury which are not essential to the individual or articles which are not essential to the nation in the sense that they either can be now or could be very shortly produced at home in substantial and sufficient quantity. We do not propose to specify these additional duties in the Bill; we propose that these duties may be imposed by Order of the Treasury after consultation with the appropriate Department, which will be the Board of Trade or the Ministry of Agriculture or other Departments concerned. But the Treasury will not take the initiative in this matter. It would be extremely undesirable to put the selection of articles to be made dutiable or the rates of duty to be levied, into the discretion of a single minister. I am quite sure that his life would very soon be made intolerable by the demands which would be addressed to him, but in addition to that it might be thought that the decisions of such a minister had been influenced by political considerations.

Accordingly, it is proposed to set up an independent advisory committee, consisting of a chairman and not less than two, or more than five, other members. . . .

I now come to the position of the Empire countries in connexion with this change in our fiscal system. The Committee is aware that next July the Imperial Conference is to be held in Ottawa, when the economic relations of the members of the British Commonwealth will be discussed. His Majesty's Government attach the utmost importance to that Conference, and they intend to approach it with a full determination of promoting arrangements which will lead to the greater increase of inter-Imperial trade. I have no doubt that the Dominions would no more question our right to impose duties in our own interests with the object either of raising revenue or of restricting imports than we have questioned theirs to do the same, but considerations of that kind have to be weighed against the advantages to be obtained from preferential entry into Dominion markets, even though they should involve some surrender of revenue or some lessening of the reduction of imports; and since until we meet the Dominion representatives we shall not be in a position to estimate the advantages or the disadvantages on either side, and since we desire to mark at every stage our wish to approach this Conference in the true spirit of Imperial unity and harmony, we have decided that so far as the Dominions are concerned—and in this arrangement we include India and Southern Rhodesia also—neither the general nor the additional duties shall become operative before the Ottawa Conference has been concluded.

After the Conference its results can be embodied in whatever modification of these duties may have been agreed upon. I am confident that this decision of his Majesty's Government will be welcomed by the Dominions in the same spirit in which it has been made. . . .

The Colonies, the Protectorates, and the Mandated Territories are in a somewhat different position from that of the Dominions. They lie, for the most part, in tropical or semitropical latitudes; they have scarcely any manufactures of importance; and their products, which are for the most part fruits and vegetables, seeds, and nuts used for expressing oils, and fibres, are not of a kind which compete with the home products of this country. Anyone who has visited those parts of the British Empire will know that they are characterized by an intense loyalty to the British connexion. In their times of prosperity they have always been large buyers of British goods, partly by means of voluntary preferences on the part of the inhabitants, partly by means of preferences deliberately arranged in their fiscal system. . . . We propose that all produce from all Colonies, Protectorates, and Mandated Territories shall be completely exempt from either the general or the additional duties. We have confidence that this great new departure in British policy will be most warmly welcomed throughout the Empire. I have no doubt it will evoke an immediate response, but I attach even greater importance to the stimulation of the prosperity and the increased purchasing power of customers of ours who have shown that they always had the will, if they have not always had the power, to buy the bulk of their requirements from the Old Country.

I should like to touch for a moment on the provisions in connexion with trade with foreign countries. They are of two kinds. The first deals with the case where the treatment accorded to goods coming from this country as compared with that accorded to goods coming from other countries amounts to discrimination against the United Kingdom. The Board of Trade will be authorized, with the concurrence of the Treasury, to impose a duty which may amount to as much as 100 per cent. in addition to the existing duties upon any goods coming from the offending country which may be specified in the Order. I am sure we all hope it will never be necessary to put that provision into operation. On the other hand, I think the Committee will be inclined to agree with me that we are less likely to have causes of complaint of this kind in future if we have the power to extend the principle of reciprocity to which I have alluded.

The second provision is designed to facilitate the lowering of tariff barriers in foreign countries by offering to reduce our own in return for an advantage of that kind. In this case also the initiative lies with the Board of Trade, which will conduct the negotiations, and on a recommendation from the Board of Trade the Treasury will have the power to direct the removal or the fixing at a lower rate of any goods from the particular country concerned which may be specified in the order. We attach a good deal of importance to this provision as a bargaining factor. I should like to take the opportunity of stating clearly that we do not intend to conclude any arrangements of this kind with any foreign country until we have made our agreements with the Conference at Ottawa.

There is one point to which, as in duty bound, we have throughout devoted our particular and serious attention—namely, the avoidance of anything that might entail a serious rise in the cost of living. After careful calculation, checked over and over again by competent observers, we have satisfied ourselves that there is no danger of anything of the kind in our proposals. There are at present very large stocks of food-stuffs in the world which are being pressed upon the market by the sellers at prices which have very little relation to their cost of production. But apart from that, and apart also from the effect that a tariff may be expected to have upon the value of sterling, our calculations have convinced us that there is no likelihood under these proposals that the cost of living could rise to a higher level than has already been attained more than once in the course of the last eighteen months. But I hope the Committee will not forget that really the essential point is the value of sterling, and if by our proposals we can correct the adverse balance of trade, if we can attract foreign capital to come to this counrty to be invested in British factories, if we can check the withdrawal of foreign short-term balances by the restoration of confidence, then indeed we shall have got a most valuable insurance against a rise in the cost of living which might well be far greater than anything that could conceivably come out of the imposition of a tariff. If there be any here who will say that we are not going fast enough, and who would seek to plunge us headlong into a system of high protection, I would say to them that these proposals do not represent a compromise between protectionists and free-traders. In fact we are not agreed. These proposals represent a carefully thought out plan, one which we who believe in the proposals, we who belong to different parties believe to be in the best interests of the nation and best adapted to its present condition and to its present relations with the world as it exists to-day. It may be, I dare say it is, imperfect in its details, but I am convinced that it will be accepted by reasonable men as a practical working plan by which we may gradually hope to rebuild the prosperity of our country.

Now I hope I may be excused if I touch one personal note. There can have been few occasions in all our long political history when the son of a man who counted for something in his day and generation has been vouchsafed the privilege of setting the seal on the work which the father began, but had perforce to leave unfinished. Nearly twenty-nine years have passed since Joseph Chamberlain entered upon his great campaign in favour of Imperial Preference and Tariff Reform. More than seventeen years have gone by since he died without having seen the fulfilment of his aims, and yet convinced that, if not exactly in his way, in some modified form his vision would eventually take shape. His work was not in vain, but

time and the misfortunes of the country have brought conviction to many who did not feel that they could agree with him
then. I believe he would have found consolation for the bitter-
ness of his disappointment if he could have foreseen that these
proposals, which are the direct and legitimate descendants of
his own conception, would be laid before the House of Commons which he loved in the presence of one and by the lips of
the other of his two immediate successors by whom his name
is carried on.

We have seen how time brings its changes to the financial policy
of a country. Financial policy must always be dependent on other
factors over which it has little or no control. *Why is it that Politics
is now largely a question of Economics?*

The answer is given in the following extract from Walter Elliot's
Rectorial Address to Aberdeen University in 1934. It will not only
help us to understand why the idyllic picture sketched by Hobson is an
impossibility in the world of to-day; it will also serve to introduce the
next section of our enquiry, in which we shall try to discover how far
the practical application of economic principles can promote the welfare
of the state.

WALTER E. ELLIOT

THE ENDLESS ADVENTURE

GOVERNMENTS to-day find that the most insistent of
their problems at home are the relations of the State—
the community as a whole—to the groups and individuals concerned in the production and distribution of wealth within
their boundaries. Abroad, they find problems more insistent
still, from contacts with other States, other Governments,
throughout the world. Governments, and States, are no longer
merely geographical or political units, but are economic units

which every kind of intercourse—industrial, agricultural, or commercial—has to take into consideration.

Some say that this is due to the War, and some that it is due to madness amongst rulers, which will shortly disappear. It is not so. It is a development inherent, but concealed, in the whole industrial development of the last 150 years which we call the Industrial Revolution. It could not have been averted, and cannot be averted, without a complete transformation of the psychological make-up of the average mortal. We may rule a psychological transformation out of account for our immediate future, and deal with men as they are.

If the problems with which we are dealing are really inherent in the structure of our century, and not merely madness, they demand the most meticulous examination. Is there any factor specially producing a change in our outlook to-day? Yes. One in particular. Production to-day is becoming decentralized, international trade becomes less and less an interchange of specialized lines of production, and more and more a competition on similar lines. This is in sharp contrast to the trend of international trade in the last hundred years, when production became highly specialized, and centralized itself in a small group of industrial areas and nations. This change comes about partly from ordinary human desires, and partly from the powers of modern science. The ordinary human cause is simply that no one likes to admit that he is unable to do something that he sees to be within the powers of his neighbour. Furthermore, unemployment, which is merely one of the signs of the increasing leisure of our times, makes it less important that everything should be done at the maximum possible speed (and only at this speed), and allows, and indeed compels, the idle hands to try out continually something or anything they can do. These experiments require the concurrence of the consumer as well as the producer, since cheapness is not to be the final criterion. The consumer can only give his consent through his political organization, which is the State. Thus the national unit is born.

The powers of modern science tend to ensure that, given determination, it becomes more and more feasible for the old specialized lines to be produced anywhere in the world, or to be replaced by others just as good. Thus the national unit becomes possible. I do not say desirable, but it does become possible.

It is vital to grasp this. We have been told so often that the whole world is every day becoming more and more interdependent that we are apt to brush aside any examination of the points where that is not true. But there are many points where it is not true. Any parroting of formulae will lead us to disaster, since situations change and formulae remain the same. The formula of the continually increasing interdependence of the world requires qualification as much as any other. You have heard that formula so often that you will not believe there is another side to it unless I give you examples.

I will give you three, drawn literally from the air around us. In the nineteenth century a great trade was built up with South America in a new and important commodity—nitrate for fertilizer. Ships were built, sailed the ocean to the coasts under the Andes, the nitrate was brought home, spread on our fields, production increased, and all, including the economists, were happy. Steel rails went out and nitrate came back, import and export returns went up, large fortunes were made in financing loans to the countries abroad which produced the nitrate, international lending improved, and the economists were happier still. Meanwhile, the scientists were at work— ignorant fellows who had never read the beautiful arguments about international trade. " Air " they said " is mostly nitrogen. There is thus a column, mainly of nitrogen, between forty and sixty miles in height, balanced on every one of the fields to which this nitrate is being so laboriously carried. . . . Do you really want nitrates? " they said to Europe. And Europe said, " Why, naturally ". And the scientists said, " Do you mind if we get it at home? " And the agriculturists said (in a low voice so as not to be overheard by the economists),

"Not at all". Meanwhile the loans floated, and the ships sailed, and fought their way out from Liverpool to Cape Horn under a canopy of nitrogen nine thousand miles long and sixty miles deep, battled round Cape Horn against a torrent of nitrogen blowing at fifty miles an hour, loaded up in South America with nitrogen, came spinning home on the wings of the wind, 78 per cent. nitrogen, all the way to Britain again—till suddenly a scientist turned a switch, an electric arc began to sizzle, and nitrate began to fall like snow out of the air upon the very regions to which these ships were hurrying. Now, was this good for Trade? It was good for production. It was bad for Trade. Europe was henceforward self-contained, if it desired, for nitrate fertilizers. And note that this was brought about without either lowering the quality of the nitrate—for nitrogen is nitrogen all the world over—or lowering the standard of living of those who used it. For it was cheaper than ever.

You will see the same factors at work to-night if you look inside and outside any one of half a dozen shops in Union Street. Electric-light bulbs within the shop typify the interdependence of humanity, the whole illumination coming from a filament of heated tungsten or some other rare-metal alloy, only to be obtained in some distant corner of the earth after the floating of the appropriate loan, and the building of the appropriate railway, with its appropriate Ordinary Shares, its First Preference, its Second Preference, and all the other appropriate preliminaries to default. But look outside the shop and see a dazzling electric light of a novel kind—the Neon sign. Neon is a constituent of the air about us—there is enough neon in this hall to light it all for ever, and as fast as it is carried away more will flow in to take its place. I do not say that the problems of lighting have all been solved in this sense yet, or that filament lamps will become obsolete and never be used again. But I do say that it is the old lamp and not the new which demands interdependence of nations, international lending, and all the paraphernalia of the nineteenth-century economics which was handed out to the people like a revelation from Sinai.

I do not need to detain you with the third example in detail. I need only say that the chemists are now handling artificial plastics, the new artificial resins and gums, by which they make a wood of their own which can be moulded and cut and hold its form and texture for ever—a wood which was originally not even gum, but gas, acetylene gas such as we used to burn in the headlights of our motor-bicycles, and such as we can produce anywhere where there is chalk and coal, so that we need worry no more about walnut or maple, or the mahogany which took our forefathers to the West Indies.

There is yet another whole section of the world's work where interdependence is no such certain sequence as it was once assumed to be. That is the section of foreign investment.

I do not wish to develop this theme, for we are discussing government and not finance. But these factors, the power of science to make anything anywhere, the determination of men to try everything everywhere, and a growing doubt as to whether foreign loans in many parts of the world are not simply free gifts which we should do as well to keep for ourselves, have produced and are producing a change so fundamental in our outlook that it might almost be described as the third stage of the Industrial Revolution. The first stage was, so to speak, the drilling of a bore hole and the tapping of a great subterranean source of power by the people who made this venture. The second, which we have just lived through, was the piping off of that power to undeveloped nations as capital development, financed by unrepaid loans. The third stage is the check and flood-back as the bore-holes in other countries strike oil in their turn, and the pipes begin to fill up from the far end also.

That is only half the problem. The other half is the problem of citizenship. The general explanation of to-day's crisis as " the War " and " the madness of rulers " are only valid in so far as the War, by opening a volcano of destruction, stimulated the pace of development everywhere, and in so far as " the madness of rulers " has not yet found a way by which people will sit with folded arms and see their work, by which they mean their place as citizens, carried out by others. The psychological reconstitution necessary for the smooth working of that process has not even been envisaged by the pundits who cheerfully advocate courses which would make it essential.

The Endless Adventure of government has become the problem of problems, the real riddle of the Sphinx.

The reason for this is immediate fear, fear both of war and of peace. There is an atmosphere of insecurity throughout the world which weighs on us all. That atmosphere of insecurity comes from the 20 million unemployed far more than from any other single cause. The fear which unemployment spreads has deep and widespread roots—the fear of losing man's place as a citizen far more, I believe, than the fear of privation. Because of the psychological effects of unemployment, States determine to keep their people at work even when that work can demonstrably be done more cheaply in other places and by other hands. Partly because the world is so large, partly because the processes of industry and finance are so difficult to follow through, and so impossible for the experts to explain (in any fashion upon which they will all agree), the movement towards smaller self-contained units, as against the World-Unit or World-Market, has recently spread very fast. Indeed the conscious defence of a self-contained isolation has begun, a philosophy which has been called Autarchy, or self-organization, with, as a unit, the Autarchic State. It is because in these smaller units a man feels more assured of his place as a citizen. We need not sneer if he dresses himself in some special uniform and goes through some special ritual gestures. He feels that at any rate he is differentiated from the 1800 millions of the world's inhabitants, and that, if trouble comes, his crowd, his chaps, his comrades, his gang, will not let him down.

The best criticism of this doctrine, so far, comes from the typists, those mirrors of the subconscious, who usually metamorphose the title word into "The Antarctic State" or "The Autarchaic State", both very revealing epithets. They are perhaps unnecessarily harsh.

Organization is essential if we are to meet the uneasiness and insecurity of the present day. But organization must choose some field within which to organize. The alternatives are to organize the whole world at once, or to organize smaller units and gear them up to each other as soon as time and hard thinking will permit. Those of us who are working at this task now have to use both methods.

Clearly the lesson of facts is that home development in agriculture, in industry, in employment, is essential and inevitable. We have to make certain that it does not mean the shutting down of intercourse overseas. But that will require thought and forbearance. It cannot be done haphazard, nor can it be done by what is called, in a jargon phrase, " sweeping away the barriers ". The barrier to Chilean trade, as I have shown, is the nitrate works at Billingham in County Durham. You cannot sweep that away; and if you did the unemployed would build it up again. But men thought of nitrate, and men thought of Billingham. Given good-will, men will make this knowledge unite and not divide them.

When, however, we pass from theory to practice we shall get neither sympathy nor understanding from the pundits. The pundits, especially the advanced, the up-to-date, the prophetic ones, divide their time almost equally between clamouring for organization and sneering at it when it appears. Not one of them has even written a paper on the disappearance of the Supreme Economic Council; not one of them ever encouraged the Empire Marketing Board while it ran, or lifted a finger to prevent its passing. But there is nothing to trouble us in that. By hit and miss, by trial and error, we shall go again to the work. The world was left in no such happy and ideal state either before, during, or after the Great War, as to leave us no responsibility save to sit round with folded hands and exclaim " How beautiful! "

The nineteenth-century citizenship, the citizenship of the consumer, will not by itself suffice very long once the minimum levels of consumption have been reached and secured. The unemployed man, even given a dole which will keep him alive, even given a vote by which he can change a Cabinet, does not feel himself fully a man. That is what is behind Hitler, that is what is behind Roosevelt, that is what drove our people by hundreds and thousands up and down the stricken areas to vote actually for a reduction in their pittances of consumption, in the desire that somehow, and in some fashion, the other half of their lives, their lives as producers, should be fulfilled as well.

The revolution in Europe, which is, I firmly believe, a great and inevitable stage of the Industrial Revolution, is at work in Britain. As always, in all revolutions we have to do it ourselves, and better than anyone else. I think it possible that in the formulae we have worked out, and are working out, for co-operation both at home and abroad, we may be as far ahead of the rest of the world as we were in the forties of last century with the formulae of industry—coal, iron, steel, steam engines, looms, ships, and chemicals. If anyone can organize co-operation among States we can organize co-operation among States. There are States scattered throughout the world which are our own flesh and blood, with whom we have worked so long that one whole range of friction, the friction of war-danger, does not even come over the horizon. War-danger amongst the British Dominions has been altogether rooted out from our minds. Economic danger, the danger of isolation, of non-contact, is present to all who consider the present state of affairs. But we have a generation of common effort behind us to help us solve it. No other group of States in the world has as much.

We must not be afraid. Production, industry, government, citizenship itself, all have to be recast, or restated in the idiom of our own time. The remoulding that other lands have undertaken has been decreed for us also.

BOOK III

WORK AND WELFARE

WORK AND WELFARE

WE have seen how wealth is produced, and how its exchange and distribution is made possible by means of money. And we have already seen how the welfare of the state depends on the economic views and actions of the government in power. This direct application of economic theory to the problems of national welfare will be our main concern in the remainder of this volume.

"Annual income twenty pounds, annual expenditure nineteen nineteen six, result happiness" said Micawber. "Annual income twenty pounds, annual expenditure twenty pound ought and six, result misery." Does this apply to the state as it does to the individual?

Before we can begin to consider this question we must have a clear idea of *what constitutes national income*. This is given in the following extract from *The Social Framework* by J. R. Hicks, Drummond Professor of Political Economy at Oxford University since 1952.

J. R. HICKS

NATIONAL INCOME

THE methods of computing the social output which are commonly employed depend on a very important economic principle, which is concerned with the close relationship between the value of the net social output and the total of the incomes of members of the community. When this principle is applied, as we usually want to apply it, to calculating the national output of a nation, there are a couple of snags which complicate the argument; after our study of the national capital, the reader will not be surprised to learn that these snags are due (1) to the existence of obligations to and from abroad, (2) to the economic activities of the government. We shall deal with these snags in due time, but for the present it will simplify things if we leave them out of account. In the rest of this chapter we shall make the unreal assumptions that there are no economic relations with persons or bodies outside our community, and that the economic activities of the State can be neglected. When these assumptions are made, the argument is easier to follow; there is not much harm in making simplifications of this sort if we propose to fill in the gaps later on.

Subject to these assumptions, the principle we have to establish is very simple. It states that the value of the net social output of the community and the sum of the incomes of its members are exactly equal. The social output and the social income are one and the same thing.

It will be convenient to begin with a special case in which this principle is directly obvious. Let us suppose that the whole of the productive system of our community is organized in a single giant firm, which controls all the capital equipment, and employs all the labour. This is very much the situation which would exist in a perfectly socialist community; the whole economic system of such a community would consist of a single firm, in which the State would own all the shares. We need not here suppose that the State owns the shares, as we do not want to bring the State in the picture just yet; we will suppose that the shares belong to a body of private share-holders, who may thus be regarded as the indirect owners of the capital equipment.

The net social output and the net output of our Firm are then one and the same thing. It consists, as we know, of the total amount of Consumption Goods and Services produced, *plus* Net Investment, which is the increase in capital equipment brought about by the year's production. The wages of labour have to be paid out of the value of this output; but all the rest is profit, belonging to the shareholders. The wages of labour are the incomes of the labourers; the profit left over is the income of the shareholders. The value of the social output is thus equal to Wages *plus* Profits; and Wages *plus* Profits equals the sum of incomes. The net social output equals the social income.

The same equality can be tested out along another route,

by considering the way in which the incomes are spent. People will spend part of their incomes on buying consumption goods and services (buying them, of course, from the Firm, so that a part of its output is accounted for in this way); the rest they will save. Now when we say that a person saves a part of his income, we do not mean that this part of his income is not spent; saving is the opposite of consumption, not the opposite of spending. When a person saves, he uses a part of his income to make an addition to his assets; he is still saving, whatever form the additional assets take. Thus one possible way for a person to save would be by purchasing new equipment directly, and adding it to the assets in his possession at the end of the year. If we supposed that all the savings took this form, then it would be easy to see that the social income would purchase the social output. The part of the social output which consisted of consumption goods and services would be bought out of consumption expenditure; the part which consisted of the net investment would be purchased out of savings. Income as a whole would purchase output as a whole; we should have social income equalling social output along this route too.

Further, it is obvious that the equality would not be disturbed if we were to suppose that the savers, after acquiring the new equipment in this way, did not retain it in their possession, but lent it back to the Firm. The social income would still have purchased the social output; but the Firm would retain control of the new equipment, issuing shares in exchange for it. The additional assets of the savers would now take the form of shares; the shares would be a liability to the Firm, but the Firm's assets and liabilities would still be equal, as they should be, because the Firm would have the new equipment, equal in value to the shares, added on to its assets. The Firm's balance-sheet would still balance.

In order to arrive at this last situation, it would obviously be unnecessary for the actual goods, which constitute the new equipment, ever to pass directly into the hands of the savers. The savers might use their savings to acquire shares directly, and the Firm might issue the shares for them to acquire, without the new equipment ever changing hands. If the value of the shares issued was equal to the value of the savings, it would also be equal to the value of the net investment. The Firm's assets and liabilities would still balance; the savers would have acquired shares to the amount of their savings, while the goods which constitute the net investment would be retained by the Firm and added to its capital equipment.

So long as we assume that the whole of the capital equipment of the community is controlled by the single Firm, it is this last form which we ought to suppose the saving to take. People save by acquiring shares in the Firm; but the creation of the shares is only the reverse side of the accumulation of additional equipment by the Firm. When a person saves, he acquires the right to receive some part of the profit which will be earned by using the additional equipment which is being produced. He uses a part of his income to acquire a share in the indirect ownership of that new capital equipment.

Let us look back at the combined balance-sheet of firm and shareholders, which was given in the last chapter, and see how it is affected by saving. Taking figures more appropriate for a giant Firm, we should have, at the beginning of the year

	Liabilities	Assets	
Firm:	Shares £1000 million	Real Equipment	£1000 million
Shareholders:	-	Shares	£1000 million

At the end of the year

	Liabilities	Assets	
Firm:	Shares £1050 million	Real Equipment	£1050 million
Shareholders:	-	Shares	£1050 million

The extra £50 million of shares held by the shareholders are their savings; the extra £50 millions' worth of Real Equipment is the Net Investment. Since the Firm's assets and liabilities must be equal *at both dates*, the savings must be equal in value to the net investment.

Thus the fact that people save by acquiring titles to the ownership of parts of the new equipment, instead of by acquiring new equipment directly, does not disturb the relationship between the social output and the social income. That relation can be summed up in the following very important equations.

On the earning side

Social Output $=$ Wages + Profits $=$ Social Income

On the spending side

$$\text{Social Income} = \frac{\text{Consumption}}{\text{Saving}}^{+} = \frac{\text{Consumption}}{\text{Net Investment}}^{+} = \text{Social Output}$$

These equations will remain valid in spite of all the further complications which we shall take into account in the rest of this chapter.

It will be convenient, as a next step, to take into account some complications which can be allowed for while still supposing that industry is organized in a giant Firm.

In the first place, we have hitherto been assuming that the Firm pays out to its shareholders the whole of the profits which it earns, that the shareholders then save part of the incomes they get in this way, and that they lend these savings back to the Firm. In practice, a firm might be inclined to short-circuit this process, and to keep back part of its profits, instead of distributing all the profits to the shareholders directly. In such a case, what effectively happens is that the shareholders are compelled to save a part of the incomes which are due to them; additional shares may not be issued, but the shares previously outstanding will increase in value, because of the additional capital goods which they represent. The undistributed profits have to be reckoned as part of the social income; they are really part of the incomes of the shareholders, although they are not usually reckoned as such, because the shareholders do not get them into their own hands. They have to be reckoned into that part of the social income which is saved; there is a part of net investment corresponding to them, as there should be.

Secondly, we have been assuming hitherto that private people can hold in their personal possession no sort of capital goods, not even consumers' capital goods, such as houses. If we allow them to possess such things as houses, then the rents of these houses have to be reckoned as part of the social income, income derived from a form of capital which is not in the possession of the Firm. (It will be remembered that we are reckoning the use of the houses as part of the social output.) Expenditure on paying the rents of houses is of course a part of consumption. The building of new houses is a part of investment; we may suppose that the actual building is carried out by the Firm, but the part of its output which consists of new houses is sold off to private people, just as the consumption goods are sold off, and not lent back to the Firm, like other investment goods. If private people spend some part of their incomes in buying new houses, they are adding to the assets which they will have in their possession at the end of the year, just as they would do if they acquired shares; consequently income spent in buying new houses is a part of saving. The new houses are to be looked on as a part of new equipment, which is retained in direct private ownership, and not handed back to the Firm in return for shares.

Thirdly, we have been assuming that all labour is employed by the Firm. This is not very convenient in the case of some of the direct personal services. If we allow some of the people who provide direct services to be working on their own account, not for the Firm, we have to distinguish a part of the social output, consisting of these services, which is not part of the output of the Firm, and also to distinguish a part of the earnings of labour which are not wages paid by the Firm. The income spent on these services is a part of consumption, so it finds its place in the table without any difficulty.

Let us now consider what alterations have to be made in our equations to allow for these three complications which we have been discussing. On the earning side, instead of Wages plus Profits, we must write Earnings of Labour *plus* Profits *plus* House Rents; and these in turn can be further divided up. So we have the following equivalent columns:

Social Output	Net Output of Firm*	Wages paid by Firm*	Earnings of Labour	Social Income
		plus Profits of Firm* paid out to shareholders *plus* Undistributed* profits	Profits of Capital *plus* House rents	
	plus Services of Labour not employed by Firm	*plus* Earnings of Labour not employed by Firm		
	plus Use of house-room	*plus* House rents		

On the spending side, consumption and saving can be similarly divided up, so that we have as our other set of equivalent columns:

Social Income	Consumption of* goods produced by Firm	Output of consumption goods and services	Consumption	Social Output
	plus Consumption of other labour services			
	plus Consumption of house-room			
	plus Saving spent on buying new houses*	*plus* Output of new houses sold to savers		
	plus Saving lent to Firm*		*plus* Net Investment	
	plus Saving in the form form of undistributed profits*	*plus* Net new equipment of Firm		

These expanded tables are exactly the same in principle as our earlier tables. They still show the social income being earned in the production of the social output, and being spent in buying the social output.

We are now in a position to drop our assumption of the giant Firm. In the tables we have just given, the part played by the giant Firm is exactly the same as that played in reality by all the firms which compose industry and commerce, when they are taken all together. Our Firm is simply the whole collection of actual firms rolled into one. And we can see the part which this whole collection of firms actually plays in the earning and spending of the social income, by looking at the place of the single Firm (marked out by the starred items) in the above tables. On the earning side, the net output of the Firm is equal to the wages it pays out, *plus* its profits (distributed and undistributed). On the spending side, the net output of the Firm is purchased (1) out of consumption expenditure, so far as it consists of consumption goods; (2) out of saving, so far as it consists of new consumers' capital goods, such as houses; (3) out of saving, so far as it is offset by lending to the Firm; (4) out of saving, so far as it corresponds to undistributed profits. This is the position of the single giant Firm, as it appears in the tables; but this is also the position of the whole collection of firms which compose the real world of industry and commerce, *when they are all taken together*. This we shall now proceed to show.

The new points which emerge when we pull apart our giant Firm into the multitudinous separate firms, large and small, which correspond to it in reality, are only two in number. On the one hand, we have to take account of the materials which are produced by one firm and sold to another, which uses them in its own production. These materials do not come into the picture, so long as industry and commerce are supposed to be amalgamated into one single Firm, because the passing on of materials from one stage of production to another is then a purely internal matter within the Firm. When the firms are pulled apart, the sale of materials looks just the same to the firm which sells them as any other sort of sale does. But since we have also to take into account the purchase of the materials by the firm which uses them, the sale and purchase of such materials will cancel out when all firms are taken together.

The other point which has to be taken into account when we have more firms than one is the possibility that a part of the shares (or other obligations) of one firm may be owned, not by private persons who are shareholders, but by another firm. If this happens, a part of the profits of the one firm will be paid out to the other firm; but here again, when all the firms are taken together, these transferences of profits will cancel out. The only profits left will be those which are actually paid out to private persons, or which remain as un-distributed profits. A further consequence of this possibility is that savings lent to one firm may not be used as a means of increasing the capital goods in the possession of that firm, but may be lent again to some other firm. (An obvious example of this is the case of the banks.) These re-lendings, too, will cancel out when all firms are taken together.

Thus the separation of firms makes absolutely no difference to our general argument. All transactions between firms cancel out, when all firms are taken together, as they have to be for calculation of the *Social* Income or Output. But it will never-theless be instructive to show in detail how the cancellation proceeds, by looking at the way in which firms do actually calculate their profits in practice. Firms calculate their profits by drawing up a profit-and-loss account; what we have now to show is the way in which the profit-and-loss account of a particular firm finds its place in those general accounts of the whole community, whose nature we have been investigating in this chapter.

The profits which are earned by a firm from the production of a particular year equal the value of its output *minus* the expenses to which it has been put in order to produce that output; but in the case of a firm which has obligations (shares or bonds) owing to it from other firms, the interest or dividends received from these other firms may also make a contribution to the firm's profits. The expenses of producing output include (1) wages and salaries; (2) cost of materials used up in order to produce the output; (3) cost of services, such as transport and insurance, provided by other firms; (4) depreciation of the fixed capital equipment. The profit left over after these expenses have been covered is due to the owners of the firm's capital equipment, or to people who have lent money to it with which the equipment has been acquired; thus some parts of the profit may have to be paid out in rent of land or buildings (hired directly), or in interest on borrowed money; what remains is available for distribution to the firm's shareholders, though a prudent management will usually not distribute the whole of the residue, but will keep back some part of it to add to reserves.

A typical profit-and-loss account could therefore be set out in the following form, which is substantially equivalent to that used in practice (the figures are only for purposes of illustration):

Expenses	£		£
Wages and salaries	5000	Value of output	10,000
Cost of materials	2000		
Transport, insurance etc.	250		
Depreciation	750	Interest and dividends received from other Firms	500
Profits:			
Rent of land or buildings	500		
Interest to bondholders	500		
Dividends to shareholders	1000		
Undistributed profit	500		
	10,500		10,5000

Since the two sides add up to the same figure, we can rearrange this account in another way, which is more convenient when we want to be able to consider all the firms in a community together. The account which follows has identically the same significance as that just given.

	£		£
Wages and salaries	5000	Value of output	10,000
Profits	2500	*less*	
less		Cost of Materials	2000
Interest and dividends		*less*	
received from other firms	500	Transport, insurance, etc,	250
		less	
		Depreciation	750
	7000		7000

This new way of writing the account has the advantage that the columns now add up to a total which is of great economic significance. The £10,500 to which the first account added up is not a figure which would have any significance except to the firm itself; the £7000 which comes out as the total when the account is written in the second form is the net output of the firm—its contribution to the net output of the community. If the accounts of all firms were written in the second form and the totals added together, we should get as a result the net output of all firms together—the net output of industry and commerce, which corresponds to the net output of the giant Firm in our previous tables.

We can check up this correspondence on either side of the account. On the left-hand side, the net output of the firm is wages *plus* profits *minus* interest and dividends received from other firms. When all the net outputs are taken together and the totals added up, the parts of profits which are paid out to other firms will cancel out against the corresponding receipts by the other firms. The only profits which will be left are those which are paid out to private persons (shareholders, bondholders, or landlords), and those which remain as undistributed profits. The net output of all firms taken together is thus equal to:

> Wages and salaries
> *plus* Profits paid out to private persons
> *plus* Undistributed profits.

But the total of these is just what the total of wages *plus* profits would be if industry were organized as a giant Firm; and we have seen that this is equal to the net output of industry and commerce.

Now look at the right-hand side. Here we have a similar cancelling-out to perform, because of the services performed by one firm for another, and because of the materials sold by one firm to another. The transport, insurance, etc., which figure among the expenses of production for most ordinary firms are part of the output of such firms as railway companies and insurance companies, and cancel out against that output. Materials which are produced by one firm within the year, and used up by another firm within the year, are reckoned in the output of the first firm and in the cost of materials for the second; thus they also cancel out when the firms are taken together. But some of the materials which are produced during the year will not be used during the year, but will be added to stocks; some of the materials used during the year will not have been produced during the year, but will be taken from stocks. Thus all materials will not necessarily cancel out.

When we have performed the cancellations, the sum totals of the right-hand sides for all firms taken together will come out as follows:

> Value of output of consumers' goods
> *plus* Value of new fixed capital produced
> *less* Depreciation of fixed capital
> *plus* Value of materials added to stocks
> *less* Value of materials taken from stocks

which can also be written

> Value of output of consumers' goods
> *plus* Net investment in fixed capital
> *plus* Net investment in stocks of materials

This is easily recognizable as the net output of consumption goods and investment goods produced by industry; that is, it is the net output of industry as before.

Thus the net output of industry and commerce is equal to the sum of the wages and profits derived from industry and commerce; and the other elements in the social output (direct labour services, services of houses) have already been accounted for. Subject to the assumptions which we made at the beginning of this chapter, the equality between social income and net social output seems to be fully checked up.

The methods which are commonly used by statisticians for the calculation of the national output (or national income) now suggest themselves at once. Although there are certain corrections which have to be introduced when the simplifying assumptions are dropped [These are discussed in later chapters of Mr. Hicks's book.] the connexion between net national output and the sum of incomes remains close enough for it to be possible to approach the same problem from either side, from the side of output or from the side of income.

Probably the best method, if it can be employed, is the *income method*, which proceeds along the route of adding up the incomes of all the members of the community. But in order to be able to use this method, we need to have adequate information about incomes; for Great Britain, that information does exist, since the Ministry of Labour collects information about the earnings of most wage-earners, and the incomes of most people who are not wage-earners are classified in the accounts of the Income Tax. The gap which is left to be covered by indirect estimates is therefore a fairly narrow one. The best estimates of the national income of Great Britain are therefore made by the income method, though other methods have been used, and their results are in any case useful as a check.

The second method is the *Census of Production method*. On this method the problem is approached from the output side. If there exists a census of production for the year in question, the net outputs of most firms can be calculated from it, and have only to be added together. Estimates have to be made for the sorts of production not included (or not satisfactorily included) in the census, and these are inevitably less reliable; nevertheless a good estimate of the net national output can often be reached in this way. Calculations of the national incomes of many foreign countries are made in this manner; they vary a great deal in reliability, according to the completeness of the statistics on which they are based. Very good estimates have been made by the production method for such countries as the United States and Sweden; but there are many countries where production statistics, as well as income statistics, are so inadequate that all estimates of their national incomes are more interesting than trustworthy.

A third method, which should perhaps be added to the list, is the *expenditure method*. The social income, on the side of spending, is equal to the value of consumption *plus* saving. An estimate of the value of consumption can sometimes be made by using statistics of retail trade; information can sometimes be got about some, at least, of the channels of saving. If these figures are available, a rough estimate of the national income can be made from them. The expenditure method is less reliable than the other methods, but since its results ought to square with those got by the other methods, it is useful as a check. And estimates of the value of consumption and saving are of course exceedingly interesting in themselves.

As a first approximation it seems reasonable to suppose that the national income will vary directly with the number of workers employed. In former days when unemployment increased, most governments imitated Micawber, and just waited for something to turn up. Now they often place the maintenance of full employment at the head of their programmes. Let us study this problem of unemployment more closely. It is a problem which vitally effects the lives and happiness of millions of people, so we must consider it, even if we find it is not so simple as we had hoped.

There are various kinds of unemployment. What we call " frictional " unemployment is the sort that cannot be avoided, and that few people want to avoid: it is the unemployment due to workers changing their jobs, or to changes in public wants and fashions. Then there is the cyclical unemployment which mounts rapidly in a trade depression, but disappears again as soon as business improves. We shall see later which trades suffer most from this plague. Finally there is what is called structural or technological unemployment which came into prominence during the period between the wars, and which seems to be the modern equivalent of the unemployment caused in the early stages of the industrial revolution by the introduction of labour-saving machinery.

In so far as both cyclical and structural unemployment are quite involuntary, the theories of the classical economists cannot be applied to them. Adam Smith did give us a picture of a country where trade was declining, and there was general poverty and want, but he never thought of the possibility of a country being prosperous on the whole, yet with millions of its workers vainly waiting for jobs.

What, then, is the meaning of modern unemployment on this grand scale ? The answer is given by Middleton Murry in the following extract from a series of talks which he broadcast, and which were later published under the title *Europe in Travail.*

J. MIDDLETON MURRY

THE MEANING OF MODERN UNEMPLOYMENT

IT is only natural that the spread of advanced industrialism over Europe should have set in motion a process of social disintegration. The advent of a machine technique, the development of modern power production, is by far the most revolutionary happening in the recorded history of man. We may guess at comparable advances in the technique of human living; but they belong to pre-history. The impact upon mankind of machine production is so staggering that I can well believe it may take man centuries to accommodate himself to it.

Now what this accommodation of man to the machine really involves is a revolutionary development of his social intelligence and his social morality. At present, the machine has merely shattered his traditional social morality. We are, quite rightly, horrified at the things that are done in totalitarian societies. They show that our precious notions of personal liberty can be annihilated overnight. But if we stand back a little, we cease to be surprised. We can see that it was inevitable that the advent of the machine should have caused a collapse of the traditional social morality of Europe. For a traditional social morality is not an abstract and conscious thing: it is a natural growth arising from a settled mode of life. Social morality depends upon a settled mode of life. If the mode of life is for ever being ruthlessly changed, no social morality can endure. And what the machine has caused and is always causing is an upheaval in all settled modes of life. Take an elementary example: the characteristic act of modern enterprise. Suppose I decide to set up a factory for making one of the million gadgets now considered necessary to civilized living. Being an enlightened man who believes in rural surroundings and the rest of it, I establish my factory in the heart of the country and build a model village. My workers, being equally enlightened, belong to their trade union and receive a fixed wage; more money for shorter hours than any of the farm labourers around. Straightway the whole moral and material economy of that section of the countryside receives a fearful shock. A process of social disintegration sets in.

This social disintegration—absolutely inevitable in a machine society without planned central control—reaches a sort of scientific purity in the body of the permanently unemployed. Prior to the impetus given to our industry by armaments production, this amounted to at least two million men and women. How are we to understand, what significance are we to attach to this great body of our fellow-human beings ?

What do they represent ? What are they ? On the positive side, they represent a portion of the vast saving of human toil that has accrued to society as a whole by the general adoption of machine production. For the truth is that society can easily carry the financial burden of keeping alive these two million adult workers who have no work. The general standard of living is unaffected. If finance alone were in question, there would be no difficulty at all in making a more generous provision for the unemployed than we actually do. Unfortunately, other things than finance *are* in question. The allowance to the unemployed has to be kept below the average wages earned by the lowest ranks of the employed: or there would be no inducement to these last to work at all.

The real burden of unemployment is not the financial burden, though many still believe that it is. The real burden is different, and far more oppressive, not merely to the man with social imagination, but to society as a whole. For whereas this huge saving of the labour formerly required to keep society alive might be spread throughout the commonwealth to which it in fact belongs, it is concentrated in this unfortunate body of men and women.

If we could look at it quite simply, we should see that the situation is fantastic. Suppose a small society of a hundred men and women live in some sequestered part of the earth, growing their food, feeding their flocks, spinning, weaving: suppose a small steam-engine is introduced into the community. Would it not be entirely monstrous if ten of the members whose previous work in pumping, sawing, thrashing, and the like was now unnecessary were just condemned to do nothing at all ? It would not be tolerated for a day either by the unfortunate ten or the remaining ninety. The ten men would be set to a new job. They would build and decorate a school or a church, or a reading-room, or a theatre. In other words, the unemployment created by the introduction of that steam-engine would be welcomed as a great gift, and would be promptly turned to the increase of the true health and wealth of the community. And so we see what unemployment really is: namely, the liberation of human capacity for the further development and enrichment of the life of society as a whole.

By saying that that is what unemployment really is, I mean that is what it would be if our society had not become so unwieldy that the sense of the community as a whole is lost. As things are, unemployment is nothing of the kind. It is a curse to society, because it is a curse to the unfortunate people upon whom it is inflicted. They are not allowed to work at all. Their manhood is condemned to rot. So that what could and should be one of two things: either a new and joyful freedom shared by every working member of society, or a new embellishment of the common life—either a new spiritual or a new material enrichment—is turned into a slow but certain gangrene of the commonwealth. But so long as the fatal philosophy of the nineteenth century clings to and clogs all our thinking, we cannot remedy this. I mean the individualistic philosophy which believes that it is through the material enrichment of the individual that the community is enriched; that there is a miraculous " harmony of interests " whereby, if everyone struggles to get all he can in his own way, the maximum happiness of society as a whole is secured. The bottom has dropped out of that philosophy. But we hardly realize it, and certainly as a nation we have not found another one. The national mind is perilously suspended somewhere between the old philosophy it has half-abandoned, and the new one it has not yet discovered. I still come across stubborn residues of the old false philosophy, fairly gleaming with moral unction. The dole is a very wicked thing, because it encourages people in idleness! If a man is unemployed, it is his own fault. But there is probably by now a great majority who do not take this unchristian view. They do recognize that the unemployed are unemployed because there really is no work for them to do, and they do acknowledge that it is a national responsibility to maintain them. But there they stop. The full human truth they will not face: namely, that systematic under-nourishment of a man and his family is bad enough, but the sense of being no use at all to his fellow-men is absolutely devastating. Nine times out of ten it just breaks a man.

The reason why they will not face this is that the situation is too difficult to remedy. There are two possible ways of using that waste and wasting human energy—either by employing it in existing industry and so giving the rest of the workers more leisure, or by setting it to work on new enterprises of positive national importance—the embellishment of the common life, of which I just spoke: but each of these demands a revolutionary change in our social and economic organization, a sacrifice of vested interests, a new sense of social responsibility. We can do nothing real for these unfortunate victims of our false social philosophy unless we put the health of the whole community first, and our own advantage second. We are not prepared to do that. So we turn to these unfortunate people and say: " We are very sorry, but the rules of our society condemn you to decay ".

And this is what they reply: " Without work, without the feeling that he belongs to the community of his fellow men and is of use to it, the life, the pride, the heart of a man perishes within him. In us is incarnate the triumph of your false society and its doom. We are the acid test of your society. You claim to be a Christian society. Our existence denies it. What society of Christian men would watch its brothers perish? You claim to be a society of free men. Our existence denies it. What free man would choose the slow starvation of his soul and body on the dole? Now you promise us work. You promise us that we shall soon be received back into the body of society, we shall again be fellows among our fellow-men. And why? Because you are at war. In us you behold the hidden truth of your society; for we are those for whom your war is peace, and your peace is war."

What answer can we make? Shall we say that because we can do nothing for them in peace, we will remain for ever at war? If that is all we can say, we are doomed, and we deserve to be. What reply, then, shall we give? Surely, nothing less than this: that we will not rest until we have found the way to bring them back to life and fellowship—not in war only, but in peace. If we must wage this war, we shall save our souls alive only by waging that other, harder, and more glorious war of which our great English prophet spoke:—

> " Bring me my bow of burning gold!
>   Bring me my arrows of desire!
> Bring me my spear! O clouds, unfold!
>   Bring me my chariot of fire!
>
> I will not cease from mental fight,
>   Nor shall my sword sleep in my hand,
> Till we have built Jerusalem
>   In England's green and pleasant land."

There are two extant solutions of the problem of unemployment. The one with which we are familiar is our own. I will call it the democratic-negative solution. The most important thing to be said about it is that it is not a solution at all. To keep the unemployed man without work, and merely to maintain him at a lower level of subsistence than the lowest paid of the employed, is only a palliative or drug. It deadens the social pain, it does not cure the social disease. What he needs is work; what society needs of him is work. " Joyful work, and fearless rest ", as William Morris used to say, are required to make a man a man. Deny a man that, or the nearest approach to it that existing society can offer, and you deny him real membership of society: you have made him an outcast.

But, it is said, democracy cannot give him this. The determination to give everybody work would involve such a re-organization of society and such a system of control that the majority of men would reject it. If that is true, it is true for one or both of two reasons: either because it is impossible in a democracy really to educate public opinion to a change which challenges so many selfish interests; or because those whose duty it was to educate opinion have shirked the duty. I believe that the task of educating opinion in a democracy to such a change is tremendous; but not absolutely impossible. If it is really impossible, mark well the consequence. If a democracy cannot rise to the determination to bring back the outcast unemployed to full membership of society, the day of democracy is over. Whatever virtues it may have had in the past, it is now incapable of dealing with its own central problem. On what solid ground could it claim to be superior to totalitarianism, which does deal with it?

For the second solution to the problem of unemployment is the totalitarian—positive. The totalitarian leader says to the unemployed: " You shall be reintegrated into society. Democracy stands in the way. Then down with democracy! The vested interests refuse? Give me political power, and I will show what the point of a revolver will do to budge the vested interests." And this positive, forthright, ruthless, social will prevails, though it may for the moment appear to be the will of a numerical minority, because it corresponds with the half-formed desire of the mass-man. At this point of European history we need not bother our heads with the distinction between Fascism and Communism. Europe is long past theory now: the revolutions have happened. We know that Communism can be as brutally nationalist as Fascism. The rough truth of the matter is that Fascism is the Communism of a capitalist democracy.

National socialism is a better name for it, though I hesitate to use it for fear of being misunderstood. In order to become effective in an industrialized democracy, socialism has to become nationalistic. The reason for this is simple. The nationalistic nation, the warlike nation—Britannia ruling the waves or *Deutschland über alles*—is the only idea of society as a whole which as yet has reality in the mind and heart of modern man. He has lost his universal religion. To ask him now to think, still more to feel, internationally is to ask for the moon. Socialism that is conceived as anti-national simply has not a dog's chance.

Nationalism is the dynamic by which the necessary social integration is accomplished under totalitarianism. The unemployment problem is solved by militarizing the whole nation. Unlike the democratic palliative, this solution really is a solution. The unemployed are brought back into the living community; they feel that social justice is being done to them. This social justice may be less than that required by abstract theory; but it satisfies the expectation of the former outcast. His expectation is much more modest and more reasonable than fiery advocates of the class-war believe.

But the price paid for this social reintegration in totalitarianism is the organization of society on a war basis. . . .

I am patriotic enough to believe that my country is capable of something better—something positive and distinctive, in return for the tremendous privileges she has enjoyed in the past. *Noblesse oblige.* The abstract outline of this positive and distinctive form of social reintegration emerges from what we have been saying. In contrast to a totalitarian national socialism, it must be a democratic national socialism. Let us take that to pieces. National—why not? Indeed it must be, if what I have said is true: namely, that nationalism supplies the only possible mass-dynamic to-day for conscious social integration. But nationalism is of different kinds, or different ages. Ours is old, and it is defensive. Defensive nationalism is not enough; yet it cannot be aggressive; yet it must be positive and creative. The solution of the dilemma is simple. It consists in the resolve that it is unworthy of this great nation that it should have to wait upon a war it did not wish to wage to bring the unemployed back into the living body of the nation. Of this unworthiness we as a nation repent.

Democratic? Why not? Is it really beyond our power to come to this repentance and this resolve of our own free will? Have we really to wait till it is enforced upon us? Have we not the moral energy to determine, as free men, that we will organize ourselves for war against the vile and ignominious conditions we inflict upon our fellow-men? Surely, we have.

Socialism? Is that the rub? When all Europe is moving in that direction with the speed and strength of an avalanche? When, if one thing is certain about the future, it is that collectivism in one form or another is coming to every nation? The question is simply how we will have it—totalitarian and brutal, or democratic and liberal and human. But we can get this last only by making up our minds that we will have it in our way, on our own moral initiative, and not at second-hand. The resolve that the unemployed shall be brought back into the body of society, not passively by the compulsion of war, but actively by the social will of the nation, means a kind of socialism. If you can't bear the word, you need not use it. I shall speak instead of a new social discipline—by which I mean a habit of action based on the conviction in every section of society that the welfare of the community as a whole takes precedence over the advantage of the individual.

This conviction we profess to have, in time of war. Perhaps we have. But whatever degree of the conviction comes to us in time of war is not enough for our purpose now. It comes to us automatically, like the war-time absorption of the unemployed. Just as that simply will not do, neither will that war patriotism do. We need the patriotism of peace. We have to pass from the passive to the active. Neither dare we wait for peace to begin. If we wait for the peace, we shall find ourselves incapable of peace, and cling like spent swimmers to our organization for war lest worse befall. Our national democratic social discipline for peace must begin now.

After that general view of the problem, let us take a closer look at this " technological " type of unemployment. It was much talked about before the war when the " rationalization " of industry was so fashionable. This rationalization had been forced on many industries by rapidly increasing costs, among which the high wages secured by some trade unions figured prominently. It was to a large extent an attempt to reduce the ratio of costs to production, not by reducing wages, but by increasing the output per unit of labour. *Why did " rationalization " increase unemployment?*

The answer is given by Sir Theodore Gregory, Professor of Economics in the University of London from 1927 to 1937, and Economic Adviser to the Government of India from 1938 to 1946. This lecture is an extract from his Presidential Address to the Economics Section of the British Association in 1930.

SIR THEODORE GREGORY

RATIONALIZATION AND TECHNOLOGICAL UNEMPLOYMENT

THROUGHOUT the world a conscious process of re-organization is taking place, involving both the structure of industry and the methods of production. To this process the name of rationalization has been given. It is many-sided, but among the characteristic results of the rationalization process are: a growing control over the market, a growing standardization of process and output, and an increasing—in some cases, a very largely increasing—output per worker.

Since the rationalization movement is international in character, and, since it undoubtedly results in most cases in a reduction of cost per unit of output, no single country engaged in international trade under competitive conditions can hope to contract out of its consequences, good and bad, except at the expense of its international trade. This is in itself a sufficient reason for pushing ahead with rationalization in this country.

In the short run, rationalization is not a remedy for unemployment, but, on the contrary, is itself a factor in making for unemployment, except to the extent that it stimulates demand in the constructional and equipment industries. But since a loss of markets due to progressive reductions in prices by rationalized industries in other countries also adds to the volume of unemployment in this country, the short-run evil of unemployment in this country changes in character, rather than grows in volume. Industries are in part depressed because local costs of production are too high and unemployment ensues. Rationalization reduces costs, but, until the lower costs have helped the industries in question to regain their market *and expand it*, unemployment will remain. But unemployment resulting from rationalization is a lesser evil than unemployment resulting from relative inefficiency.

In the long run, since rationalization effects a lowering of real costs, then, given a desire for a rising standard of life, there is no reason to suppose that the volume of unemployment will not again fall. But, in the absence of any definite knowledge of the elasticities of demand for different products, we cannot foretell in what directions an increased demand for labour will manifest itself. The occupied population in the future is likely to be less " industrialized " than in the immediate past: and the growth of trades and occupations outside the narrow concept of " industry " will continue as rationalization proceeds.

The most optimistic view of the situation must take into account the fact that a grave transfer problem is involved, and that monetary and other circumstances having nothing directly to do with the rationalization problem may accentuate the difficulties of transition. The first and most obvious step in the direction of ameliorative measures must therefore be an increase in the mobility of the working population.

In estimating the probable duration of unemployment resulting from rationalization, account has to be taken, not only of the state of technical knowledge, but of the movement of the population. Since rationalization produces its most striking results when the aggregate demand for a product continually increases, a stationary population (and the most advanced nations are tending to stationariness of population) places a limit to the expansion of output in each of the several directions in which the economies of large-scale production are most strikingly displayed. At the same time the decline in the number of new entrants into industry, which is to be expected over the next few years, will diminish the immediate pressure. But it is quite possible that the normal level of unemployment will be higher in the future than in the past: in which case, unemployment will cease to serve as an index of material well-being. The paradox of a rising standard of life with a higher level of unemployment may well be the result of the present tendency in industry.

On the other hand, there are not wanting examples to show that demand for new products and services can be stimulated very quickly, provided they are sufficiently cheap: and there is therefore no reason to fear that we shall all " starve in the midst of plenty ".

There is an obvious relationship between the progress of rationalization on the one hand and the possibility of a shorter working day and higher earnings from labour on the other. The rise in the standard of living and the shorter hours which have characterized the progress of industry in the last hundred years were both conditioned by increased productivity.

A shorter working day and higher wage rates are, of course, frequently defended, not on the legitimate ground that society can afford them with increasing productive powers, but on the ground that they are *direct* means for reducing unemployment, because they " spread work " and stabilize " working class purchasing power ". Unless accompanied by increasing productivity, however, they are incapable of achieving these results: for a shorter working day without a larger output would either involve lower wages or rising costs per unit: and rising money wages without increasing productivity would also result in disequilibrium. But given increasing productive powers, it is possible to lower prices to the consumer and pay the same wage as before for a shorter day or, with the same lower cost to the consumer, pay a higher wage for the same working day. Growing productivity, in fact, gives society a margin to " play with," and this margin is the source out of which unemployment can be relieved. But we have no right to assume that the process works without friction or that the fears of the workers are based entirely on " prejudice and error ". In the end, one must rest one's hopes on the known elasticity and responsiveness of capitalistic society: an organization which was capable of surviving the shocks of the War and post-War period is hardly likely to perish because it is learning to turn the arts of production to still better use in the future than it did during the last 150 years.

It was hoped that this technological unemployment would be merely a temporary phase, and that the reduced costs made possible by rationalization would quickly lead to a bigger and a wider market, as had happened in the early days of the industrial revolution. But this hope proved vain, and the world was faced with the queer problem of poverty in the midst of plenty. It seemed as though the extension of machine-manufactures to all civilized countries had resulted in a state of over-industrialization, and many people began to think that Marx's prophecy about the inevitable breakdown of the capitalist system was about to be realized. The machinery of production had been developed far more quickly than the machinery of distribution and marketing. A clever salesman could earn more than a clever technician, but even with his help the markets necessary to absorb the full production of the machines could not be found. The efforts of the various governments to stimulate the trade of their own countries were not very successful, and the main result was a decline in international trade. So that highly industrial countries like Great Britain had a permanent army of unemployed, while peasant countries suffered from what is called " concealed unemployment "—the crowding on to the land of more workers than it really needed, or could properly support.

To the unemployment of structural or technological type, that due to cyclical causes was added in the worst years. What is the explanation of this? Let us ask G. D. H. Cole to tell us *what happens in slumps*.

G. D. H. COLE

WHAT HAPPENS IN SLUMPS

THE unemployment which devastated the capitalist world so soon after 1918 had, on the face of the matter, two aspects. A good deal of it appeared to be due to the collapse of the demand for exports, which threw workers in the coal, cotton, and other exporting industries out of work, and, by destroying their purchasing power, reacted adversely on the demand for the products of other industries. A good deal of it appeared to be due to the fall in the orders for capital goods, as business men, losing faith in the prospect of the consuming market, almost ceased to buy new machinery, even for the replacement of worn-out or obsolescent machines. The slump affected other branches of production besides these: indeed, there was no industry or service that it did not affect. But it affected these two groups most of all.

If we look back on the history of earlier depressions, or forward to the even more devastating depression of 1930 and the following years, we shall find the same thing happening. In Great Britain and other industrial countries, the heaviest blows have fallen, in one slump after another, on two groups of industries—those producing largely for export and those producing instruments of production and other constructional goods. This is a common feature of nearly all depressions, as they affect industry. Although the demand for all classes of goods and services undergoes some reduction when times are bad, the heaviest reduction occurs in these two overlapping fields—for of course some exports are machines or other kinds of capital goods. The home demand for consumers' goods falls off as a rule much less than either the demand for exports or the demand for capital goods.

This is what happens to industry. In agriculture things usually take a somewhat different course. The demand for foodstuffs as a whole varies much less between good and bad times than the demand for most other things; and the demand for the cheaper kinds of foodstuffs varies least of all. Men must eat, and when their incomes are reduced they usually economize on other things sooner than go short of food—if they can get it. One would suppose, therefore, that the agricultural producers would find themselves in a relatively favourable position during a slump, and would be able to take advantage of the cheapening of industrial products while maintaining the prices of their own. Nothing could be further from the truth. The volume of agricultural output usually stays relatively high, even if it does not actually increase, during periods of depression; but, even if the demand for foodstuffs falls only a little, agricultural prices usually slump even more catastrophically than the prices of industrial goods, so that the purchasing power of agricultural commodities over industrial products falls off sharply, accentuating the decline in foreign trade. In particular, the prices of agricultural raw materials suffer a devastating decline.

This sharp fall in agricultural prices occurs partly because agricultural producers can neither combine easily to control the prices of their produce nor speedily cut down the amounts produced. Output is indeed in the short run dependent much more on the chances of harvests than on any deliberate action of the producers, who can act only within the conditions set by the natural rhythm of the seasons and the established practices of crop rotation and combined production of animal and vegetable products. Faced with a shortage of demand, actual or expected, the industrial employer can in most cases rapidly contract his output and discharge the workers he no longer requires. The farmer cannot act so quickly, nor when he does act can he so easily adapt his labour force to the changed conditions of the market—above all when he is a peasant or family farmer, employing little or no labour beyond that of his own household.

Indeed, the farmer may in many cases react to a depression not by reducing his output, after the manner of most industrial employers, but by producing more. If he is a man of small resources, as most farmers are, he must sell his crops or his beasts without delay, even if he has not been compelled in effect to sell or mortgage them before they were grown. He depends on what he gets from the year's crops for re-stocking his farm, for buying such industrial goods and food-stuffs as he needs, for paying his rent, if he is a tenant, or his mortgage interest, and for meeting the claims of the tax-gatherer and in many cases the money-lender. He must have cash at all costs; and if the price of his produce falls, his first reaction is to attempt to grow or raise more in order to maintain his cash income. In doing so, he of course worsens the market conditions; for the more he offers for sale, the less per unit he is likely to get. But it will not help him to refrain from in-creasing his output, unless his competitors do the same—and for the basic agricultural commodities the number of his competitors is legion, because these commodities are sold in a world-wide market, made up of millions of small producers, as well as a few large ones, in many different countries.

This helps to explain why, despite the fact that the con-sumption of foodstuffs is usually well maintained during a slump, their prices fall off so much. The millions of agricultural producers are in a weak bargaining position, both because of their sheer numbers and because they are scattered over many lands. Many of them try to improve their situation by joining together in Agricultural Co-operative Societies, among which the Canadian Grain-growers' Co-operatives are important, for the collective marketing of their produce. But unless such methods can become general, in all the large exporting coun-tries, and unless the Co-operative Societies can be induced to follow a common policy in all countries, the power of the farmers, even collectively, to influence market conditions is severely limited. The Canadians cannot well afford to hold out for a higher price than the Argentinians are prepared to accept for grain of equal quality; for if they do, their grain will remain unsold and they will have to incur the heavy costs of storage, nor will they find it easy to borrow the cash which their farmer-

members must have in order to carry on at all. Of course, if
all the wheat available were wanted by the consumers without
delay, this situation would not arise. The farmers would be
able to hold out for a reasonable price without fear of having
their crops left on their hands. But all the grain is not wanted
at once; there is usually a large carry-over in store from
previous harvests. If the farmers try to hold out, the dealers
use up the stocks without replacing them, leaving the producers to bear the costs of storage. There are usually enough
needy sellers to bring the prices of basic foodstuffs tumbling
down in a depression, despite the maintenance of consumption.
And, of course, consumption is maintained partly because
prices do fall so far. The buyers can buy as much as before,
without using on foodstuffs any larger fraction of their reduced
incomes. They may even consume more—those who are
still in work—and yet spend a smaller proportion of their
incomes.

Farm incomes, then, are apt to fall drastically in a slump—
above all, the incomes of peasant producers, who are least in a
position to protect themselves. In countries which habitually
import foodstuffs, the agricultural producers are often protected by their Governments, which restrict imports and take
measures to raise the domestic prices of wheat and other
agricultural products far above the world level. This, however,
only makes matters worse for the agriculturists of the food-
exporting countries, by narrowing the markets where conditions are already adverse. Naturally, one consequence is that
the peasants in these countries have to cut down almost to
nothing their purchases of industrial goods—especially of
imported goods, which become impossibly expensive as the
Governments of the agricultural countries impose high tariffs
on them, partly to protect home industries, but also partly in
order to balance their international accounts. For the fall in
agricultural prices reduces the yield of the exports from these
countries, leaving them with less foreign money to cover their
purchases of imports after meeting such debts as they owe

abroad to foreign owners of capital. This decline in the purchases of industrial goods by the agriculturists deepens the
depression in the industrial countries; and further depression
in these markets helps to force agricultural prices down further
still.

Thus industrial and agricultural depression interact, showing themselves in unemployment in the industrial areas, but in
the agricultural areas rather in a general fall in the standard
of living far below its normally low levels. Prices fall in both
agricultural and industrial areas; but the fall in agriculture is
usually the greater, because agricultural production is not cut
down, at any rate until the slump has continued for a considerable time.

We have already seen a part of the reason why depression
in the industrial countries falls with special severity on the
exporting industries. It is not only in agricultural countries that,
when market conditions become adverse, attempts are made
to cut down imports to the greatest practicable extent. In the
industrial countries also, manufacturers demand increased
protection, in the hope of mitigating the effects of the fall in
demand on the sales and prices of their own products; while
the fall in exports creates exchange difficulties similar to those
which arise in the agricultural States, and makes the Governments concerned ready to listen to the claims of the manufacturers. Thus, periods of world depression are usually
periods of increased restrictions on foreign trade, as each
country attempts to protect its own nationals against the effects
of the general worsening of economic affairs. These practices,
when one country after another resorts to them, lose most of
their effectiveness from the standpoint of each of the countries
concerned; for countries cannot prosper by not taking in one
another's washing.

What results is a general shrinkage in the volume of world
trade, and therewith of world production and employment as
well, wherever countries allow the volume of employment to
be regulated by the conditions of the market. No one country,

however, dares give up its beggar-my-neighbour policy as long as others persist in the same courses, for fear of having its market flooded with imports which will throw more of its own workers out of jobs, and will also dislocate its balance of payments. This was what happened to a considerable extent in Great Britain in 1931, as a consequence of the world crisis; and it led this country to abandon its traditional policy of Free Trade, and take to Protectionism instead, in addition to giving up the gold standard. Whether these measures were really necessary—either of them or both—we need not pause to consider just now. Our present concern is that each country's attempt, in time of depression, to protect its own home market is bound to cause a severe contraction in the amount of world trade. This reacts with particular seriousness on the industries which produce manufactured goods for export—including both capital and consumers' goods; for as a rule countries find it much easier to dispense in bad times with imports of manufactures than to curtail their normal imports of raw materials or foodstuffs to the desired extent— especially if the prices of such goods fall much more sharply than the prices of manufactures.

The second group of industries in the industrial countries which suffers in an exceptional degree when depression sets in is that which produces mainly capital goods for the home market or for export. Unemployment and the fall in production are in general much more severe in the industries which make " capital goods " than in those which make consumers' goods for everyday use. In more technical language, " investment " declines more than " consumption ", despite the fall in consumption which follows upon the loss of purchasing power by those who are thrown out of work. Such industries as shipbuilding, iron and steel manufacture, heavy engineering, and, as a rule, building, suffer a much greater decline in activity than such industries as food processing, clothing, printing, and the lighter metal trades, which work mainly for the consumers' market.

[Figures are given in Professor Cole's book showing the increase in unemployment in eight groups of industries between 1929 and 1931-3. Industries making capital goods (steel, shipbuilding, constructional engineering, etc.) had the largest increase; then came export industries; then those making durable consumers' goods (building, furniture, etc.); and then the industries serving other industries (coal-mining, chemicals, etc.). Production of food and of clothing for everyday use showed the smallest increase in unemployment.]

The reasons for these sharp differences in the incidence of general depressions on industries and services of different types are not difficult to see. The demand for capital goods, in the sense of instruments of production, such as factories, machinery, ships, and the materials used in making them, is what is technically called a " derived " demand: it depends on the expected demand for the final consumable products which these instruments of production or transport can be used to make or to carry about. The amounts which owners of capital are prepared to invest, or business men to borrow from them for investments, obviously depend on the expectations of profit which they entertain. If effective demand for goods and services in general is expected to expand, that is a reason for buying more machinery, etc., in order to be able to make a profit out of catering for this demand; whereas, if demand is expected to fall off, that is a strong reason for refraining from such investment. In other words, the demand for investment goods depends on the current capitalist views of the prospects of the markets for consumers' goods; for all products either are consumers' goods or are destined to help directly or indirectly in making consumers' goods, or to be exchanged for them. Consumption is the only end of production; and it would be mere folly to pile up instruments of production in the absence of expected means of disposing of their products.

In bad times, then, the amount of " investment " falls off sharply, because the prospects of profitably enlarging, or even of maintaining, the sales of consumers' goods and services grow less, or disappear. It may seem that, if the sums withheld from " investment " were applied instead to the buying of additional quantities of consumers' goods and services, no harm would be done, and the volume of production and employment would be unaffected. This, however, is not what actually happens; nor, if it did, would the effects be negligible. The trades producing consumers' goods and services could not at short notice expand their output to meet this large shift in demand: nor could the workers displaced from the investment industries shift over suddenly to quite different skills. A puddler cannot turn suddenly to making puddings, or a machine-maker into a maker of boots. An attempt suddenly to expand greatly the demand for consumers' goods, in face of a sharp decline in the demand for investment goods, would in practice leave plant, business ability, and skilled labour derelict in the declining trades, and would at the same time force up costs of production and prices in the expanding trades, which could largely increase their output at short notice only at rising costs. Thus, even if all the income withdrawn from investment were transferred promptly to consumption, serious dislocation would arise.

All the income is not, however, thus transferred. The agencies which would have spent money on investment goods do not as a rule, when they reduce investment, increase consumption instead. If Imperial Chemical Industries decides to refrain from building a new factory, it does not expend the sum withheld on champagne for its directors; nor does it pay this money out in higher dividends to its shareholders—much less in higher wages to its employees. It treats the money as capital, and *holds it in reserve*—or, in other words, does not spend it at all, until it thinks the time has come for resuming active investment in the light of improving market prospects. " Investment ", however, will fall off, not merely in proportion to the expected fall in the demand for consumers' goods, but much more. If the sales of consumers' goods fall off at all, or are expected to fall off, the demand for means of making or transporting such goods will be likely to fall off much more sharply, because most manufacturers or transport undertakings will be able to make do with the instruments of production or conveyance which they already have, without buying additional ones or even replacing all those which wear out or become obsolete.

A slump in one country does not benefit other countries. It is not as though a competitor had gone out of business, but as though a good customer had done so. The maintenance of full employment is therefore a matter of great international importance, and the United Nations Organization asked a group of economic experts to submit a report on National and International Measures for Full Employment. Mr. E. Ronald Walker, Economic Adviser to the Australian Department of External Affairs, was chairman, and the following brief quotations from the Report gives us an answer to the question, *What is the key to the problem of unemployment?* It will help to make the fuller exposition which follows it more easy to understand.

UNITED NATIONS DEPARTMENT OF ECONOMIC AFFAIRS

THE KEY TO THE PROBLEM OF UNEMPLOYMENT

THE key to an understanding of the problem of effective demand lies in the recognition of the fact that in a private enterprise economy the decisions to save and the decisions to invest are to a considerable extent independent of each other; this is also true of the current revenue and expenditure of the government, as well as of the level of exports and imports. Thus the rate of investment depends heavily on the extent to which existing capital equipment is utilized, and the expectations of the rate of profit that can be earned in the future with the aid of new equipment. Decisions to save, on the other hand, maintain a fairly stable relation to current income, this relation depending on the habits of individuals, and on the share of business profits ploughed back into industry. In the same way, government tax revenue is highly dependent on the level of income, since a change in the community's income will affect government tax receipts (at given rates of taxation) more than proportionately. Government expenditures, on the other hand, do not necessarily vary with income, and may even vary in a contrary direction. Finally, the level of imports varies with the level of incomes of the importing country, while exports depend largely on the incomes of other countries.

These factors and their interaction explain why at times the community is unable to secure full utilization of its resources. Assuming for the moment that taxation is equal to government expenditures, and that imports are equal to exports, the principle can be illustrated by the interaction of decisions to save and decisions to invest. When savings decisions exceed investment there is a deficiency in the aggregate demand for goods and services, and some of the output currently produced will remain unsold (or sold at unremunerative prices), which, in turn, will necessarily cause a tendency towards contraction in the level of production and incomes. Since, however, savings largely depend upon the level of incomes, the contraction of incomes in itself tends to reduce savings, and thus to eliminate the excess of supply over demand. When, conversely, the decisions to invest exceed current savings, the aggregate demand for goods and services will exceed the current supply, and incomes will tend to rise. This in turn will tend to increase savings until the rise in incomes reaches a point at which the excess of demand for goods and services over the supply is eliminated.

Similar forces of contraction and expansion in the economic system result also from the activities of the government and the movement of foreign trade. A change in the rate of government expenditure at given rates of taxation, or a change in exports relatively to imports at given rates of exchange, sets up the same forces of expansion or contraction in the economic system, as a change in investment decisions relatively to savings.

We have seen that a slump is felt most keenly by the firms which supply either goods for export or those for production and construction —capital goods, as they are called. And it has also been suggested that the slump really begins when the business men who normally buy or rent these capital goods reduce their demand for them because they cannot see a reasonable chance of a satisfactory profit from an investment in them. If this is so, if we have found one of the main causes of a slump, *Can we take action to prevent a slump developing?* Can we use our knowledge to prevent this curse of unemployment?

Keynes was the first great economist to declare, roundly and with conviction, that we could so use our knowledge. And he backed up his conviction with an economic argument of great strength and subtlety. Here is the crux of it, taken from his epoch-making book: *The General Theory of Employment, Interest, and Money.* Frankly, this is not easy reading, but it is so important that the effort required to follow it closely will be amply rewarded.

J. M. KEYNES (LORD KEYNES)

THE GENERAL THEORY OF EMPLOYMENT

WE have now reached a point where we can gather together the threads of our argument. To begin with, it may be useful to make clear which elements in the economic system we usually take as given, which are the independent variables of our system and which are the dependent variables.

We take as given the existing skill and quantity of available labour, the existing quality and quantity of available equipment, the existing technique, the degree of competition, the tastes and habits of the consumer, the disutility of different intensities of labour and of the activities of supervision and organization, as well as the social structure including the forces, other than our variables set forth below, which determine the distribution of the national income. This does not mean that we assume these factors to be constant; but merely that, in this place and context, we are not considering or taking into account the effects and consequences of changes in them.

Our independent variables are, in the first instance, the propensity to consume, the schedule of the marginal efficiency of capital and the rate of interest, though, as we have already seen, these are capable of further analysis.

Our dependent variables are the volume of employment and the national income (or national dividend) measured in wage-units.

The factors, which we have taken as given, influence our independent variables, but do not completely determine them. . . .

There will be an inducement to push the rate of new investment to the point which forces the supply-price of each type of capital-asset to a figure which, taken in conjunction with its prospective yield, brings the marginal efficiency of capital in general to approximate equality with the rate of interest. That is to say, the physical conditions of supply in the capital-goods industries, the state of confidence concerning the prospective yield, the psychological attitude to liquidity and the quantity of money (preferably calculated in terms of wage-units) determine, between them, the rate of new investment.

But an increase (or decrease) in the rate of investment will have to carry with it an increase (or decrease) in the rate of consumption; because the behaviour of the public is, in general, of such a character that they are only willing to widen (or narrow) the gap between their income and their consumption if their income is being increased (or diminished). That is to say, changes in the rate of consumption are, in general, in the same direction (though smaller in amount) as changes in the rate of income. The relation between the increment of consumption which has to accompany a given increment of saving is given by the marginal propensity to consume. The ratio, thus determined, between an increment of investment and the corresponding increment of aggregate income, both measured in wage-units, is given by the investment multiplier.

Finally, if we assume (as a first approximation) that the employment multiplier is equal to the investment multiplier, we can, by applying the multiplier to the increment or decrement in the rate of investment brought about by the factors first described, infer the increment of employment.

An increment (or decrement) of employment is liable, however, to raise (or lower) the schedule of liquidity-preference; there being three ways in which it will tend to increase the demand for money, inasmuch as the value of output will rise when employment increases even if the wage-unit and prices (in terms of the wage-unit) are unchanged, but, in addition, the wage-unit itself will tend to rise as employment improves, and the increase in output will be accompanied by a rise of prices (in terms of the wage-unit) owing to increasing cost in the short period.

Thus the position of equilibrium will be influenced by these repercussions; and there are other repercussions also. Moreover, there is not one of the above factors which is not liable to change without much warning, and sometimes substantially. Hence the extreme complexity of the actual course of events. Nevertheless, these seem to be the factors which it is useful and convenient to isolate. If we examine any actual problem along the lines of the above schematism, we shall find it more manageable; and our practical intuition (which can take account of a more detailed complex of facts than can be treated on general principles) will be offered a less intractable material upon which to work.

The above is a summary of the General Theory. But the actual phenomena of the economic system are also coloured by certain special characteristics of the propensity to consume, the schedule of the marginal efficiency of capital and the rate of interest, about which we can safely generalize from experience, but which are not logically necessary.

In particular, it is an outstanding characteristic of the economic system in which we live that, whilst it is subject to severe fluctuations in respect of output and employment, it is not violently unstable. Indeed it seems capable of remaining in a chronic condition of sub-normal activity for a considerable period without any marked tendency either towards recovery or towards complete collapse. Moreover, the evidence indicates that full, or even approximately full, employment is of rare and short-lived occurrence. Fluctuations may start briskly but seem to wear themselves out before they have proceeded to great extremes, and an intermediate situation which is neither desperate nor satisfactory is our normal lot. It is upon the fact that fluctuations tend to wear themselves out before proceeding to extremes and eventually to reverse themselves, that the theory of business *cycles* having a regular phase has been founded. The same thing is true of prices, which, in response to an initiating cause of disturbance, seem to be able to find a level at which they can remain, for the time being, moderately stable.

Now, since these facts of experience do not follow of logical necessity, one must suppose that the environment and the psychological propensities of the modern world must be of such a character as to produce these results. It is, therefore, useful to consider what hypothetical psychological propensities would lead to a stable system; and, then, whether these propensities can be plausibly ascribed, on our general knowledge of contemporary human nature, to the world in which we live.

The conditions of stability which the foregoing analysis suggests to us as capable of explaining the observed results are the following:

(i) The marginal propensity to consume is such that, when the output of a given community increases (or decreases) because more (or less) employment is being applied to its capital equipment, the multiplier relating the two is greater than unity but not very large.

(ii) When there is a change in the prospective yield of capital or in the rate of interest, the schedule of the marginal efficiency of capital will be such that the change in new investment will not be in great disproportion to the change in the former; i.e., moderate changes in the prospective yield of capital or in the rate of interest will not be associated with very great changes in the rate of investment.

(iii) When there is a change in employment, money-wages tend to change in the same direction as, but not in great disproportion to, the change in employment; i.e., moderate changes in employment are not associated with very great changes in money-wages. This is a condition of the stability of prices rather than of employment.

(iv) We may add a fourth condition, which provides not so much for the stability of the system as for the tendency of a fluctuation in one direction to reverse itself in due course; namely, that a rate of investment, higher (or lower) than prevailed formerly, begins to react unfavourably (or favourably) on the marginal efficiency of capital if it is continued for a period which, measured in years, is not very large.

(i) Our first condition of stability, namely, that the multiplier, whilst greater than unity is not very great, is highly plausible as a psychological characteristic of human nature. As real income increases, both the pressure of present needs diminishes and the margin over the established standard of life is increased; and as real income diminishes the opposite is true. Thus it is natural—at any rate on the average of the community—that current consumption should be expanded when employment increases, but by less than the full increment of real income; and that it should be diminished when employment diminishes, but by less than the full decrement of real income. Moreover, what is true of the average of individuals is likely to be also true of governments, especially in an age when a progressive increase of unemployment will usually force the State to provide relief out of borrowed funds.

But whether or not this psychological law strikes the reader as plausible *a priori*, it is certain that experience would be extremely different from what it is if the law did not hold. For in that case an increase of investment, however small, would set moving a cumulative increase of effective demand until a position of full employment had been reached; while a decrease of investment would set moving a cumulative decrease of effective demand until no one at all was employed. Yet experience shows that we are generally in an intermediate position. It is not impossible that there may be a range within which instability in fact does prevail. But, if so, it is probably a narrow one, outside of which in either direction our psychological law must unquestionably hold good. Furthermore, it is also evident that the multiplier, though exceeding unity, is not, in normal circumstances, enormously large. For, if it were, a given change in the rate of investment would involve a great change (limited only by full or zero employment) in the rate of consumption.

(ii) Whilst our first condition provides that a moderate change in the rate of investment will not involve an indefinitely great change in the demand for consumption goods our second condition provides that a moderate change in the prospective yield of capital assets or in the rate of interest will not involve an indefinitely great change in the rate of investment. This is likely to be the case owing to the increasing cost of producing a greatly enlarged output from the existing equipment. If, indeed, we start from a position where there are very large surplus resources for the production of capital-assets, there may be considerable instability within a certain range; but this will cease to hold good as soon as the surplus is being largely utilized. Moreover, this condition sets a limit to the instability resulting from rapid changes in the prospective yield of capital-assets due to sharp fluctuations in business psychology or to epoch-making inventions—though more, perhaps, in the upward than in the downward direction.

(iii) Our third condition accords with our experience of human nature. For although the struggle for money-wages is, as we have pointed out above, essentially a struggle to maintain a high *relative* wage, this struggle is likely, as employment increases, to be intensified in each individual case both because the bargaining position of the worker is improved and because the diminished marginal utility of his wage and his improved financial margin make him readier to run risks. Yet, all the same, these motives will operate within limits, and workers will not seek a much greater money-wage when employment improves or allow a very great reduction rather than suffer any unemployment at all.

But here again, whether or not this conclusion is plausible *a priori*, experience shows that some such psychological law must actually hold. For if competition between unemployed workers always led to a very great reduction of the money-wage, there would be a violently instability in the price-level. Moreover, there might be no position of stable equilibrium except in conditions consistent with full employment; since the wage-unit might have to fall without limit until it reached a point where the effect of the abundance of money in terms of the wage-unit on the rate of interest was sufficient to restore a level of full employment. At no other point could there be a resting place.

(iv) Our fourth condition, which is a condition not so much of stability as of alternate recession and recovery, is merely based on the presumption that capital-assets are of various ages, wear out with time and are not all very long-lived; so that if the rate of investment falls below a certain minimum level, it is merely a question of time (failing large fluctuations in other factors) before the marginal efficiency of capital rises sufficiently to bring about a recovery of investment above this minimum. And similarly, of course, if investment rises to a higher figure than formerly, it is only a question of time before the marginal efficiency of capital falls sufficiently to bring about a recession unless there are compensating changes in other factors.

For this reason, even those degrees of recovery and recession, which can occur within the limitations set by our other conditions of stability, will be likely, if they persist for a sufficient length of time and are not interfered with by changes in the other factors, to cause a reverse movement in the opposite direction, until the same forces as before again reverse the direction.

Thus our four conditions together are adequate to explain the outstanding features of our actual experience;—namely, that we oscillate, avoiding the gravest extremes of fluctation in employment and in prices in both directions, round an intermediate position appreciably below full employment and appreciably above the minimum employment a decline below which would endanger life.

But we must not conclude that the mean position thus determined by " natural " tendencies, namely, by those tendencies which are likely to persist, failing measures expressly designed to correct them, is, therefore, established by laws of necessity. The unimpeded rule of the above conditions is a fact of observation concerning the world as it is or has been, and not a necessary principle which cannot be changed.

Yes, that is the important point. The economic laws which have worked to produce the brief boom and long slump, together with the chronic unemployment of the past half-century, are not irresistible natural laws which cannot be overcome. We have seen that slumps arise when entrepreneurs take a gloomy view and act on a pessimistic hypothesis, but, as Keynes himself says, " If we consistently act on the optimistic hypothesis, this hypothesis will tend to be realized ; whilst by acting on the pessimistic hypothesis we can keep ourselves for ever in the pit of want "

What a caustic commentary on human skill and foresight if the very caution which led our business men to " go steady " when they felt that a trade recession was due proved to be the cause producing what they most dreaded! In any case it would seem that full employment can be maintained if we are willing to pay the price. *What is the price of full employment?*

The answer is given by Seebohm Rowntree whose long life was filled with a very intense interest in social problems. His address was broadcast in 1944, and this will explain the topical allusions of the opening paragraphs.

SEEBOHM ROWNTREE

THE PRICE OF FULL EMPLOYMENT

I SAW a cartoon the other day of a shop assistant showing a soldier a sample of the civilian clothing outfits which are being provided for men when they are demobbed. " It's complete " he explained " even to the back collar stud! Now can you think of anything that has been forgotten," he asked " anything more that a man will need? " " Yes," replied the soldier " he'll need a job." Thousands of men are asking to-day: " Am I going to get a decent job when this war is over, or am I going on the dole for years, as my dad did? Because if I am, I sometimes wonder what I'm fighting for."

It is tremendously important that every man and woman in the Forces, or working in war factories, should know that there is no need to be fearful about the future, and I want to tell you why. You have heard about trade cycles—how trade is always moving up and down just like a swing—up to a boom or down to a slump, so that whenever trade has become really good, you could be certain that very soon a depression would set in, which would probably last for years. Now when the last war ended, the experts who were studying the question did not know what caused these trade cycles, and so naturally they did not know how to cure them. But during the last few years they have learnt a good deal more, both about the causes and about the cure. Let us see what they have learnt.

First, that if you are to prevent unemployment from spreading, you must tackle it the moment the symptoms of a depression appear, and that these are almost certain to appear first in the industries engaged in making capital goods, such as machinery, buildings, ships, and so on. The moment this occurs the State must take steps to ensure that people go on spending money on capital goods, so that the workers engaged in producing them may be kept in work. Second, that the steps taken must be adequate. The half-measures we tried during the last great depression are useless. Third, that the State need not hesitate to borrow whatever money is necessary to check a depression. Fourth, and this is very important, that the State acting alone cannot cure unemployment. This will need the active co-operation of all those engaged in industry, agriculture, and commerce.

So we see that there are three sets of people who must get busy if trade depressions are to be avoided: the State, employers, and workers. Let us first see what the State must do. You know that in war-time trained observers, with the help of scientific instruments, are constantly on the look-out for approaching enemy aeroplanes. Just in the same way an expert body, furnished with all necessary statistical information, must be constantly on the look-out for the first signs of a trade depression, so that the necessary defensive measures may be taken instantly. Directly they observe that the community is investing in capital goods less than is necessary to keep the workers employed, the Government must see that the gap is quickly filled up. This may be done in many ways, such, for instance, as temporarily increasing the tax allowance in respect of depreciation of plant, or making it possible for firms to borrow money at low rates of interest, or encouraging people to invest through action taken by a National Investment Board.

If these methods fail to absorb the money people are saving instead of spending, the State and local authorities must themselves invest up to the needed amount, increasing their usual expenditure on such objects as house building, slum clearance, and the provision of improved water and electrical services. Why, it may well be asked, wasn't such action taken between the wars? It was not taken because we did not realize the importance of acting as soon as the first symptoms of trade depression appear. We allowed it to become so widespread before we did anything about it that checking it would have involved an expenditure by the State much greater than could be met out of the year's revenue.

At that time it was held by economists and the Treasury and financial pundits generally that, in times of peace, the national Budget must at all costs be balanced every year, and that if once the Government started spending beyond its income, it was heading for national bankruptcy. Thus when unemployment had become severe, with the inevitable result that revenue from taxes declined, the Government, in order to balance its Budget, increased taxation and cut down expenditure ruthlessly. It spent less on armaments, on education, on social security, on slum clearance, and on a host of other things. Such economy campaigns were carried through three times between the wars, with the result that unemployment was increased rather than reduced. At the same time that this fatal policy was being pursued, the Government spent a little money on public works, but nothing like enough to absorb the unemployed labour. It spent so little because of the belief that on no account must money be borrowed for such a purpose.

To-day it is held by all responsible people that this policy was entirely wrong and that there is absolutely no reason why the finances of the State should not be run on the same lines as those of business. In business you may prudently borrow money to an unlimited extent so long as it is lucratively invested, and you need never pay off the money you have borrowed. It would have been impossible to build up the great industrial enterprises of to-day on any other lines. This, then, is the revolutionary change that has taken place in our way of thinking. This is the chief reason why I am confident that we can conquer unemployment. This is why it need not be " the same as last time ".

Well, that is all about the steps the State must take if we are to conquer unemployment. But do not let us for one moment imagine that we can leave the matter to the State acting alone. There are two other groups of people who have got to play too. Without the help of employers and workers, unemployment cannot be cured. Let us see what they must do. Taking the employers first, the answer to this question may be summed up in a sentence. It is that their aim should always be to sell " a lot for a little rather than a little for a lot ". All practices which aim at limiting the supply of goods or services so as to make them scarce and therefore dear must cease, for they are opposed to the public interest and lead to unemployment. If employers who now adopt such practices will not give them up of their own accord, then, in my opinion, they should be made to do so by law. Cartels, combines, and trade associations may, and often do, serve a useful purpose, but only in so far as they succeed in offering to consumers a wider variety and better value for money in the goods they produce or distribute than can be offered by independent producers or retailers. All practices which stand in the way of the cheap and easy passage of goods from producer to consumer must also cease. We must lessen the gap between the price the producer gets for his goods and the price the consumer has to pay for them. So far from taking things easy when trade is good because profits are then easy to come by, employers must aim at the highest possible degree of efficiency in their businesses, not just for the sake of extra profits, but so that they may sell cheaply and command large sales, both at home and abroad. Jobs as managers and directors must go to those who can do them most efficiently: no favouritism must be shown to the sons and cousins and personal friends of existing directors.

Now what about the workers? They also will be called upon to give up those practices that lower industrial efficiency, for instance the unreasonable limitation of the number of workers allowed to enter a given trade so as to create a scarcity value for the services of those already employed in it. Or by demanding that more workers shall be employed upon any given job than are necessary. Or by doing less work, day by day, than could reasonably be expected from them. . . . Such practices increase the cost of production and lead to unemployment. I know that there are reasons for them and am reminded of the lad's reply to an impatient lady, for whom his father was doing a bricklaying job. She asked him " Whenever will this job get finished? " and he replied " Well, mum, Dad's gone off now after another job. If he gets it, your job'll be finished to-morrow. If he doesn't, heaven only knows when it *will* get done! "

Then again the workers must be prepared to be mobile. Of course, this is not to say that they must be constantly moving about. The need for this will rarely occur, but they must be willing to do so if there is no chance of work in the town where they live, and suitable employment is available elsewhere. In the same way, they must be willing to change their occupation if necessary. This will sometimes mean that trade union rules must be made more flexible so that workers may more easily pass from one trade to another. The rules that work of a given kind may only be done by members of a particular trade union although it could be done equally well by others must be discontinued, for they usually mean that jobs cost much more than they need. If the fear of unemployment is removed, the reason for those rules will largely disappear.

Then it is essential that workers shall not take advantage of a state of full employment to refuse to submit to reasonable shop discipline, nor must they demand wages so unreasonable as to dislocate industry and to produce an increase in selling prices and therefore in the cost of living. Don't misunderstand me. I am not advocating a policy of low wages. On the contrary, I want to see them as high as possible, but if they are forced up so high that employers are obliged to raise their selling prices, the workers as a whole will not be any better off. What they gain as producers they will lose as consumers. Moreover, high selling prices will lessen our chance of selling goods abroad, and we must remember that we must have a large export trade if we are to have full employment at home with a rising standard of living.

I can well believe that you may think the price I am suggesting is a heavy one. It is: but if, as a result of paying it, full employment can be stabilized, the benefit to all concerned, whether valued in terms of income or of freedom from anxiety, will be so great that we shall all feel that we have got a good bargain. And there's one other thing. The most unanswerable charge that fascism has ever brought against democracy is that it has never succeeded in finding a remedy for unemployment. Under fascism this is done through the exercise of a strict and cruel discipline. Under democracy discipline is still needed, but it must be self-imposed, and it is not always easy to discipline oneself, for it means being willing to place the interests of the community ahead of one's own selfish interest. But the fact is that democracy just won't work unless men are prepared to act unselfishly. We are, in very truth, members one of another, and only in a spirit of brotherhood can universal prosperity be attained.

A natural question to ask now is how much a policy of full employment will cost the tax-payer. It used to be said, with considerable vigour, and sometimes a fair show of justification, that the worst thing that could happen to money was for it to fall into the hands of the public authorities. But if these authorities are going to take over the main responsibility for seeing that the country remains prosperous, then they must be able to control a large proportion of the national income. This brings us face to face with the question of taxation, and once again we had better study the subject from its foundations. *How have our modern Tax Ideals developed?*

The answer is given by Ursula Hicks in the following extract from her book on *Public Finance*, one of the well-known series of Cambridge Economic Handbooks.

URSULA K. HICKS

THE DEVELOPMENT OF MODERN TAX IDEALS

IN the sixteenth and seventeenth centuries tax revenue was derived from two sources, a variety of partial taxes on expenditure, and a general tax on wealth. At the beginning of the period most of these partial taxes were on imported goods, and according to current theory, lay outside general distributional considerations, because they were regarded as paid by importers, and earmarked for naval expenditure. As the needs of the revenue increased and the customs duties were multiplied, this theory could no longer be plausibly maintained, and the distributional aspect of taxes on imports had to be considered. For the most part it was aimed to concentrate them on " nice and delicate things ", such as silk, wines, and tobacco, from the taxation of which the poor could not be expected to derive much hurt.

The chief interest of distributional theory was with the general tax on wealth. This had been reformed by Henry VIII under name of " The Subsidy ". Liability was fixed at 4s. in the £ on income, or alternatively at 2s. 8d. on the capital value of the source of income. The tax was considered to fall mainly on the rich or " the middle sort ". A gradual process of totally exempting the poor is discernible and appears to have been complete by the accession of Elizabeth. Unfortunately, the public service was incapable of maintaining the intention of the Subsidy, and before the end of the century contributions had become "stereotyped" (tied to conventional assessments). The result of this was a progressive fall in the amount of revenue collected.

The revenue needs of the Civil War gave rise to a series of attempts to rejuvenate the Subsidy; the most important of these was the Parliamentary "Monthly Assessment" of 1645. This time the income basis was adopted for all assessments; but in order to simplify the administration, as many taxpayers as possible were assessed by rank or station, only the remainder being directly assessed on salary or other income. In order to secure prompt collection it was thought necessary to allow the local assessors to use their judgment as to the most appropriate method of assessment, and presently it was found necessary to allocate a fixed minimum revenue to each district. This soon led to a hopeless degeneration in the tax, and gave rise to great unevenness of burden between different parts of the country.

This second deterioration of the general tax on wealth made it necessary for further reform to be attempted in the reign of William III when the needs of the revenue once again became pressing. The new "General Aid" was again in intention a proportional tax "according to yearly profits". In practice it was assessed in three ways, directly on salaries, indirectly in respect of income from moveable property by imposing a percentage on the capital value, and finally, in respect of income from real estate by collecting tax from the tenants, who stopped it out of the rent. It soon became apparent that it was still beyond the powers of the authorities to collect tax on income from personal property, so that in fact the Aid became a Land Tax. Throughout the eighteenth century it remained an important source of revenue; and it is still paid (but has no longer any fiscal importance) on certain old houses in respect of which it has never been redeemed by a capital payment.

It seems clear from these efforts that in the sixteenth and seventeenth centuries it was the intention of the legislature to raise an important part of the revenue by a general tax proportional to ability to pay; from contemporary writings it would seem that it was customary to pay some attention to family circumstances as well as to wealth. The fact that what emerged was a partial tax on income from real property was due partly to the relative ease with which income from this source could be assessed and the tax collected. At the same time land remained by far the greatest source of income until some way through the nineteenth century, so that the greater part of the receipts of an effectively general tax would also have come from land. The partiality of the tax does not seem to have been a source of serious complaint until well on in the eighteenth century.

There is no doubt that these " general " taxes were mainly paid by the wealthy, and the poor were virtually exempt. The result of sixteenth- and seventeenth-century policy was to fix the doctrine that income was the proper standard of equitable tax distribution.

In the later seventeenth and early eighteenth centuries the strain on the exchequer of long periods of war required the discovery of another source of revenue. This was found in the imposition of taxes on home-produced goods known as excises. During periods of exceptional strain (such as under the Commonwealth and again in the Marlborough wars), excises were freely imposed on commodities which were largely bought by the poor (especially beer, leather and salt). At first accepted because of the dire needs of the exchequer, and then condoned because of their impartiality, it was later argued that after all the excises were not distributionally unsatisfactory, because rich households made larger per head purchases of taxed commodities than poor families. Only a few of the clearest brains perceived that the excises were still unsatisfactory unless the rich bought *proportionately* more than the poor, which was not very likely.

A more serious argument in favour of taxes on general consumption was derived from Locke's political philosophy which became fashionable in the eighteenth century. This put forward the concept of the State as a voluntary association for the sole purpose of providing for the primary collective wants. Since all must share these wants it was just that each should contribute to their satisfaction, no matter how humble his station. This view was never universally accepted; in Parliament (which consisted mainly of landowners) there was always lively interest in the welfare of the poor, the class to which most members' tenants belonged, and a consequent reluctance to tax them.

The view that tax contributions should be assessed in accordance with ability to pay was thus never completely overthrown, but for a large part of the eighteenth century the flame burnt less brightly than at any other period of our fiscal history. Nevertheless, about the middle of the century, when the strain on the revenue was eased, the taxes imposed were in fact less regressive. Excises on commodities in general use were reduced to very low rates, and greater reliance was placed on high rate taxes on luxury goods. The eighteenth century approved of such taxes not merely because distributionally they were more acceptable, but also because they regarded them as to some extent optional; the manner in which he would make his contribution to the revenue might in some sort be left to the discretion of the taxpayer. Only an age of light revenue needs could have failed to realize that services cannot be paid for by optional taxes.

Towards the end of the century, when the needs of the revenue were once more expanding, new taxes were again required. This time the choice fell on a series of external indications of wealth, such as the number of hearths or windows in houses. Such things were easy to assess, and ownership might be assumed to be roughly proportional to wealth. These taxes undoubtedly represented a return towards the old tradition. The small houses were completely exempt; and the window tax was even assessed at slightly higher rates as the number of windows increased.

At the end of the eighteenth century there set in a period of severe financial strain similar to that which had occurred a century previously. Once again tax ideals were thrown overboard in a scramble for revenue. Excises of all sorts were introduced, and continued in operation throughout the Napoleonic wars. They were once again condoned as a war necessity, but it is not improbable that they served something of the same function during the war as the purchase tax of 1940, in restraining consumption which would have been in competition with the war effort.

The imposition of the new excises on top of the hearth and window taxes, the remains of the " optional " taxes, and various other remnants from earlier ages, reduced the tax structure to the utmost confusion. Owing mainly to the degeneration of the old taxes, up to 1797 the revenue was never sufficient to cover more than a minimum satisfaction of the primary collective wants and the interest on new war borrowing. The persistent prejudice against the inequity of general taxes on wealth (as they had so far been imposed) prevented any solution from being found, until Pitt finally succeeded in persuading Parliament to return to the general taxation of wealth in the form of an income tax.

Pitt's income tax of 1797 was enormously more effective than any previous general tax. It produced revenue above expectation, and what was still more remarkable, instead of degenerating after a few years in the manner of all previous taxes, the longer it was in operation the more revenue it produced. This was no doubt partly due to the rise in money incomes during the war, but it also revealed a new efficiency in the revenue authorities.

Like the earlier general taxes, the income tax aimed broadly at an impartial proportionality in distribution; but it took definite cognizance of family circumstances by a system of rebates, and the lower incomes were assessed a reduced rate. Returns of income were not compulsory, but declarations had to be made in order to claim these allowances. These returns were a substantial aid to correct assessment, and still more important, they formed a precedent for the later compulsory returns, which as experience has abundantly shown, are a *sine qua non* of an equitable and effective income tax.

In spite of its greater efficiency, the generality of Pitt's income tax was still suspect. It did not succeed in catching the profit incomes adequately, and the main burden still fell on land. This was one reason, perhaps the main reason, for the bitter opposition which it aroused, and which led to its suspension at the earliest possible moment after the war. Although the first income tax vanished in 1816, and every effort was made to obliterate its traces, few people believed that it would not return. The door had once more been opened wide on the old tradition of taxation in accordance with ability. None of the Victorians seriously questioned its validity, although they inherited from the eighteenth century the partially contradictory principle that all should contribute to the expenses of government. It is only in the most recent period that these two ideals have been successfully reconciled.

THE SUBSIDIARY AIMS OF TAXATION

Once the income tax was gone, the tax structure inevitably sank back into something like its eighteenth-century distribution. Thus, in 1828, over 70 per cent. of the revenue came from Customs and Excise, over a quarter being derived from duties on food and non-alcoholic drinks, and a considerable part of the rest from excises on bricks, glass, hides and other commodities which certainly affected the working class. This tax structure probably bore at least as heavily on the poor as that of the late seventeenth and early eighteenth century, but it differed from it in an important manner, in respect of the subsidiary aims to be achieved by the revenue. It will be convenient to turn aside to discuss the change of opinion in

this respect before proceeding to trace the modern development
of the distributional ideal.

From the middle of the seventeenth century an increasing
desire to serve economic ends by differential import and export duties is discernible. At first the main objective was to
encourage the import, and discourage the export, of raw
materials which might serve to stimulate employment at home.
Gradually, the direct protection of home industries and the
encouragement of exports came to attract more attention.
In the eighteenth-century period of revenue ease Parliament
was able to experiment widely with differential duties designed
to reach the " productional optimum " by favouring particular
interests. As usually happens, many of these attempts over-
reached themselves.

A striking example of an unlooked-for consequence of the
encouragement of industry by the State was the effect on the
home production of alcohol of an import duty. In the eighteenth century the protection afforded to the manufacture of
spirits resulted in such an enormous increase of output, and
fall in prices, that the spread of gin drinking among the working
class alarmed and shocked the whole country. (It was a case,
as the phrase went, of " drunk for a penny, dead drunk for
tuppence ".) The result of this fiasco was the inauguration
of the now traditional British policy of drastic excises on
intoxicants, with the express purpose of reducing consumption. Already in 1828 a third of the revenue was derived from
alcohol and tobacco (the latter duties had also something of a
sumptuary purpose). As we have seen, this policy has been
continued without intermission right up to the present day,
not, as must be acknowledged, without considerable advantage
to the revenue.

Of greater economic importance were the duties imposed
on imports, with the purpose of protecting the balance of payments. It would seem that in the latter half of the eighteenth
century a severe strain was felt on the exchanges; this manifested itself in a series of crises, and in high and fluctuating

interest rates. The causes of the pressure were complicated, they were compounded partly of the strain of successive wars, partly of the weakness of the Dutch exchange (due to the gradual impoverishment of that country) and the consequent efforts of Dutch nationals to repatriate funds hitherto invested in England.

The customs duties with which the eighteenth century attempted to meet this trouble were clumsy and no doubt inefficient. Adam Smith viewed the tax structure of his day with great disfavour, and no doubt he was right in believing (in effect) that the innumerable duties and subsidies seriously distorted the allocation of resources, and so hindered the approach to the productional optimum. In principle Pitt was also in favour of tariff reduction, but during the war period the state of the exchanges did not allow of any relaxation; indeed the suspension of cash payments by the Bank of England signalled the final collapse of the balance of payments.

Not long after the end of the war, however, Huskisson was able to effect an enormous simplification of the tax structure without any appreciable loss of revenue. This was a reform entirely in line with Smith's doctrine; but it also paved the way for the later reduction of duties on the path to free trade. Nevertheless the repeated exchange crises of the early nineteenth century, and their obvious relation to abnormal food imports (consequent on bad harvests at home), reveal that the balance of payments remained precarious until near the middle of the nineteenth century. It is probable that the most important economic effect of the Corn Laws was their restriction of imports.

From the 1860's the balance of payments was never in serious danger until after 1925. The Victorians, accustomed to rapidly expanding markets and to an unprecedented rate of capital accumulation, looked back incredulously at an age which had thought it sensible to multiply customs duties, and even to attempt to prevent the export of coin. In our own times, faced again with a deterioration in the balance of payments, we may look more kindly on an age when governments had to meet a very difficult international situation with whatever clumsy and primitive weapons lay to their hands.

Although the successive repeal of protective duties (culminating in that of the Corn Laws in 1846) led eventually in the circumstances of the mid-nineteenth century to a substantial increase in the national income and in the standard of living, it entailed for the time being a serious loss of revenue, which sooner or later would have to be made good. Reluctantly it was realized that this implied the return of the income tax. Thus it was that in 1842 Pitt's income tax came back, on the strict understanding that it was a temporary reserve for emergencies. It was soon perceived, however, that many of the old objections to it had lost weight. Partly owing to the increased skill of the Inland Revenue, partly to the rising morality of the business world, the assessments could no longer be accused of partiality. Gladstone continued to the end of his days to affirm that the income tax was only temporary, but the fact remains that when he might have abolished it he refrained from doing so.

THE ACCEPTANCE OF THE PROGRESSIVE PRINCIPLE

The principle that a substantial part of the revenue should be raised by means of a tax which paid prime attention to ability to pay, was thus firmly and finally established. The remaining stage of interpreting " ability " as satisfied only by progressive taxation was delayed for a few more decades. Sir William Harcourt's progressive death duties of 1894 were the first step along the new road, but the tax structure as a whole remained strictly proportional up to the second decade of the twentieth century. Yet the concept of progressive taxation, and the policy of bringing about a more egalitarian distribution of income through public finance, were no more than logical extensions of the traditional tax ideals. It is possible to trace the gradual emergence of the modern outlook from at least an early stage in the nineteenth century.

Up to the end of the eighteenth century the progressive idea (if we can call it such) was confined to the (very persistent) attempts to lighten the tax burden of the working class. The choice of excises falling outside the range of working-class purchases, and the exemption limits of the hearth and window taxes, are illustrative of these attempts. In the " reduced rate " on small incomes of Pitt's income tax, it is perhaps possible to detect a small further step; historically it did prove to be the first link in the chain of a fully progressive income tax. This tenderness for the poor was based on humanitarian grounds, and was not supported by logical argument; indeed there was a total failure to produce any argument which could stand up to Locke's contention that all should contribute to the expenses of the State.

About the turn of the eighteenth century, however, economists were arguing that the poor should be exempted from taxation on strictly economic grounds. Since (by common assumption rather than by factual demonstration) the poor lived on the margin of subsistence, any rise in prices, such as that due to the taxation of commodities which they purchased, would drive them below the margin. If employers did not increase wages to compensate for the tax, the supply of workers would decline. In either case British production costs would rise and our international competitive position would be damaged. It was an argument that no doubt reflects the unfavourable terms of trade of the early nineteenth century, but it did provide a logical basis for the many who wished to treat the poor generously on humanitarian grounds.

On the whole Adam Smith reflected the eighteenth-century point of view in being relatively uninterested in distributional questions, yet it is evident from other parts of his book that he was extremely interested in welfare problems. It is probable that in his view progress towards the " productional optimum " (which would be fostered by a reduction in restrictive duties) would improve the lot of all rapidly more than conscious redistribution. Among his contemporaries, however, there were already some who demanded that taxation should be used " to remedy the inequality of riches as much as possible by relieving the poor and burdening the rich ".

By the middle of the nineteenth century such a leading economist as Mill was prepared to support progressive taxation so long as the object could be obtained without taxing " industry and economy ". He was apprehensive of the effect of a progressive income tax on investment (a very real danger in the days of small-scale private business), but he was in favour of the taxation of economic surplus (Ricardian rent), and also of progressive inheritance taxes. The first of these two alternatives was immediately recognized as being economically admirable. Since pure surplus arises as the result of forces outside the control of the individual (such as the increased demand for his labour or for the use of his property) he can have no incentive to reduce his output if the surplus is taxed away. Unfortunately, the revenue to be gained from taxes on pure surplus is in most circumstances negligible in relation to the costs and difficulties of assessment and collection.

Largely owing to Mill's support, the progressive inheritance tax became law in 1894. By that time it is clear that some degree of progressive taxation had become generally acceptable. Many Liberals would probably have been prepared for a progressive income tax almost immediately. The change in outlook owed much to the marginal analysis of the 'seventies, and its demonstration that an accurate interpretation of " ability " must take account of the fall in the marginal significance of money as income rises, so that even an " equal sacrifice " of income called for progressive rather than for proportional taxation.

A few years after Harcourt's death duties had been introduced Edgeworth was arguing not for " equal sacrifice " but for "minimum aggregate sacrifice"—which, strictly interpreted, would have implied the confiscation of all incomes over a defined level. Since both these principles required the interpersonal measurement of utilities, they were not capable of providing an objective criterion for the direction of policy (such as is provided by the modern utility criterion). Nevertheless, the general acceptance of the principle of the redistribution of incomes through public finance—which was well on the way by the end of the nineteenth century—owed much to the contemporary discussions of the economists.

At the beginning of the twentieth century it would not have taken a very well informed prophet to foretell that the next substantial strain on the revenue would see the establishment of the progressive income tax. The occasion came with the Liberal Budget of 1909, which called for large additional funds (to finance additional naval expenditure as well as new social services). Thus super-tax finally found its way into the tax structure; in 1913 it yielded £3 million, by 1920 this had already jumped to nearly £56 million.

Realization of the redistributional potentialities of public finance was greatly facilitated by a new way of looking at taxes which is first discernible in the Gladstone era. Instead of regarding each tax separately, and attempting the impossible task of choosing only those taxes which would pass all the tests, it was suddenly realized that any desired distributional result could be obtained by a compensatory structure of taxes, in which the faults of one would be offset by the virtues of another. It followed logically (although this was only later realized) that expenditure should be taken into account, or at least so much of it as satisfied wants other than the primary collective needs.

This discovery finally made it possible to resolve the dilemma between the principles that all should contribute to the expenses of government (on political and moral grounds), and that the poor should be exempt (on humanitarian and utility grounds). In Britain to-day working-class families do contribute to the costs of government; in respect of income tax it is a fully conscious contribution. Nevertheless on a balancing up of pluses and minuses there is a net redistribution in favour of the lower income groups. By appropriate alterations of the tax and expenditure policy the redistribution can be adjusted to whatever extent, or in whatever direction, is required by the criteria of policy.

The arguments which the business man brings forward against heavy taxation are known to all: it " cramps his style "; it prevents him accumulating capital from his profits for further ventures; it makes him unwilling to take risks because he will reap no appreciable benefit for himself; and it destroys initiative and enterprise because it makes the game no longer worth the candle.

But *what is the effect of taxation on the worker?* How does the wage-earner react to taxation in the welfare state of to-day? The answer is given by a great expert on P.A.Y.E., and a former Commissioner of Inland Revenue. This lecture was broadcast in 1948, so it will be understood that slight changes may have occurred since then in the actual figures quoted.

S. P. CHAMBERS

TAXATION, INCENTIVES, AND SOCIAL INSURANCE

I OUGHT, perhaps, to begin by explaining why I have grouped taxation, incentives and social insurance in my title. The argument that the present method of levying income tax discourages the will to work is, I think, familiar enough already. Social insurance comes within my scope, because there are certain affinities between the contributions levied for social-insurance purposes and the payments we make in income tax, and also because similar affinities exist between the various income-tax relief allowances and the monetary benefits given under some of our social-insurance schemes. I shall be talking first about the problem of income tax and incentives, and later about a reform of the income-tax structure, which would comprehend the contributions for social-insurance purposes.

Out of about 20,000,000 people working for a living, about 18,000,000 get less than £500 a year and most of these are wage-earners whose attitude to work is affected quite noticeably by the amount of the weekly pay packet. There are, of course, exceptions, but generally speaking that is true. The actual amount of money drawn makes a big difference; and income tax affects that amount very materially. Let me try to illustrate that by some figures. Take the case of a single man earning £6 a week or a married man earning £8 a week. Both of them pay on their overtime earnings at 7s. 6d. in the pound (that is the 9s. standard rate, less one-sixth earned income allowance). The average rate of tax on the whole in both cases is just over 2s. because part of the income is free from tax, part is charged at 2s. 6d. in the pound, part at 5s. and only a small part at 7s. 6d. But it is not the average rate that counts. It is the rate levied on the extra pay earned by extra work. For instance, two hours' extra work at 3s. an hour will bring in 6s., but after tax at 7s. 6d. in the £1, the worker keeps only 3s. 9d. Now 3s. 9d. is not much for two hours' hard work at the end of a normal working day. It does not go very far in cigarettes, or drinks, or household goods subject to purchase tax.

It is true that basic needs such as milk, bread, and meat are cheap enough to enable us to buy as much of these rationed goods as we are allowed. It is the other things that cost so much—incidental items of clothing, things from a chemist's shop, cigarettes, beer, and so on. The whole tax structure almost seems designed to make extra work worth as little as possible in extra purchasing power. When the value of extra leisure is weighed against that of the extra earnings for overtime, too often extra leisure wins. Most industrial work is arduous: much of it is exceedingly tedious; and the point comes when an hour or two off from work—or even a day off

—for recreation of one kind or another is worth more than the pay lost.

Let us then admit that high taxation discourages work. But what can we do about it? With the enormous amount of government expenditure to which we are all committed, it is no use sighing for the days when a Chancellor of the Exchequer promised to abolish the income tax and actually did abolish it. Nor is it any good attempting to throw the whole burden on to the other taxes; in many ways these other taxes are as bad, if not worse, than the income tax. What we can do, however, is· to see whether, without reducing the total tax burden, its worst influences upon the willingness to work can be removed.

Let us look first at the method of collection. Before the war the tax-payer, whether wage-earner or director, paid his tax direct to the collector on the basis of an assessment of the income of a past period—a six months' period in one case and a year in the other. In 1940 a system of deduction of tax from earnings was introduced, the tax deducted during any period being the tax due on the wages earned in an earlier period. Then in 1943 came the P.A.Y.E. system, under which the tax deducted in any week was calculated on the earnings of that week. Notice that, from the incentive angle, both earlier systems were superior to P.A.Y.E. If a wage-earner worked overtime he used to receive his full overtime wages immediately, because the tax reduction at the end of the week was already fixed by reference to past earnings. The extra tax in respect of his overtime that week would not come along for some months, and for tax purposes the earnings of the week would anyhow be merged into the earnings of all the other weeks of the half year. Thus extra earnings had so indirect an effect upon the tax bill under the collection-in-arrear or the deduction-in-arrear system that the effect of the tax on the incentive to work was negligible. Under P.A.Y.E., on the other hand, the tax deducted in any week is calculated on the earnings of that week, and therefore extra earnings attract extra tax at once—and at the wage-earner's highest rate.

In spite of these disadvantages P.A.Y.E. was introduced because on other grounds it was superior to the older methods of tax collection. Under P.A.Y.E. the heavier tax falls on the week for which the heavier pay is earned, and in weeks of sickness a tax refund becomes due automatically. P.A.Y.E. also means prompt collection and therefore more efficient and more complete collection. A further advantage of P.A.Y.E. is that in a period of rising income levels, tax collections rise immediately as incomes rise, and not after a time-lag of between nine months and two years. This latter aspect makes P.A.Y.E. quite an important anti-inflationary weapon; and if income levels ever fall it will become an anti-deflationary weapon. For these reasons the P.A.Y.E. principle has clearly come to stay.

But P.A.Y.E. is only a method of collection; its introduction did not alter the general system of taxing individual incomes. Under that system the lowest slice of income is exempted from tax as a personal allowance, to which are added other free slices for children and other dependants. The next slice of earned income is chargeable at 2s. 6d. in the £, the next at 5s., and the next at 7s. 6d. Higher rates are charged on the slices of income above £2000. The effect of this rather complicated system is that while the average rate of tax on the whole income may be low the marginal rate of tax—the tax on the last bit of earnings—is frequently 7s. 6d. in the £. It is this system of high marginal rates which is so harmful. The system was designed when the rates of tax were lower, when extra tax was separated by a convenient interval of time from extra wages, and when, in consequence, the discouragement from work was much smaller. The theory behind it was sound for the conditions then prevailing. In two important respects conditions to-day are different.

First the amount of revenue to be raised is far greater. Rules of taxation which are appropriate when less than 10 per cent. of the population pay income tax are inappropriate when, except for very low incomes, income tax is universal. Secondly, the system of allowances for children and other dependants has been rendered obsolete by the new social security laws. These allowances, together with the other personal allowances, were designed with the object of exempting from tax the basic cost of living of the taxpayer and his family, and the theory was that the part of the income which the taxpayer used for his bare living needs ought not to be taxed.

But to-day a married couple get free education and many other free services for their children. They also get a weekly family allowance in cash in respect of all the children other than the first. So some people get two cash allowances from the same Government for the same children. One of these allowances—that under the Family Allowance Act of 1945— is fixed at 5s. a week however large the taxpayer's income. The other—that under the Income Tax Acts—varies according to the taxpayer's income. But the variation is the wrong way round; the smaller the income the smaller the allowance. Look at the figures for the second child where the income is £200 a year, £350, £400, and £600. For the lowest income the cash reduction is nil, because no tax is payable anyhow. The £350 a year man gets £7 off his tax bill, the £400 a year man, £15, and the £600 a year man gets £27 off his tax bill. Taking the allowances together the effect is that although the State has assumed considerable responsibility for the cost of bringing up children, it pays the parent more when the parent's income is larger and when he is therefore not in such need of assistance.

There is clearly duplication and anomaly here. The old tax system is inconsistent with the new social insurance system. The trouble is that the two sets of allowances have grown up independently. They are separately administered by separate Departments under separate Ministers. A surgical operation on the two systems has become necessary to get rid of the malignant growth of many years. But the anomalies are not confined to the allowances. Flat contributions are collected under the National Insurance Act and the Industrial Injuries

Act, and after next July these contributions will amount to 5s. 1d. a week for the adult male worker. The employer pays another 4s. 2d. a week, and if we assume that the employer could pay this 4s. 2d. as extra wages to the employee if he did not pay it to the State this means that the real cost to the employee is not less than £24 a year.

Although these payments are called " contributions ", they are, of course, taxes, and are so described in the Government White Papers on National Income and Expenditure. They constitute a form of direct taxation which is violently regressive. That is to say, the rate of tax per pound of income goes up as the income goes down. For a worker earning £2 a week the joint contributions are equivalent to a flat tax of no less than 4s. 6d. in the £; for the £5 a week man the equivalent is 1s. 9d. in the £; for the £60 a week man it is less than 2d. in the £. So we have an income tax for which the rate in the pound goes up as income goes up, and a National Insurance contribution for which the rate goes up as the income goes down. This regression is, of course, a feature of all flat contributions. But what is so convenient as to be passable when the weekly amount is a penny or two is no longer acceptable when the weekly amount is counted in shillings.

Now, if we stand right back from all the detail of these taxes and allowances under the Income Tax Acts and the Social Security laws, two main features emerge. On the one hand the State takes money away as taxation, on the other it gives money as allowances. This suggests that the proper course would be to merge the insurance contributions with the income tax, and to merge the main income-tax allowances with the family allowances. Now that we have a Family Allowances Act and other Social Security laws, there is no sense in retaining the whole paraphernalia of personal allowances, child allowances, allowances for dependants, and so on, in the Income Tax Acts.

What could be done, and done simply, is to expand the family allowance system to cover payments for the wife, first child, and other dependants, and then exclude all these allowances from the income-tax system. On the other hand, the insurance contributions could be abolished altogether, leaving this taxing function to the income tax. This would open the way to a sweeping simplification of the income tax except for the higher ranges of incomes, which in any case constitute such a small proportion of the total number of incomes. A flat rate of 3s. in the £ on all income up to £500 a year would be sufficient to bring in about £800,000,000—which is roughly sufficient to cover not only the whole revenue of the present complicated system under P.A.Y.E. but also the contributions under the National Insurance Acts and the amount necessary to expand the family allowances as I have suggested. A flat tax of 3s. in the £ would mean that the marginal rate of tax would be made equal to the average rate, and for the extra £1 of earnings the extra tax would be 3s. and not 7s. 6d. That would be an enormous improvement. The present budget brings the 7s. 6d. down to 7s. 2d., which shows how little can be done to bring down the rate of tax on overtime earnings by merely adjusting the allowances under the present system.

How much the flat rate of tax should be would depend upon budgetary factors which change from year to year, and the 3s. rate which I have suggested is little more than an illustration, although in fact it is just about the rate which would leave the whole budgetary position substantially unchanged this year. The individual taxpayer will not, of course, be in exactly the same position as before. For example, a single man earning £250 a year pays at present £20 in income tax and about £13 in national insurance contributions—a total of £33 excluding employer contributions. At a flat 3s. in the £ he would pay £38. That is a little more, but his marginal rate of tax drops from 7s. 6d. in the pound to 3s. in the £: he will get 17s. in the £ in cash out of every extra £ he earns.

A change of this kind would mean a great simplification of both the income tax and the national insurance. For nearly

18,000,000 people a vast amount of form-filling, assessment, and other complicated tax work under P.A.Y.E. would be abolished. Employers would also be relieved of a mass of detailed work under P.A.Y.E. and would also be relieved of all the work of stamping millions of National Insurance cards. In the place of these complicated operations the employer's task would be confined to deducting tax at the flat rate in all cases and paying it over to the Inland Revenue. For a radical reform of this kind there are, of course, many details to be filled in, but given the relatively broad and simple aims on the one hand and cash allowances on the other, a fundamental reform of this kind must, I feel, be tackled sooner or later.

The present complicated system of income-tax allowances has outlived its usefulness, and the system of stamping insurance cards has also had its day. These old horse 'buses are now obsolete; and although we admire the work of those who built these systems for their day and generation, we must recognize that much of what they did has ceased to have any meaning, and that the time has passed when further tinkering with these out-worn administrative machines is good enough. In the industrial world, research and development render much of our time-honoured machinery obsolete. Courage is required to scrap it. Perhaps still greater courage is required to scrap the accumulated junk of old and obsolete administrative machinery with its extravagant calls upon man-power, and to replace it by new labour-saving machinery designed to handle, not the light tasks of the nineteenth century, but the much heavier tasks of the twentieth.

Yes, our taxation system does seem to be out of date, and it does not take sufficient notice of the fact that there seems to be for most people, in the words of Sir Josiah Stamp, " a standard amount of total earnings which the worker will exert himself greatly to reach, but will not exert himself greatly to exceed".

We come now to the fashionable panacea of the moment: planning. The swing of the pendulum from the nineteenth-century preference for *laissez-faire*, both in politics and in economics, has led to the popularity of this movement. Even before the war the opinion spread that any institution which had grown up or evolved in a haphazard or natural way must be grossly imperfect. And, to quote F. A. Hayek: " To bring order to such a chaos, to apply reason to the organization of society, and to shape it deliberately in every detail according to human wishes and the common ideas of justice, seemed the only course of action worthy of a reasonable being ".

In the economic field it is obvious that every individual has to plan. So has every firm, and the bigger the firm the greater the need for wide planning. Surely it is only logical to carry this idea to its ultimate conclusion, and to apply the planning principle to the state itself.

Why is centralized planning a superior form of economic organization to that of free enterprise? The question is Evan Durbin's, and here is his answer in an extract from *Problems of Economic Planning*. The paper from which it is taken was originally published in 1935, and this will explain some of the topical allusions.

E. F. M. DURBIN

THE CASE FOR PLANNING

THERE are three charges which have been brought against Planning—both by professional economists and by business men. It has been argued that a Planned Economy will be a muddled economy because it will lack the automatic guide to productive activity provided by a pricing system; that it will lack the necessary incentives to secure efficient management; and that it will be unable to make adequate provision for the future. These are serious charges and must be considered.

The first of them—that Planning will lead to chaos because it lacks the automatic guidance of prices—can be advanced in two forms. It may either be said that a Planned Economy cannot have a pricing system because the institutions of central control render accurate prices impossible, or that although prices can exist their guidance *will not*, in fact, be followed by a Planning Authority. These two versions of the argument are radically different. The first assumes that there is some logical contradiction between prices and central control, while the second argument must be based upon social and psychological assumptions. It could only be justified by a demonstration that people will necessarily be foolish and pigheaded in a society which has chosen to control its economic life. It is of the greatest interest to notice that the arguments of *laissez-faire* economists have recently shifted their emphasis sharply from the one trend of argument to the other. This is so for three reasons:—

(*a*) In the first place, Russia, a centrally Planned economy, is plainly operating a price system of a sort. The Communist Party attempted in the first instance to abandon economic calculus altogether, and the result was unspeakably disastrous. The present Russian system including the Five-Year Plan is therefore one which is based fundamentally upon prices. The Plan or industrial budget is a schedule of total prices; industries are rationed in the monetary funds placed at their disposal; costs are calculated; and prices are charged for finished products at every stage. No one is saying that their price system is accurate, or that relative prices are made the sole criterion of productive policy. But that a price system can exist side by side with the central control of production is demonstrated beyond the possibility of refutation by Russian economic history.

(*b*) And, in the second place, it cannot be denied that any price system, however crude, must result in *some* kind of rational guidance as long as consumers are left free to spend their money as they please and a rough uniformity of costing practice is enforced upon all industries at once. Economists are perfectly right to insist that only the most delicate assessment of the value of economic resources in alternative uses will secure a *perfect* adaptation of production to the needs of society. But the degree of adaptation can vary very greatly, and any Planning Authority which insists upon a uniform assessment of values and costs will be able to make correspondingly wide adjustments to changing tastes and changing conditions. Even in the Russian price system where no payment is made for land or for the differences of individual efficiency within large groups of workers, it is obvious that the Central Authority could detect large divergences between the value produced and the cost incurred in any particular line of production by the tendency for stocks to change or prices to move at any given level of output. And this reasoning applies to every type of product. Crude price systems mean crude adjustment. Delicate price systems mean delicate adjustment. But it is only the absence of any price system which means no adjustment.

(c) From these two lines of investigation it must follow that there is no formal or logical contradiction between planning and pricing. It is perfectly possible for a centralized authority to order a price system to appear and to follow the guidance it necessarily gives. *There is no necessary connexion between the form of the authority by which decisions are taken and the principles according to which the decisions are made.* It would be just as sensible to argue that the organization of the medical profession under a National Council which laid down rules of professional conduct made it impossible to practise sound medicine as to affirm that the creation of a governing body for industry made it *impossible* to take wise economic decisions. It all depends upon what the Central Authority chooses to do.

Consequently the emphasis of the attack upon Planning has, in recent years, shifted back to the second charge, that, despite the logical possibility of pricing and wise planning, such wisdom will not in fact be exhibited by central authorities. I know of no reasoned defence of the view that central control will strengthen social unreason, but the two specific charges that proper incentive will be lacking and that socialist planning will be incapable of capital accumulation have been made and must be met.

The first of those charges can scarcely be sustained after the experience of authoritarian industrial management witnessed in Europe during and after the War. The sanctions against mismanagement provided by capitalism are bankruptcy and unemployment. The incentive for rapid and socially desirable activity is the hope of larger real incomes. There is no conceivable reason why a Central Authority should not impose just as strong, and even stronger, negative checks and provide the same type of positive inducement. Indeed, the experience of Planned Economies suggests that the danger with respect to negative checks is that they will be made too severe rather than too mild. The firing squad and the swamps of Siberia have featured too prominently as a reward for incompetent management in Russia, for example. And in the same way there is no reason in the nature of planning, and no great probability in practice, that differences in earnings will cease to be attached to grades of labour and skill which it is in the interests of society to develop and extend.

The only charge against Planning in which there remains the least shadow of substance is that a democratic and Socialist form of planning will find it difficult to secure funds for capital accumulation. It is obvious that the *authoritarian* economy in Russia has been guilty of *over*-saving rather than under-saving, but in this case it was possible to enforce the relative restriction of consumption by the bayonet and machine-gun. Would it be possible to do the same under a democratic régime in which Trade Union influence was strong?

It would be silly to deny that in a Socialist economy the pressure to raise wages in all industries at once would be sustained and grave. Nevertheless, if the natural desire on the part of each group of workers to increase the volume of their consumption is acceded to indefinitely, the rise in wages will eat into and finally altogether destroy the funds out of which the services of the Central Government and the building of new capital can alone be financed. The surplus arising in socialized industries must be owned by society and not by the group of workers in each industry. It must be administered by the Supreme Economic Authority for the good of the whole economy and not absorbed by the increase in the standard of living of small groups. Otherwise economic progress will cease. To this point we shall return in discussing the conditions of efficient Planning.

An investigation of the case against Planning leaves us, then, with the conclusion that, while there is no ground for supposing that it is impossible for a centrally controlled system to be as wisely guided as an unplanned system, there is one obvious danger from which a democratically controlled Socialist economy may suffer and must be saved. But we must go on to ask if there are any reasons for supposing that a Planned Economy will be *more* efficient than an unplanned? There are, in my view, at least four reasons for supposing that this will be the case:

(*a*) To begin with, a centrally controlled economy will be an economy with *open eyes*. It is the essence of an unplanned and competitive arrangement of industry that the persons who take decisions about output and investment should be blind. They control such a small fraction of the output of a single commodity, and, therefore, take into account such a small part of the industrial field, that they are not and cannot be aware of the consequences of their own actions. They are not aware of the economic results. They do not even consider social repercussions. Competitive producers, for example, will tend to install machinery with a view to increasing output without realizing that all their fellow producers will be doing the same thing and that prices will be forced down in consequence. They will, in fact, be forced below the price which would justify the increased output. Moreover, they will throw labour out of employment without any regard to the results of such a step. Since as producers they are not forced to maintain their erstwhile employees until they—the employees —have found new work, no final assessment of the cost of labour displacement is made by the private employer. Nevertheless, *society* has to bear the cost of maintaining the unemployed. Moreover, the sufferings of the displaced individuals as persons are part of the true cost to humanity of the technical change. In this and a thousand other ways the decisions taken in an unplanned economy must be short-sighted, irrational, self-frustrating and socially disastrous. There is no space to describe in detail the prejudice in favour of change, the wastage of human skill, and the continuous maladjustment which competitive industry exhibits under slowly changing conditions.

All these limitations of vision and calculation could be swept away by central control. The consequences of every decision can be estimated, however remote from the point of disturbance they may arise. Some allowance for it can then be made. When it is decided to install an electrical drill in a coal mine it will be possible to take into account not only the immediate effect upon the cost of extracting coal, but also the influence upon market price of an all-round rise in the output of the mines, the opportunities for the re-employment of displaced coal hewers elsewhere, the costs of maintaining them during the transitional period, and even some allowance can be made for the loss of skill and happiness—a loss that can be brought to no direct pecuniary assessment. A central authority, because it is central—because, that is to say, it can survey the whole industrial field—can see things no individual producer can ever see and give weight to considerations that cannot play any part in the calculations of men engaged in competing with one another. The general officers on the hill must be able to see more than the ensign in the line of battle.

(*b*) Just as there is an extension of the field of cognition over the breadth of industry, so also is there an increase in the length of foresight in time. A Central Authority can take account of processes which are occurring so slowly, or will begin to occur so far in the future, that no single producer could be aware of their existence.

A Central Authority could have foreseen the long agony of the hand-loom weavers at the beginning of last century in this country, the slow and cruel pressure upon world agriculture of more recent times, the need for a large-scale redistribution of labour in England in the 'twenties of this century; and could have made adjustments on a sufficient scale and over a long enough period to prevent much of the suffering and disharmony that have scarred our economic and social life.

A central Authority can foresee the exhaustion of raw materials, the wastage of natural resources of beauty and health and the destruction of human life which the blind scrambling of short-period plans continuously ignores. Such an Authority would, if it were in existence, foresee in our own country the tragic waste of the countryside indiscriminate building is everywhere occasioning, discern the disastrous social and economic consequences of the continual movement of industry into the south, and tackle in its greater wisdom the task of assessing the real social requirements in respect of the geographical distribution of industry and employment.

(c) One of the most important matters with which a Planning Authority will have to deal is the relation between finance and production. In no other field has the unplanned economy been less successful. The constant recurrence of depression and the instability of prosperity is one of the most marked features of capitalist society, and there is a virtual unanimity among economists that the wide movements of industrial activity are traceable to the mismanagement of the relation between credit policy and production. Moreover, the whole trend of recent thought on this subject has gone to show that, if it were possible to control one critical relation, the problem would be solved. The crucial relation is that between the savings of the public—the amount of money income which is not spent on consumption—and the money which is invested in setting up new capital. In an unplanned economy there are two sources of disequilibrium: (i) in the first place, the people who save and the people who invest are in no direct connexion with each other, and it is no one's business to see that acts of saving are followed immediately by equal acts of investment; (ii) in the second place, private banking institutions are in a position to vary the volume of investment without any reference to the course of saving. These are two sources of serious instability and are responsible between them for a very considerable proportion of the unemployment which has afflicted Capitalism throughout its history. No doubt there are purely scientific problems of great intricacy which must be resolved before we can hope to create and maintain stable prosperity. In my view, a large proportion of this necessary preliminary scientific work has been brought to a successful conclusion in recent years. But, whether that is the case or not, it is quite certain that whatever the correct monetary policy may be, it can only be enforced upon private corporations by the creation of an Authority in the financial sphere with adequate powers to over-ride all private considerations in the interest of general harmony. It is therefore safe to say that cyclical oscillation—the major cause of unemployment—will never be cured without the creation of the institutions of centralized *monetary* control. The financial field provides one of the most important opportunities for a Planned Economy to prove more efficient than an unplanned.

(*d*) Finally, there is one way in which a Socialist Economy may expect an increase in the volume and efficiency of the factors of production which is not available for any other sort of economy whatever—and that is in the attitude of the Trade Union worker to production. In an industrial world dominated by the struggle between organized property and organized labour for status and wealth, it is inevitable that all sorts of obstructive regulations should arise and " ca' canny " practices be enforced. These are, no doubt, partly due to the continuously recurring contractions in the demand for labour. But this is not wholly the case. A residuum of such resistance is wholly attributable to the dislike of the employer and the rights of property as such. There is, therefore, every reason to believe that there will be an increased willingness to relax such restrictions and to co-operate more willingly with the management side of industry when a Socialist Authority has raised the status of workers' representation and can provide full employment for the working population. No doubt too much has been made of this " change of spirit " in the Socialist apologetics of the past. The probability of conflicts between the interests of workers organized in industrial groups and the general service of society is very real. But to assert that the socialization of the means of production and distribution would release *no* new stores of vital productive energy in the labour force, would be to ignore the width and intensity of the Socialist sentiment which consciously or unconsciously animates the whole proletariat of a modern society.

If the arguments of this article are correct, it follows that, while there are no inherent and insuperable obstacles to prevent a centrally controlled economy from making wise distribution of the resources at its disposal, there are several reasons why it *could*, if it chose, make a better distribution and secure a greater volume of production. Will it do so ? The answer to that question rests with the future and is not subject to rigid prophecy. A Socialist Planning Authority will probably make use of some of these opportunities and not of others. But it is possible to lay down with some degree of certainty the conditions for the successful operation of a planned system in Great Britain.

In the *first* place, it will be essential to set up some kind of Central Authority with power over industry and finance. And this for two reasons:

(*a*) It will not do merely to create a large number of powerful but autonomous Public Corporations. This is only Planning of the first degree. It is subject to manifold dangers and limitations. It is quite true that Public Corporations operating with legally limited rates of profits will not be able to exert the same kind of monopoly pressure as a purely private body placed in the same dominating position. But it will possess the power and the motive to restrict the volume of service rendered, and to raise prices or fail to lower them, in the interests of the workers and the management in that industry. If such dangerous syndicalist tendencies are to be overruled, some authority with power to fix prices, output, and investment must be set over the Public Corporations.

(*h*) Of even greater importance, since restriction is always the child of financial stringency, is the need to control the financial mechanisms of the economy. It is of supreme urgency, if the Planned Economy is to be rendered popular and therefore stable in the midst of a democracy, to see that the early days of central control are followed by an expansion of employment and a stabilization at the higher level. This can only be done by control of banking and investment policy. The creation of a National Investment Board, the control of policy of the Joint Stock Banks and the use of the powers so acquired for the execution of a concerted plan of expansion and subsequent stabilization are, in my view, a *sine qua non* condition of successful Planning.

If this is the case, the process of socialization must begin rather than end with the creation of a Supreme Economic Authority. It does not matter whether the Authority consists of a Planning Department with a responsible Minister at the head of it, or a sub-committee of the Cabinet with the responsible Minister in the Chair, or even a number of Commissioners under general Parliamentary control, as long as the body is not too big or cumbersome, and is of a representative character. But it is of vital importance that one small body should have before it the relations between industry and industry on the one hand and industry and finance on the other. Only by this device is it reasonable to hope that the full advantages of central control can be secured.

In the *second* place, it is of great importance that an Authority with general powers should proceed upon the basis of a reasonable pricing and costing policy. Economists have been right to insist that the problem of distributing scarce resources between alternative employments exists for all economies—for a Socialist economy as much as a Capitalist. It is imperative to know what particular commodities are worth and how much they cost if any solution to the problem is to be found. As we have seen, it is not absolutely essential that the principles of costing should be accurate in every particular. They are certainly anything but accurate in existing competitive economies. The principles of costing under Socialist Planning will be less accurate in some important respects and more accurate in others. It will tend, for example, to obliterate the differences between the productivity of individuals within large groups of workers, but it will certainly assess to each type of production the general social disadvantages which private producers can shift on to the community. There is no reason why Socialist costing should not be as accurate as, or even more accurate on balance than, competitive costing—but costing there must be. If the Central Authority insists upon pricing outputs fairly, and secures uniform costing principles throughout the sector of socialized industry, the last requirement of efficiency—that of securing the distribution of labour and capital according to the differences between prices and costs—will arise. We can see the nature of this last requirement in the light of the general conclusion to which we are brought.

It has been the purpose of this article to emphasize that the importance of Planning to a democratic Socialist is two-fold. In the first place, a transference of industry to social control is the prerequisite political condition for any stable advance to a more just society. In the second place, Planning is vitally important in order to establish a more efficient economic system. This will render the approach to equality popular and, in any case, it is desirable for its own sake. In the establishment of a more efficient economy the most important single change lies undoubtedly in the cure of periodical depressions. But beyond that task, stretching out into the future when full employment is secured, there remains the double task of maintaining economic advance through the accumulation of capital and retaining the flexibility in the arrangement of the factors of production. Now, neither of these tasks can possibly be performed unless there is a willingness on the part of organized labour to adjust itself to the new conditions of national control. As we have already seen, the only way in which the accumulation of capital can be financed is by the withdrawal of part of the funds earned by socialized industries from the workers employed in them to finance the capital items in the industrial budget. Surpluses arising in socialized industries must not belong to the workers in such industries. They must belong to the State. And in the same way, if correct adjustments are to be made within the industrial structure, the vested interests of the workers in any particular industry must never be allowed to prevent contraction of employment if it is making losses or expansion if it is making profits. No one with a knowledge of Trade Union opinions and practices will doubt that this is one of the real problems of Socialist Planning.

The third, and perhaps the most important, requirement of efficient Planning is therefore the supersession in the Trade Union and Labour Movement in practice as well as in theory of the last elements of Syndicalism. All partial groups of workers by hand and brain—lawyers as well as bricklayers, postmen as well as doctors—must be prepared in the last resort to allow their own interests to be subordinated to the interests of the workers as a whole. It is scarcely necessary to point out that this does not mean that no regard is to be paid to the general human desire for stability and security. Nor does it mean that the vast majority of workers will not benefit by the processes of mutual concession that are demanded from us all. On the contrary, a rapid rate of capital accumulation

and a reasonable degree of flexibility are of vital importance for the welfare of every single worker in his nature
as a consumer. Only within these conditions can any individual
enjoy a rapidly rising standard of living. The interests of all
persons as consumers may be in conflict with the interests of
particular groups of persons as producers. What is requisite
for efficiency is that the interests of all should be served by a
continuous process of concession on the part of particular
groups. We must all mitigate our claims in order that others
may mitigate their claims against us and that by compromise
we may all live.

The efficiency of Planning depends in the last resort upon
the breadth and consistency of the Socialist faith which animates us. The organized workers who claim with justice that
the interests of the community should not be over-ridden for
the profits of the few should go on to add that those same
interests must not be over-ridden for the wages of a few. The
interests of the whole are sovereign over the interests of the
part. In society we are born; by society we must live. To
the centralized control of a democratic community our liveli-
hood and our security must be submitted. It is the business
of society to secure the welfare of all. To do so it must be
able to set limits to the welfare of each one of us.

Evidently the planning of the country's monetary policy is a most
important factor in the total planning scheme, and this has long been
done, at least to some extent, in every civilized state. In most countries
the Central Banks, which determine the conditions of the supply of
money, are state banks, directly controlled by the government in power.
Opinions differ on whether the state should regulate the ordinary
commercial banks while still leaving them in private ownership, or make
them actual state concerns, or should adopt some compromise between
these two systems.

There is a strong demand that the banking system shall be so
reformed and regulated as to ensure a supply of money rightly " man-

aged " in relation to the needs of the country's trade and industry. *Would the planned control of money alone be sufficient to ensure stability and prosperity?* Some financial experts think it might, but the following argument leads to a negative conclusion.

G. D. H. COLE

A PLANNED MONETARY POLICY

MONEY itself produces nothing; it is, except when it gets out of hand and becomes a clog upon production, no more than a means of facilitating the exchange of goods and services. Accordingly, the monetary machine should be the servant of the productive and distributive system, and should be so managed as to fit in with its needs. But it cannot be so managed if the system which it ought to serve is devoid of any coherent plan. The supply of money has always been a difficult problem; but it became infinitely harder when to the uncertainty of the supply of metallic money was added the great discovery of the bankers that they possess the mysterious power to create money out of nothing and to annihilate at will the money that they had made.

From the ills which this power to make and destroy money has brought in its train some economists have concluded that the instability of production would vanish if only this arbitrary power were taken away. We are told that if the quantity of money were absolutely fixed, prices would speedily adjust themselves to the available supply of means of payment, and we should only have to let things alone in order to ensure that every agent of production would be fully employed at a price corresponding to its real productivity. There would be no reason, we are told, for industrial activity to vary, if only the bankers were prevented from causing alternate booms and slumps by varying the supply of purchasing power.

Economists are fond of trying to demonstrate this by assuming what they call a " condition of equilibrium " in a " static " society in which no technical changes at all are supposed to occur—and sometimes even no changes at all in the demands of the population, whose number is supposed to be also unchanging. Doubtless, if such society did exist it would be a stranger to booms and slumps; for booms and slumps alike presuppose changes in the character of demand, and are closely associated with technical change. But to imagine such a society is in effect to abstract from real societies their most essential characteristics. Capitalism is in its essence a dynamic system; it is capable of being interpreted only in dynamic terms.

As soon as account is taken of technical changes and of changes in the character of demand, it ceases to be possible to regard the economic system as self-adjusting, even in the absence of monetary disturbance. For the balancing of supply and demand is no longer a matter of repeating endlessly an established routine, but of constant adaptation to new forces arising in both spheres. Every change in the direction of demand requires changes in the productive machine; and every change in relative costs of producing different things alters the direction of demand. The advocates of *laissez-faire* contend that these adjustments will be best made by letting things alone, so that the competition of the producers responds to every change in the conditions of demand and cost. But where full competition exists, the result is not equilibrium, but a continual process of trial and error, by which producers first make mistakes, and then try to correct them. This must be so, not only because producers can never know fully what the direction of demand will be, but still more because, under competitive conditions, no producer ever knows fully what his competitors are doing or proposing to do.

When competition is limited by sectional monopolies, as it is in every advanced capitalist society, this does not mend matters. The monopolist may be better equipped for anticipating the course of demand, and can eliminate the waste that arises from competitors producing too much of the same thing in ignorance of one another's doings. But ultimately no sectional monopoly is a monopoly; for consumers can substitute not merely Mr. B.'s cigarettes for Mr. A.'s, but anything they like. They can give up smoking, or smoke less, and taking to motoring, or theatre-going, or spending more on the house, or saving more and spending less, or any of a thousand other things. The possibilities of substitution are endless, and no monopolist can ever quite get away from them.

Accordingly, there is never under capitalism any assurance that supply and demand will be rightly adjusted. From this it follows that there is never any assurance that it will be worth while for business men to employ all the available factors of production. They will decide how much to produce, and how many workers to employ, by trying to hit on the level of production that will yield them the highest profit; and this may often be a level that leaves a good many people unemployed. But if once people do become unemployed, their condition tends to become perpetual; for the abolition of their purchasing power restricts the market for goods, and so makes it less worth while than before to extend the scale of production.

Under capitalism, depression tends to be self-perpetuating, quite apart from any misbehaviour of the monetary machine. But, if this is so, should not prosperity be self-perpetuating in an equal degree? For the fact that people are employed and earning incomes is a reason for continuing to employ them. This would be true in the main, if it were not for technical change. But this is constantly causing workers to be displaced by machines, under conditions which cause business men to think it most profitable not to extend production to an extent sufficient to absorb all the displaced labour. Accordingly, technical changes cause unemployment and so decrease purchasing power; and prosperity is not self-perpetuating, even apart from any fault in the management of money.

It is, of course, true that a decrease in total employment need not mean a decrease in purchasing power in terms of money; for the total prices of all the goods on the market and the total incomes of those still in employment may remain as large as before. But this is not the point, which is that the money is being exchanged against either less goods, or goods produced with a smaller expenditure of productive resources, so that a part of the power to produce goes to waste.

This tendency, inherent in capitalism, to waste productive resources, is greatly aggravated in one direction, but also alleviated in another, by the behaviour of money. The creation of additional money out of nothing, and the advancing of it in the form of producers' credits, becomes a means, by raising prices faster than costs, of inducing business men to employ resources which would otherwise have been left unused. This is so far to the good; but banks seldom stop creating credit at the right point—that is, when there are no surplus resources of production left unused—or dole it out in the right proportions to different types of producers. In a boom, credit is created till its only effect can be to raise prices without causing additional employment, and it is also so created as to lead to over-production of some things and under-production of others. There is an inflationary rise of prices; but at the same time the prices of the goods that have been over-produced begin to fall, or unsold stocks to accumulate.

At this point bankers and business men alike begin to take fright. The less foolhardy business men cut down production or orders for stock, and the banks sharply contract their loans. A crisis occurs, and most industries soon slump.

It appears, then, that if banks could be induced to create credit up to the point required to induce full employment, and then to hold the supply of credit steady at that point, there would be no need for the crisis to occur. But to hold this is to forget that credit is being maldistributed even before it becomes redundant in total amount. Bankers have not the knowledge to prevent this. They cannot have the knowledge, because, under an economic system of planless production, the necessary knowledge does not, and cannot, exist. Moreover, it should not be assumed that the banks have at all times the power to bring unemployed productive resources into use merely by the creation of additional credits. There is ample evidence that they have not, and that a policy of " easy money " may be quite ineffective in stimulating production if it is applied during a slump. For bank money is borrowed money. Even if it is available at low interest, it has to be repaid; and business men will not borrow it unless they see a prospect of profit by its use. But unless it is borrowed, and so gets into effective circulation, it cannot do its work of raising prices and demand, and so making the borrowing of it worth while. Banks can make booms when economic conditions are already favourable. They can turn booms into slumps by contracting credits. But they cannot turn slumps into booms merely by the manufacture of money. They can, however, check a recovery by refusing to manufacture it.

In fact, the power of the banks is that of abetting, or of thwarting, real economic forces arising in the sphere of production or demand, and not that of substituting their influence for these forces. It follows that, if we want to cure the instability of capitalism, we must act upon these economic forces as well as upon the monetary machine. We must set out to plan production in such a way as to ensure that all the available productive resources will be fully and continuously used; and therewith we must plan money in such a way as to fit in with our production plan.

Of course, no amount of planning will secure absolutely full use of all productive resources. Nor can a planned economy escape from the limitation that the way in which consumers will apportion their demands among different goods and services can never be absolutely known in advance. A planned economy can never be immune from errors of judgment arising from a wrong anticipation of demand. But it can eliminate errors due to lack of knowledge about the actions and intentions of other producers, not only in the same branch of industry, but in all. It can, therefore, hope to approach much more nearly than the present system to a correct anticipation of relative demands—the more so because it will certainly pursue a more equalitarian policy in distributing the final product of industry, and this will make most demands easier to foresee.

The final superiority, however, of planned production is that it makes possible a social decision to employ as nearly as possible all the available resources of production, and to make this employment continuous. For a planned economy can never be in the position of seeing a better prospect of profit in leaving a part of its resources idle, both because it will have to bear the costs of maintaining the idle resources—whereas under capitalism these do not fall directly on the employer—and also because the profit that accrues from underproducing must always be a profit at someone else's expense, and can never be a profit from the standpoint of the economy as a whole.

Within the limits laid down above, what are the conditions of a sound monetary system? First, that there shall be enough means of payment available to finance the exchange of the current production without upsetting the " national " movement of prices—by which I mean simply their movement on the assumption that money remains neutral in relation to them. In this sense, there should be neither too little money nor too much.

The correct standard for deciding how much money there ought to be is to be found in the condition of production. If factories that could be used to produce things that people need are standing idle, and workmen who could work in them are without jobs, that is a clear sign that there is too little money in circulation. The supply of money ought to be expanded up to the point at which use is being made of all the resources of production that it is worth while to use— worth while, that is, from the standpoint of our needing the things they can be employed to produce. On the other hand, if prices are being forced up because there is a monetary demand for more goods and services than the economic system can produce, that is a clear sign of a redundancy of money, and a case for reducing the supply.

Thus, ability to produce, and not stability of either prices or exchange rates, ought to be the guiding principle of monetary policy. But it does not follow that all that is needed in order to restore prosperity is simply for the banks to make available enough money to re-employ all the idle productive resources which it is really worth while to use. For, if the banks did this, and nothing else were done, there is no reason to suppose that any extra production at all would result, unless the conditions were in other respects favourable to increased industrial activity—or unless the banks took to lending money to anyone who asked for it, irrespective of his standing or of the soundness of his schemes. Potential credit becomes actual money only when someone actually uses it; and a mere increase in the potential supply of money would not in itself lead to any additional borrowing.

Secondly, then, the money required for the financing of production should be distributed to producers in accordance with the requirements of a production plan. In other words, the bank, or banks, in advancing credits must act in accordance with the requirements of the planning authorities. This matter of the right distribution of the money is every whit as important as the adequacy of the total amount. Indeed, in a planned economy it is even more important; for the danger to a planned economy is that the economic and financial machines may not work in together.

Thirdly, the distribution of the money to the final recipients of incomes through the productive system or otherwise should be in harmony with the planned production of goods and services. For clearly any planning of production implies and involves such a distribution of incomes as will cause demand to correspond as nearly as possible to what is produced. The orthodox capitalist view is, of course, the reverse of this— that what is produced ought to correspond to demand. But what is demanded depends essentially on how incomes are distributed; and I am assuming an economy that will have at its very basis a planning of the distribution of incomes. It will aim at as near an approach to equality as is consistent with the necessity for affording sufficient incentives to call out effort. It will accordingly frame a plan of income distribution upon this basis, and will make its plan of production in the light of its plan for the distribution of incomes. Within this limiting condition it will and should aim at giving the consumer the fullest freedom to spend his income on what he pleases; and it will accordingly make its production plan on the basis of giving the consumer as nearly as possible what he wants. But what the consumer does want will be itself conditioned by the prior decision of the planned economy to distribute incomes in a particular way. This distribution may be made mainly through the productive system, in the form of wages and salaries (and interest, as long as bonds earmarked against particular undertakings are allowed to survive); or it may be made to an increasing extent by way of " social dividends ", paid to all citizens quite apart from the work they do simply as shares in the social income. That is irrelevant for my present point, which is that the distribution of income, however it is made, is the fundamental determinant of the entire planning of production.

" Money " is needed, under our present system, both for buying finished goods and services and for financing intermediate exchanges. One of the chief reasons why money gets out of hand is that we use the same sort of money for these two essentially different purposes, so that it can be shifted from the one to the other, with the result of throwing the system out of balance. In a planned economy, the " money " used for financing intermediate exchanges can be kept wholly separate from the money used for final purchases, and all intermediate payments can be made in a pure money of account. Planned enterprise will draw the money it needs to pay out as final incomes from the banking system in one kind of money, and the sums it needs for intermediate payments in another; and the money of account will be exchangeable into "real" money only in accordance with the planned arrangements for the distribution of final incomes.

In a planned economy, the accumulation of capital will be a collective and not an individual matter. The incomes distributed to individuals will suffice only to buy the available supply of consumers' goods, and not the supply of producers' goods as well. Producers' goods will be regarded, as they should be, as intermediate goods, and will be bought and sold with money of account, and not with "real" money. There will be no question of "saving" outrunning "investment"; for investment will not be made out of individual saving, but out of planned appropriations of productive resources against which no "real" money will be issued to the consumers. Nor will "investment" be able to outrun "saving"; for the investment will be the saving. It will remain possible for individuals, by hoarding a part of their incomes, to create a deficiency of consumers' demand; but, as they will presumably be unable to earn any interest on their hoardings, what inducement will they have to hoard? Any tendency to hoard can be at once removed by causing "real" money to depreciate in value if it is not spent, as Gesell proposed.

Nor can there be any possibility of a planned economy saving and investing so large a proportion of its income as to cause a crisis. Doubtless, a planned economy can save and invest either too much or too little—too much to give its citizens as good a current standard of living as it can reasonably afford, or too little to provide for an adequate advance in its productive power. But there can never be any question as to the ability of a planned economy to secure an outlet in consumption for as much as it is able to produce. It can produce relatively too much of one thing and too little of another. But it cannot possibly produce more of things in general than it is able to sell; for it has unlimited power to create incomes for spending on final consumers' goods.

A capitalist society, on the other hand, can " oversave ";
for it can so distribute incomes that the recipients desire to
save and invest at a rate in excess of that which is rendered
profitable by the expansion of their will to consume. Investment can be profitable only if there is a proportionate expansion
in consumers' demand. Doubtless, the will to " oversave "
is checked in due course by the fall in profits which a limited
market for consumers' goods involves. But in view of the
instability of Capitalism, aggravated by the instability of credit,
the check may operate far too late to avoid a gross waste of
productive resources. For over-investment is not necessarily
unprofitable to the actual investor. It may only mean loss to
the owners of existing capital resources which the competition
of the new investments drives below the margin of profitable
use.

From this immense source of waste a planned economy
will be able to render itself wholly free. The determination
of the amount and direction of new investment will be made
at the same time as, and in conjunction with, the determination
of the distribution of incomes. They are indeed essentially
parts of the same process—that of deciding how much of the
current supply of productive resources shall be devoted to
meeting the current needs of the consumers, and how much to
providing in advance for their future needs.

The monetary management of a planned economy will thus
be, in its essence, a simple problem. The amount of " real "
money that will be needed will be simply that which suffices
to pay the consumers the incomes which have been allotted
to them under the planned distribution of incomes. The
amount of " money of account " that will be needed will be
simply that which suffices to finance the intermediate exchanges provided for in the plan of production. Of course,
both these amounts are relative to the price level, or the price
level is relative to them. For the prices of consumers' goods
and services must be equal in the aggregate to the consumers'
incomes; and the prices of account at which intermediate

goods change hands must correspond to the book entries which represent the credits issued in respect of them. It will, however, scarcely matter what the level of prices is—provided, of course, that the planned economy is not tied by an invariable gold standard to an international system of prices in terms of the national money. Freedom to vary exchange rates being assumed, the level of prices becomes unimportant. What do matter are *relative* prices, that is, that the prices of particular goods shall continue to be determined by the relative cost of producing them.

In a completely planned economy, it is almost true that there would be no monetary problem, but only a problem of fixing prices and incomes in the right relation to each other, and of adjusting the rates of exchange to the level required by the relative domestic purchasing powers of the various national currencies. But, of course, when we decide to adopt a Socialist economy, we shall not be able to leap at once to a completely planned system. There will remain branches of production outside the scope of planning, and forms of income outside the direct control of the planning authority. It will not be possible at once to make a complete separation between " money of account " and " real money ", because of the continued existence of these unplanned, or imperfectly planned, " sections " of the national economy; and accordingly for some time at least difficult problems of monetary management will remain in being. But the extension of planning over a large part of the economic field, provided that it includes and is based upon the planning of incomes as well as of production, will at once immensely simplify the monetary problem, by making it, as it should be, clearly secondary to the planning of production and distribution—the servant, instead of the master, of the industrial system.

In default of a planned system of production and distribution, the planning of money alone is bound to be ineffective. It may reduce the amplitude of capitalist fluctuations; but it cannot create a situation in which it will always pay best to use all the available resources of production to the fullest possible extent. Monetary management by itself may be efficacious in preventing booms; but it cannot cure slumps, and there is a danger that it may limit fluctuations only at the cost of leaving a part of the available productive resources permanently unused. For, let us repeat, money creates nothing: it is at most merely a means of facilitating exchanges. The first task for a sensibly ordered society is to decide in what proportions to distribute the right to consume, and to plan production in accordance with the demand which follows from the planned distribution of incomes. The issuing of the required monetary tokens is merely a secondary matter, which should conform to the needs arising out of the collective plan of production and consumption. To set out to regulate money without regulating the production and distribution of goods and services is to put the cart before the horse.

We have had the main general arguments for planning placed before us, and it will help us to see the picture more clearly if we take a concrete example and ask, *How should a factory site be chosen?* The answer is given by Professor Sargant Florence, one of the modern school of statistical economists who pride themselves on the accuracy of their mathematical methods.

P. SARGANT FLORENCE

"DESIRABLE SITE FOR FACTORY"

YOU have all seen advertisements published by towns or railways, advising you to put your factory, if you have any, in that highly desirable town or on that particular line. Well, we must ask ourselves what, in the national interest, is the best place for works to go to. And by national interest I mean where it is best for the works to go in the interests of all the people of the country. Under our system of free enterprise anybody with the money to buy or lease a parcel of land and to put up buildings has the right to do so almost anywhere. We take this for granted, as a matter of course. But when one thinks of the length of time these buildings will stand and of the different circumstances that may meanwhile crop up, and of the many other persons likely to be affected by the original decision to build, this placing of factories does seem rather an important matter to leave to one or a few individuals. For instance, there are factory buildings near the centre of Birmingham that are a hundred years old. When they were built, they were put on the edge of the town but now they clutter up space that should be devoted to public buildings or a fine thoroughfare for shoppers. Those who originally put up these factories probably had only their own interests in mind, and, in placing a factory, these interests are mainly what are called economic— that is, the business man hopes for a large money profit, larger than if the factory were placed anywhere else. For instance, if there is a choice of putting his factory in a large city or in the country, the business man is likely to choose the city, because he can get labour easily without building any new houses and without having to induce men to move by offering high salaries and wages, and also because railways and other transport are available. His costs are thus on the whole less in the city and his profits greater. As an economist I am popularly supposed to defend such economic motives. I am still supposed to believe faithfully what Adam Smith wrote over a hundred and fifty years ago, that by pursuing his own interest man is " led by an invisible hand to promote an end which was no part of his intention ". The business man hopes to increase his profit by finding a site that will reduce his costs and will economize his resources. This, so runs the argument, will also economize in national resources, and thus there is no need for national planning. Q.E.D.

The invisible hand will do it for you, through the profit-seeking business man.

To go back to our instance of the business man preferring the city. It might be considered a national waste, too, to build new housing for the worker in the country with new drainage, streets, electric light, and so on when such utilities already exist in the cities. By thus putting factories in the city, the community will save money and economize as well as the business man.

But the question is: What is the end which, though no part of the business man's intention, the invisible hand is going so economically to promote? For in order to achieve a good plan you must have an end clearly in view. Planning in itself is neither good nor bad till you know what the plans are for. Nazi plans, most people would agree, are worse than no plans. Now in choosing ultimate ends economists seem to me to have no right to speak with more authority than anyone else. Given an ultimate end, they can only say whether such-and-such means will efficiently serve that end.

Here, for instance, is a nice question: Should our planning be for the greatest total income, or for a more evenly spread income, even though, as a total, it is not quite so large? This is not just a conundrum to set before the Brains Trust, but I assure you, a very real practical dilemma. Ask yourselves, would you rather have in the coming year £5 a week sure, week in and week out; or would you rather have even odds, a fifty-fifty chance, on £10 or £2? The latter choice, the equal chance of £10 or £2, averages out at £6, but I believe most people would prefer the certain £5.

Now there are very much the same alternatives in the location of industry. A town may be, on the average and in the balance of chances over a number of years, wealthier if it specializes on a single industry, for there are great economies in concentrating on one job. But the town will not be safe. The particular industry specialized in may slump, like the cotton industry of Lancashire or the heavy iron and steel

industry of South Wales, the North-East Coast, and Lanark-
shire, and leave nothing else for the depressed area—the
so-called special area—to do. The towns in the area may
become ghost towns where all the social capital sunk in roads,
drains, and public utilities becomes so much idle capacity.
Half the workers in the one mobile, or foot-loose, industry
the area possesses may be unemployed. This was not unusual during the slump of 1930 to 1933. Those unemployed
have nothing but the dole, and can buy only bare needs. So
shops lose trade, and less personal services, building activities,
amusements, can be paid for. Shopkeepers, builders, and
the entertainment trades drift toward bankruptcy and have
to sack their assistants. But put your eggs in more than one
basket, and though you may lose in total industrial efficiency
—for two baskets are more bothersome to carry than one—you
gain in security. It is not for the economists to say whether
you should choose maximum average income or choose
security. But he can tell, once you have chosen, how to
achieve whichever end you want.

On the whole, the world, with its bitter experience of
unemployment in the inter-war years, is plumping for social
security. Once this lead is given, the economists can immediately say, " Right, as it is security and freedom from
the fear of unemployment that you want, here is my plan:
diversify your foot-loose industries in any one area, and
diversify them in such a way that the industries selected will
fit in with one another and give a constant load of employment. Have industries that employ men only, such as heavy
iron and steel, balanced with industries that employ women
in large proportions such as light engineering or chocolate-
making or dressmaking. Have industries that suffer from
seasonal ups and downs mixed with industries that don't—or,
better still, mixed with industries that suffer the opposite ups
and downs—downs and ups, in fact. Potteries, for instance,
seem to go slack in the middle of summer and winter, and
boom in spring and autumn. Brick- and tile-making, on the

other hand, boom in the height of summer. So if you have
both industries you get steady employment at least in three
seasons of the year. You might also mix the industries like
machine-building, which have those terrible periodic downs
that occur every ten years or so, with stable industries like
those producing foodstuffs."

And there is also another sort of mixing more important
than any of them for the industrial security of a town. That
is to mix decaying industries like, say, saddlery, with growing
industries, like wireless parts, or like ladies' handbags. Handbags are also made of leather, but, unlike saddles, are coming
into fashion.

Now let us get back to the original question of who has
been responsible for the present location of industry and
whether he is the right person to do the job in the future.
Can the business man with an eye on his own interests, who
has been responsible up to the present, be relied upon to see
that industries in any one area are balanced, dovetailed,
spliced, and generally made to fit, in order to achieve security?
I honestly doubt it. To have an accurate picture of the
degree of fluctuation, decline, or growth, and of the types of
employees of different industries, requires, I am bound to
say, highly technical knowledge: statistical analysis, the trend
of international trade, and all that. Business men are not
particularly good at reading statistics of trades other than
their own, or of following the politics of nations other than
their own. They are indeed quite human. Even if he knows
the facts, it may not be to the business man's own interest
to mix industries. As a business man he is out for profit for
himself or his shareholders, and it will pay him to put his
factory where other factories in the same industry are found.
The social security of any given area will not concern him.
If his industry slumps, it will slump wherever he is placed.

Social security is not, of course, the only objective of modern
schemes of planned industrial location. There is the desire
for a mixture of town and country outlook, which would

clamp down on the further growth of London, where people live so far from any green and pleasant land, that life in the country positively gives them the creeps. And what is true of London applies almost equally to the string of towns in Southern Lancashire or Birmingham and the Black Country.

If we are to mix town and country; if we are to leave a bit of the country in the form, say, of green belts round a town and to " disperse " industries into the country or country town, then we may have to sacrifice some economic advantage to individual businesses for the sake of social advantages to the community as a whole. It is not for the economist to veto this, he must simply record, as far as he can, the probable extent of the sacrifice. However, some of the bills of costs presented by the economists, though stiff, may be thought worth while for the sake of creating the diversity of industries that gives greater security, health, and amenity. Parliament agreed before the war to spend several million pounds in broadening the basis of industry in the special areas which had up to then specialized in coal-mining and the heavy metal industries. It was thought worth this money to give the areas a variety of lighter industries on which to fall back when the heavy industries slumped, as they so often do. Planning legislation has to some extent restricted the sites within a town where a business man can build a factory. I am not talking, however, of the so-called zones where a factory is allowed to go within a town once that town is chosen, but of the choice of the town or district itself. In this wider problem the business man still has unrestricted choice.

I have said that towns have tended to specialize in certain industries for sound economic reasons. That is to say, the reasons were economically sound to the business men of the single industry who put their factories there. They did so because they knew that they could always find labour in that town skilled in their particular trade; that they could always find auxiliary trades making the accessories and components which their particular industry wanted, and could always find the sort of services (transport, repairs, marketing, banking) that their particular trade wanted. But though sound for the individual factory owner, this specialization—or localization as it is called—is not necessarily sound from the standpoint of the town itself. Nor is the localizing of industries a cure-all for every economic ailment. I am not a quack doctor. My medicine does prevent one area dying of the disease of industrial slump when other areas are fit and well. But it does not prevent a widespread, mild attack of the disease.

On the whole, our larger towns—Glasgow, Birmingham, Manchester, Leeds, and of course London—are towns of mixed industries; whereas our smaller towns—Bolton, Merthyr Tydfil, Stoke-on-Trent, Kidderminster, Motherwell—are often towns of one industry. But one can effect a fairly happy compromise by the device of small satellite towns each specializing in a certain industry. If one of these industries slumps, the citizens of the town that slumps with its industry are not too far away from the other towns to travel there for work; but they are far enough away to have a green belt of country between the towns. If you cannot manage such satellite towns, you can hit upon some middling size of town that will be large enough to have several manufacturing industries, each on an economic scale, but not too large to lose touch with the country. One must not belittle the economic advantages of a town specializing in an industry. But there is no reason why every medium-sized city should not have a second and perhaps a third string to its industrial bow.

People get confused by such words as the planning or moving of industry. We have not got a clean slate, and to clean it completely and start all over again by physically moving factories would be frightfully costly. It is in fact very seldom that the equipment of a factory is moved from one place to another. What happens when an industry shifts is that the factories in one place fail to grow or even decline and fall, while factories in the same industry but in another place, start up, grow, and spread. In a democratic country we cannot force manufacturers to settle their factories in any one place. But we can stop the starting or extension of factories in places that don't meet national needs, and can offer instead alternative sites in selected areas. We can also help to close down old, outworn, and obsolete factories, being careful to clean up the mess they leave. The useful life of the average factory is not really so very long. Just as every seventy years the population is in fact quite a different lot, so just by taking care of new industrial *births* we may in thirty or forty years have materially changed the industrial face of Britain.

Faith in planning was in many cases a logical development from the belief in the efficiency of the big firm. People saw smaller businesses being swallowed by big ones, and they saw the big ones reducing prices (perhaps only for a time, but let that pass) and they said that obviously the large concern was more efficient than the small one. They even found economic arguments to support this theory based on a law of " increasing returns ". Was this conclusion justified? *Does bigness make for efficiency?*

The answer is given by Mr. S. R. Dennison, Lecturer in Economics at Cambridge University.

S. R. DENNISON

DOES BIGNESS MAKE FOR EFFICIENCY?

I AM often struck by the irony implicit in an argument which must be familiar to everyone. Because some development or other in our affairs is said to be inevitable, then, it is claimed, we must do all in our power to bring it to pass. This seems to me to presume that if we did not exert our efforts, the inevitable would not happen. In fact, of course, ideas can often have a powerful influence on the course of events. Many things are made inevitable only because they are believed to be so.

I want to try to demonstrate that this argument can be applied to one of the most widely held economic beliefs of our time. It is this—that an economic organization on a large scale must be efficient, and that the trend towards bigger organizations is inevitable. Entangled with this belief is the view that the planning of economic affairs by a central authority is superior to a system of free enterprise, not only because the central authority will take better decisions, but also because production will be carried on more efficiently. Here is the basis of the promise of the higher standard of living held out to us by the believers in economic planning. There are many reasons why I believe this promise to be illusory; but I am concerned here mainly with one—that the identification of large size with efficiency is contrary to both general reasoning and specific evidence.

First of all we must be clear on the meaning of " efficiency ". The essential idea is simple, but it is often obscured and neglected. As an approximation, efficiency consists of achieving a given result with the greatest economy of effort. It means producing with the minimum real costs in capital, labour, materials and so on. I am aware that my brother economists could immediately state a dozen qualifications to this formulation—that is why I referred to it as an approximation. But I will keep to it as a general rule valid enough to make any departure from it require specific justification.

Let us pose our problems with this definition in mind. Is a large firm efficient? However many highly paid officials it employs, however up to date its system of cost accounting, and so on, does it use less resources for a given production than are required by a smaller concern? A smaller concern does not have the same elaborate organization, hierarchy of officials, and all the rest, simply because it does not need them; they are, in fact, the costly necessities of bigness, worth while only if they are more than offset by other economies in production which are not available to the smaller producer.

There are some branches of production where great technical economies can be got by large-scale operation. The examples usually quoted are electricity generation, rail transport, iron and steel and the motor-car industry. In fact, they are quoted so often that one sometimes wonders if there can be many others. They seem to be exceptional in that great economies can be got by using large units of capital equipment. This is not found in many other industries; a large cotton mill, for example, does not have bigger and better spindles than a small one; it simply has a larger number of spindles, and there are in fact no technical economies of the kind which can be got from a big electric power station or a big blast furnace. There is a great deal of evidence to show that the economies of mass-production are not nearly so general as is commonly supposed. We can use the reports of the Working Parties to illustrate this point. The Working Parties have been investigating various British industries, and they have almost invariably reported that the large factory has no greater access to economies in production than the comparatively small factory. For example, the boot and shoe industry is one in which manufacture is said by the Working Party to be " carried on under conditions which increasingly approximate to mass production ". Yet out of a total of more than 800 factories there are only fourteen which employ more than 1000 workers each; the majority have less than 200 workers each. In spite of this, the Working Party concluded that " the general level of efficiency is such that we do not find any striking and far-reaching economies that could be made by reorganization "

In the United States, it has been estimated that mass-production is technically appropriate for about one-third of the goods produced there. The proportion in Britain is almost certainly less than this. The manufacture of goods accounts for not much more than one-third of our total activity; mass-production methods are still less appropriate for the other two-thirds, including agriculture, the distributive trades, and all the various personal and other services. So, in all, perhaps one-eighth of our economic system is appropriate for large-scale organization, if that is needed to secure the economies of mass-production. As we have seen, however, mass-production does not necessarily mean huge organizations; the scale needed for its full exploitation may, in fact, be quite modest. In certain directions, moreover, technical progress is on the side of the small unit. Electric power, for instance, though it needs a big unit for its efficient production, has almost certainly reduced the size needed for optimum efficiency in many other branches of production.

The large concern may, of course, be able to secure certain commercial economies for which a single factory would be too small. In certain cases these other economies may be of considerable importance. But there are also diseconomies of size, which increase with the growth of the scale of operations. The root problems are those of management and control. Those writers who like to solve problems by stating them are wont to refer to co-ordination as the answer to all difficulties. It is not—it is itself a main problem to be solved. A large organization must necessarily delegate duties and responsibility to many people. But if the organization is to mean anything at all, there must be consistency between the actions of all these individuals who are of necessity acting independently in their separate spheres of responsibility. This consistency can be achieved only by reference to a common centre, where one individual must take the final decisions. In consequence there must be constant consultation and a great deal of duplication of effort. And the results may be unsatisfactory compromises. For, of course, each individual must know more than anyone else about his own immediate field of action, and the supreme head, the co-ordinator, has to take decisions on very generalized information; he may well come to judge on the merits of the man who puts the case rather than on the merits of the case itself—or I should have said the merits of the case as they are presented to him.

Moreover, however elaborate the systems of checks and controls, there will be room for waste and mismanagement which never gets known at the top. Various administrative systems are just so many attempts to secure effective control by the centre without at the same time stifling all independent action and initiative. They can never overcome the fundamental dilemma, that there is a choice between decentralization, with its freedom to exercise initiative, and co-ordination, with its fitting of the separate parts into a centrally determined scheme. In practice some form of compromise has to be reached.

At bottom, the limit to efficient size depends upon individual human ability to comprehend and control the details of a complex whole. The " best " men, who are now so much in demand to run new State organizations, are very scarce, and even when they can be found, their abilities are not unlimited. It certainly seems that at least the very big firms are too large to be operated at optimum efficiency. This has long been recognized by those who ought to know best. Here, for example, is the Chairman of General Motors, the largest industrial concern in the United States: " In practically all our activities we seem to suffer from the inertia resulting from our great size. It seems to be hard for us to get action. . . . There are so many people involved and it requires such a tremendous effort to put something new into effect. . . . Sometimes I am forced to the conclusion that General Motors is so large and its inertia so great that it is impossible for us to be leaders." This was in 1925; since then General Motors have adopted the only satisfactory solution to the problem—that is, to give up the attempt and to divide itself into a number of virtually autonomous units bound together by relatively loose control from the centre. Its example has been followed by others, and not only by the giants. The nice co-ordination and smooth-running efficiency of the large concern is something which exists only in the imagination of the economic planners; those who have first-hand experience are more aware of the difficulties, the wastes, and the imperfections.

These considerations apply with added force to national-ized industries. Nationalization is advocated, and adopted, for reasons too numerous for me to discuss here. But much seems to be expected from a single control of a whole industry, to secure the blessings of co-ordination. The first step is thus the creation of a large new administrative machine—on top, of course, of that already existing in the firms which comprise the industry. Given the promise that the industry has to be controlled, such a machine is, of course, necessary. But if my diagnosis is correct, the blessings of co-ordination are, in fact, illusory, whereas the problems created by the simple fact of the establishment of a huge organization will become very obvious. The nationalized industry has, moreover, cer-tain features which are likely to intensify the disadvantages of bigness—the scale of operations will be greater than that of any private concern, the controlling body has special monopol-istic powers, and the form of organization adopted creates ill-defined and divided responsibilities.

Widening our perspective, we have the attempt to control in detail the major part of our economic life. The delays and frustrations which are now so familiar are not accidental but inherent in the scale and complexity of the system. And it would need a good deal of imagination to contend that the results are always satisfactory and worth the price.

A committee sponsored by the Fabian Society has recently stated that " there may be only two choices: to agree to less Government activity, including planning; or to watch the economic life of the country slow down ". I think that this is true. But the committee decided that " neither alternative is acceptable "—which is characteristic of this school. Their answer lies in better organization of the higher Civil Service, with improved recruitment and new methods of training. This is again to solve the problem by stating it: the Civil Service cannot cope with the tasks imposed upon it? Very well, we must reform it so that it can. And while this is being propounded, from many quarters, the First Commissioner of the Civil Service has been expressing concern at the low quality of many of the entrants now coming forward. Of course, the planners will have an easy answer to that one—we must start by reforming the Civil Service Commission.

It is a quarter of a century since one writer predicted this very thing, showing that when a system of State economic controls began to break down under its own weight, the cry would go up that the administrators must be chosen differently and trained in new ways. In truth, these problems are not to be solved by even the most radical reforms of the Civil Service. They are insoluble, for they are the result of organization too big to be effectively controlled by mere human abilities.

If all this is true, you may well ask: Why are large organizations so characteristic of the modern economic system? One answer is that they are not. For example, only about one-quarter of the total number of workers in manufacturing industries are in firms with over 1000 workers each, and in many industries comparatively small firms lead the way in efficiency and enterprise. In many services, such as the distributive trades, the small unit is, of course, predominant. The real answer, however, is that large organizations are deliberate creations. There is nothing inherent in our modern economy which makes them inevitable. This is so obvious for nationalized industries that it hardly seems worth saying. In private industry, the giant firms usually result from conditions other than a search for increased efficiency, one important reason being an attempt to create monopoly, and all that this implies.

This, I think, is tacitly recognized in the Bill to investigate and control monopolies which was introduced in the House of Commons in March 1948. A Monopolies Act could be a useful piece of legislation. But there are various legal and institutional elements in our present society which can favour monopoly, and without changes in these, any direct effort to check monopoly can have only limited effect. Moreover, nationalized industries, and apparently other statutory organizations, are excluded from the proposed legislation. We still have the belief that the large organization must be more efficient than the small one, and that co-ordination is superior to what is usually called the chaos of competition.

I suggest that our only hope of securing a rise in our standard of living depends upon the restoration of the freedom of competitive enterprise. As Lord Keynes once wrote, " The advantage of the decentralization of decisions and of individual responsibility is even greater, perhaps, than the nineteenth century supposed ". It is greater in so far as the economic world has become more complex, more dependent on specialization. We have, in fact, developed far beyond the stage when human ability can successfully control economic life in the way envisaged in overall planning. It is not the system of free enterprise which has been rendered obsolete by the economic developments of the past 200 years. It is overall State planning which is out of date, which belongs to an earlier and simpler economic world.

It is by no means an easy task to create conditions under which competition could perform its essential functions and at the same time to correct the important disharmonies (such as heavy unemployment or extreme inequality) which we all recognize must not be allowed to exist. It is a task which demands much positive action by the State, both to ensure that competition is able to work effectively and justly, and to secure that its benefits are used to give minimum standards for all. It is something which has never been done before. But it is not, I think, impossible; and, unlike the dream world of some planners, it does hold out some real promise of economic and social improvement.

Perhaps bigness does not always mean efficiency, but even then planning cannot yet be condemned.

The great economic problem which we all have to solve is, to quote Professor Hayek again, " the distribution of available resources between different uses ". " The economic problem arises as soon as different purposes compete for the available resources. And the criterion of its presence is that costs have to be taken into account. Cost here, as anywhere, means nothing but the advantages to be derived from the use of given resources in other directions." We can all understand that. " Counting the cost " is an occupation with which we are all too familiar. But we must do it if we are going to make a wise use of our income. And the business man must do it on a bigger scale if his business is to be efficient. You will remember the " Principle of Substitution " which we considered when we were studying production. Surely then, if every individual, every business man, must plan the distribution of available resources between competing uses, it is still more essential for the state to do the same.

Professor Hayek does not think so. The fundamental question, he says, is whether it is possible under the complex conditions of a large modern society for a central authority to solve the economic problem of distributing a limited amount of resources between a practically infinite number of competing purposes. He first stated the question in his *Collectivist Economic Planning* (1935) and he answered it with a decided and vigorous negative in *The Road to Serfdom* (1944) from which the following extract is taken.

F. A. HAYEK

IS PLANNING INEVITABLE?

I T is a revealing fact that few planners are content to say that central planning is desirable. Most of them affirm that we can no longer choose but are compelled by circumstances beyond our control to substitute planning for competition. The myth is deliberately cultivated that we are embarking on the new course not out of free will but because competition is spontaneously eliminated by technological changes which we neither can reverse nor should wish to prevent. This argument is rarely developed at any length—

it is one of the assertions taken over by one writer from another till, by mere iteration, it has come to be accepted as an established fact. It is, nevertheless, devoid of foundation. The tendency towards monopoly and planning is not the result of any " objective facts " beyond our control, but the product of opinions fostered and propagated for half a century till they have come to dominate all our policy.

Of the various arguments employed to demonstrate the inevitability of planning, the one most frequently heard is that technological changes have made competition impossible in a constantly increasing number of fields, and that the only choice left to us is between control of production by private monopolies and direction by the government. This belief derives mainly from the Marxist doctrine of the " concentration of industry ", although, like so many Marxist ideas, it is now found in many circles who have received it at third or fourth hand and do not know whence it derives.

The historical fact of the progressive growth of monopoly during the last fifty years and the increasing restriction of the field in which competition rules is, of course, not disputed— although the extent of the phenomenon is often greatly exaggerated. The important question is whether this development is a necessary consequence of the advance of technology, or whether it is simply the result of the policies pursued in most countries. We shall presently see that the actual history of this development strongly suggests the latter. But we must first consider in how far modern technological developments are of such a kind as to make the growth of monopolies in wide fields inevitable.

The alleged technological cause of the growth of monopoly is the superiority of the large firm over the small, due to the greater efficiency of modern methods of mass production. Modern methods, it is asserted, have created conditions in the majority of industries where the production of the large firm can be increased at decreasing costs per unit, with the result that the large firms are everywhere underbidding and driving out the small ones; this process must go on till in each industry only one or at most a few giant firms are left. This argument singles out one effect sometimes accompanying technological progress; it disregards others which work in the opposite direction; and it receives little support from a serious study of the facts.

[Professor Hayek goes on to question the alleged superior efficiency of the large firm which we have already considered above.]

The assertion that modern technological progress makes planning inevitable can also be interpreted in a different manner. It may mean that the complexity of our modern industrial civilization creates new problems with which we cannot hope to deal effectively except by central planning. In a sense this is true—yet not in the wide sense in which it is claimed. It is, for example, a commonplace that many of the problems created by a modern town, like many other problems caused by close contiguity in space, are not adequately solved by competition. But it is not these problems, like those of the " public utilities ", etc., which are uppermost in the minds of those who invoke the complexity of modern civilization as an argument for central planning. What they generally suggest is that the increasing difficulty of obtaining a coherent picture of the complete economic process makes it indispensable that things should be co-ordinated by some central agency if social life is not to dissolve in chaos.

This argument is based on a complete misapprehension of the working of competition. Far from being appropriate only to comparatively simple conditions, it is the very complexity of the division of labour under modern conditions which makes competition the only method by which such co-ordination can be adequately brought about. There would be no difficulty about efficient control or planning were conditions so simple that a single person or board could effectively survey all the relevant facts. It is only as the factors which have to be taken into account become so numerous that it is impossible to gain a synoptic view of them, that decentralization becomes imperative. But once decentralization is necessary, the problem of co-ordination arises, a co-ordination which leaves the separate agencies free to adjust their activities to the facts which only they can know, and yet brings about a mutual adjustment of their respective plans. As decentralization has become necessary because nobody can consciously balance all the considerations bearing on the decisions of so many individuals, the co-ordination can clearly not be effected by " conscious control ", but only by arrangements which convey to each agent the information he must possess in order effectively to adjust his decisions to those of others. And because all the details of the changes constantly affecting the conditions of demand and supply of the different commodities can never be fully known, or quickly enough be collected and disseminated, by any one centre, what is required is some apparatus of registration which automatically records all the relevant effects of individual actions, and whose indications are at the same time the resultant of, and the guide for, all the individual decisions.

This is precisely what the price system does under competition, and which no other system even promises to accomplish. It enables entrepreneurs, by watching the movement of comparatively few prices, as an engineer watches the hands of a few dials, to adjust their activities to those of their fellows. The important point here is that the price system will fulfil this function only if competition prevails, that is, if the individual producer has to adapt himself to price changes and cannot control them. The more complicated the whole, the more dependent we become on that division of knowledge between individuals whose separate efforts are co-ordinated by the impersonal mechanism for transmitting the relevant information known by us as the price system.

It is no exaggeration to say that if we had had to rely on

conscious central planning for the growth of our industrial system, it would never have reached the degree of differentiation, complexity, and flexibility it has attained. Compared with this method of solving the economic problem by means of decentralization plus automatic co-ordination, the more obvious method of central direction is incredibly clumsy, primitive, and limited in scope. That the division of labour has reached the extent which makes modern civilization possible we owe to the fact that it did not have to be consciously created, but that man tumbled on a method by which the division of labour could be extended far beyond the limits within which it could have been planned. Any further growth of its complexity, therefore, far from making central direction more necessary, makes it more important than ever that we should use a technique which does not depend on conscious control.

While there can thus be little doubt that the movement towards planning is the result of deliberate action and that there are no external necessities which force us to it, it is worth enquiring why so large a proportion of the technical experts should be found in the front rank of the planners. The explanation of this phenomenon is closely connected with an important fact which the critics of the planners should always keep in mind: that there is little question that almost every one of the technical ideals of our experts could be realized within a comparatively short time if to achieve them were made the sole aim of humanity. There is an infinite number of good things, which we all agree are highly desirable as well as possible, but of which we cannot hope to achieve more than a few within our lifetime, or which we can hope to achieve only very imperfectly. It is the frustration of his ambitions in his own field which makes the specialist revolt against the existing order. We all find it difficult to bear to see things left undone which everybody must admit are both desirable and possible. That these things cannot all be done at the same time, that any one of them can be achieved only at the sacrifice of others, can be seen only by taking into account factors which fall outside any specialism, which can be appreciated only by a painful intellectual effort—the more painful as it forces us to see against a wider background the objects to which most of our labours are directed, and to balance them against others which lie outside our immediate interest and for which, for that reason, we care less.

Every one of the many aims which, considered in isolation, it would be possible to achieve in a planned society, creates enthusiasts for planning who feel confident that they will be able to instil into the directors of such a society their sense of the value of the particular objective; and the hopes of some of them would undoubtedly be fulfilled, since a planned society would certainly further some objectives more than is the case at present. It would be foolish to deny that the instances of planned or semi-planned societies which we know do furnish illustrations in point, good things which the people of these countries owe entirely to planning. The magnificent motor roads in Germany and Italy are an instance often quoted—even though they do represent a kind of planning not equally possible in a liberal society. But it is equally foolish to quote such instances of technical excellence in particular fields as evidence of the general superiority of planning. It would be more correct to say that such extreme technical excellence out of line with general conditions is evidence of a misdirection of resources. Anyone who has driven along the famous German motor roads and found the amount of traffic on them less than on many a secondary road in England, can have little doubt that, so far as peace purposes are concerned, there was little justification for them. Whether it was not a case where the planners decided in favour of " guns " instead of " butter " is another matter. But by our standards there is little ground for enthusiasm.

The illusion of the specialist that in a planned society he would secure more attention to the objectives for which he cares most is a more general phenomenon than the term of specialist at first suggests. In our predilection and interests we are all in some measure specialists. And we all think that our personal order of values is not merely personal, but that in a free discussion among rational people we would convince the others that ours is the right one. The lover of the country-side who wants above all that its traditional appearance should be preserved and that the blots already made by industry on its fair face should be removed, no less than the health enthusiast who wants all the picturesque but insanitary old cottages cleared away, or the motorist who wishes the country cut up by big motor roads, the efficiency fanatic who desires the maximum of specialization and mechanization no less than the idealist who for the development of personality wants to preserve as many independent craftsmen as possible, all know that their aim can be fully achieved only by planning—and they all want planning for that reason. But, of course, the adoption of the social planning for which they clamour can only bring out the concealed conflict between their aims.

The movement for planning owes its present strength largely to the fact that, while planning is in the main still an ambition, it unites almost all the single-minded idealists, all the men and women who have devoted their lives to a single task. The hopes they place in planning, however, are not the result of a comprehensive view of society, but rather of a very imited view, and often the result of a great exaggeration of he importance of the ends they place foremost. This is not o underrate the great pragmatic value of this type of men in a free society like ours, which makes them the subject of just admiration. But it would make the very men who are most anxious to plan society the most dangerous if they were allowed to do so—and the most intolerant of the planning of others. From the saintly and single-minded idealist to the fanatic is often but a step. Though it is the resentment of the frustrated specialist which gives the demand for planning its strongest impetus, there could hardly be a more unbearable— and more irrational—world than one in which the most eminent specialists in each field were allowed to proceed unchecked with the realization of their ideals. Nor can " co-ordination ", as some planners seem to imagine, become a new specialism. The economist is the last to claim that he has the knowledge which the co-ordinator would need. His plea is for a method which effects such co-ordination without the need for an omniscient dictator. But that means precisely the retention of some such impersonal and often unintelligible checks on individual efforts as those against which all specialists chafe.

Yes, it does seem as though Planning has its drawbacks. Adam Smith had probably never heard the word used as it is used to-day, but he had his own opinion on the idea, and a very strong opinion it was, too: " The statesman who should attempt to direct private people in what manner they ought to employ their capitals would not only load himself with a most unnecessary attention, but assume an authority which could safely be trusted to no council and senate whatever, and which would nowhere be so dangerous as in the hands of a man who had folly and presumption enough to fancy himself fit to exercise it."

In the opinion of the " man in the street " the main argument for planning is that it can prevent unemployment, and that, under the Labour government in Britain in the years after the war, it did prevent unemployment. Perhaps there would have been little unemployment in any case with such a world-wide demand for goods and services which had been unprocurable during the war years. And if unemployment should arise under a system of planning it will have an even worse effect on the unemployed than it used to have. The feeling of being " unwanted " will be much more bitter when the decision has been made, not by some blind force, but by one's fellow-men. However, J. M. Keynes was a firm believer in the possibility of preventing widespread unemployment by prompt government action. " Planning " for him meant some central management, more particularly of finance, but the leaving of all details of production to individual enterprise and initiative. Given some people wanting goods and others wanting work, what is to stop the government satisfying both? *How much does Finance matter?* The answer is given in the following brief talk, broadcast in

1942. It will remind us of Keynes's revolutionary ideas on monetary policy.

J. M. KEYNES (LORD KEYNES)

HOW MUCH DOES FINANCE MATTER?

FOR some weeks at this hour you have enjoyed the day-dreams of planning. But what about the nightmare of finance? I am sure there have been many listeners who have been muttering: "That's all very well, but how is it to be paid for?"

Let me begin by telling you how I tried to answer an eminent architect who pushed on one side all the grandiose plans to rebuild London with the phrase "Where's the money to come from?" "The money?" I said. "But surely, Sir John, you don't build houses with money? Do you mean that there won't be enough bricks and mortar and steel and cement?" "Oh no," he replied; "of course there will be plenty of all that." "Do you mean" I went on "that there won't be enough labour? For what will the builders be doing if they are not building houses?" "Oh no, that's all right," he agreed. "Then there is only one conclusion. You must be meaning, Sir John, that there won't be enough *architects*." But there I was trespassing on the boundaries of politeness. So I hurried to add: "Well, if there are bricks and mortar and steel and concrete and labour and architects, why not assemble all this good material into houses?" But he was, I fear, quite unconvinced. "What I want to know" he repeated "is where the money is coming from." To answer that would have got him and me into deeper water than I cared for, so I replied rather shabbily: "The same place it is coming from now". He might have countered (but he didn't): "Of course I know that money is not the slightest use whatever. But, all the same, my dear sir, you will find it a devil of a business not to have any."

Had I given him a good and convincing answer by saying that we build houses with bricks and mortar, not with money? Or was I only teasing him? It all depends what he really had in mind. He might have meant that the burden of the national debt, the heavy taxation, the fact that the banks have lent so much money to the Government and all that, would make it impossible to borrow money to pay the wages of the makers of the raw material, the building labour, and even the architects. Or he might have meant something quite different. He could have pointed out very justly that those who were making houses would have to be supported meanwhile with the means of subsistence. Will the rest of us, after supporting ourselves, have enough margin of output of food and clothing and the like, directly or by foreign trade, to support the builders as well as ourselves whilst they are at work?

In fact was he really talking about money? Or was he talking about resources in general—resources in a wide sense, not merely bricks and cement and architects? If the former, if it was some technical problem of finance that was troubling him, then my answer was good and sufficient. For one thing, he was making the very usual confusion between the problem of finance for an individual and the problem for the community as a whole. Apart from this, no doubt there *is* a technical problem, a problem which we have sometimes bungled in the past, but one which to-day we understand much more thoroughly. It would be out of place to try to explain it in a few minutes, just as it would be to explain the technical details of bridge-building or the internal combustion engine or the surgery of the thyroid gland. As a technician in these matters I can only affirm that the technical problem of where the *money* for reconstruction is to come from can be solved, and therefore should be solved.

Perhaps I can go a little further than this. The technical problem at the end of this war is likely to be a great deal easier to handle than it was at the end of the last war when we bungled it badly. There are two chief reasons for this. The Treasury is borrowing money at only half the rate of interest paid in the last war, with the result that the interest paid in 1941 on the new debt incurred in this war was actually more than offset by the relief to national resources of not having a large body of unemployed. We cannot expect that the position will be so good as this at the end of the War. Nevertheless, if we *keep* good employment when peace comes (which we can and mean to do), even the post-War Budget problem will not be too difficult. And there is another reason also. In 1919 public opinion and political opinion were determined to get back to 1914 by scrapping at the first possible moment many of the controls which were making the technical task easier. I do not notice to-day the same enthusiasm to get back to 1939. I hope and believe that this time public opinion will give the technicians a fair chance by letting them retain so long as they think necessary many of the controls over the financial machinery which we are finding useful, and indeed essential, to-day.

Now let me turn back to the other interpretation of what my friend may have had at the back of his head—the adequacy of our resources in general, even assuming good employment, to allow us to devote a large body of labour to capital works which would bring in no immediate return. Here is a real problem, fundamental yet essentially simple, which it is important for all of us to try to understand. The first task is to make sure that there is enough demand to provide employment for everyone. The second task is to prevent a demand in excess of the physical possibilities of supply, which is the proper meaning of inflation. For the physical possibilities of supply are very far from unlimited. Our building programme must be properly proportioned to the resources which are left *after* we have met our daily needs and have produced enough exports to pay for what we require to import from overseas. Immediately after the war the export industries must have the first claim on our attention. I cannot emphasize that too much. Until we have rebuilt our export trade to its former dimensions, we must be prepared for any reasonable sacrifice in the interests of exports. Success in that field is the clue to success all along the line. After meeting our daily needs by production and by export, we shall find ourselves with a certain surplus of resources and of labour available for capital works of improvement. If there is *insufficient* outlet for this surplus, we have unemployment. If, on the other hand, there is an *excess* demand, we have inflation.

To make sure of good employment we must have ready an ample programme of re-stocking and of development over a wide field, industrial, engineering, transport, and agricultural—not merely building. Having prepared our blueprints, covering the whole field of our requirements and not building alone—and these can be as ambitious and glorious as the minds of our engineers and architects and social planners can conceive—those in charge must then concentrate on the vital task of central management, the *pace* at which the programme is put into operation, neither so slow as to cause unemployment nor so rapid as to cause inflation. The proportion of this surplus which can be allocated to building must depend on the order of our preference between different types of project.

With that analysis in our minds, let us come back to the building and constructional plans. It is extremely difficult to predict accurately in advance the scale and pace on which they can be carried out. In the long run almost anything is possible. Therefore do not be afraid of large and bold schemes. Let our plans be big, significant, but not hasty. Rome was not built in a day. The building of the great architectural monuments of the past was carried out slowly, gradually, over many years, and they drew much of their virtue from being the fruit of slow cogitation ripening under the hand and before the eyes of the designer. The problem of pace can be determined rightly only in the light of the competing programmes in all other directions.

The difficulty of predicting accurately the appropriate pace of the execution of the building programme is extremely tiresome to those concerned. You cannot improvise a building industry suddenly or put part of it into cold storage when it is excessive. Tell those concerned that we shall need a building industry of a million operatives directly employed—well and good, it can be arranged. Tell them that we shall need a million and a half or two millions—again well and good. But we must let them have in good time some reasonably accurate idea of the target. For if the building industry is to expand in an orderly fashion, it must have some assurance of continuing employment for the larger labour force.

I myself have no adequate data on which to guess. But if you put me against a wall opposite a firing squad, I should, at the last moment, reply that at the present level of prices and wages we might afford in the early post-War years to spend not less than £600 million a year and not more than £800 million on the output of the building industry as a whole. Please remember that this includes repairs and current painting and decorations and replacements as well as all new construction, not merely on houses but also on factories and all other buildings. That, for what it is worth, is my best guess. It covers the activities of private citizens, of firms and companies, of building societies, as well as of local authorities and the Central Government. Now these are very large sums. Continued, year by year, over a period of ten years or more, they are enormous. We could double in twenty years all the buildings there now are in the whole country. We can do almost anything we like, *given time*. We must not force the pace—that is a necessary warning. In good time we can do it all. But we must work to a long-term programme.

Not all planning is expensive. Take the talk of two months ago about planning the countryside. Nothing costly there. To preserve as the national domain for exercise and recreation and the enjoyment and contemplation of nature the cliffs and coastline of the country, the Highlands, the lakes, the moors and fells and mountains, the downs and woodlands furnished with hostels and camping grounds and easy access—that requires no more than the decision to act. For the community as a whole the expense is insignificant. Or take the question of compensation, which Mr. Osborn discussed so clearly and so fairly a fortnight ago. Compensation uses up no resources. It is out of one pocket into another and costs nothing to the community as a whole.

Even the planning of London to give space and air and perspective costs nothing to the nation's resources and need not involve a charge on the Budget. There is heaps of room, enough and more than enough, in a re-planned London. We could get all the accommodation we need if a third of the present built-up area was cleared altogether and left cleared. The blitz has uncovered St. Paul's to the eyes of this generation. To leave it so will cost nothing to the community as a whole. To build may be costly. Let us offset that expense by a generous policy, here and there, of *not* building.

Where we are using up resources, do not let us submit to the vile doctrine of the nineteenth century that every enterprise must justify itself in pounds, shillings, and pence of cash income, with no other denominator of values but this. I should like to see the war memorials of this tragic struggle take the shape of an enrichment of the civic life of every great centre of population. Why should we not set aside, let us say, £50 million a year for the next twenty years to add in every substantial city of the realm the dignity of an ancient University or a European capital to our local schools and their surroundings, to our local government and its offices, and above all, perhaps to provide a local centre of refreshment and entertainment with an ample theatre, a concert-hall, a dance-hall, a gallery, a British restaurant, canteens, cafés, and so forth. Assuredly we can afford this and much more. Anything we can actually *do* we can afford. Once done, it is *there*. Nothing can take it from us. We are immeasurably richer than our predecessors. Is it not evident that some sophistry, some fallacy, governs our collective action if we are forced to be so much meaner than they in the embellishments of life?

Yet these must be only the trimmings on the more solid, urgent, and necessary outgoings on housing the people, on reconstructing industry and transport, and on re-planning the environment of our daily life. Not only shall we come to possess these excellent things. With a big programme carried out at a properly regulated pace we can hope to keep employment good for many years to come. We shall, in very fact, have built our New Jersualem out of the labour which in our former vain folly we were keeping unused and unhappy in enforced idleness.

Suppose we agree that a certain amount of planning is desirable, or even necessary. Then comes an even more important question. *What are we to plan for? Security or Efficiency?* Is it possible to plan for one without giving full consideration to the other? The case for efficiency is outlined below in a radio talk by Sir Geoffrey Crowther. This was the last of three talks on " Wealth and Welfare ". In the second talk he had pointed out that " there are three main things that you can try to do with your economic machine ". You can aim at high production, which is the only possible basis for a high standard of living. Or you can aim at stability and the avoidance of slumps ; at full employment in other words. Or you can aim at security and the elimination of poverty from any cause whatever. All three objects, he said, were desirable, and all three were possible, but we had been tending to forget the need for efficiency in our pursuit of stability and security.

SIR GEOFFREY CROWTHER

THE WAY BACK TO SOLVENCY

A FORTNIGHT ago I argued that the British economy had become in these recent years very stiff and un-adaptable to changing circumstances. It is still capable of a high output of goods, but only at a very heavy cost. It may seem to most people that our present circumstances are not too bad, but hidden in them there are real risks. I do not want to exaggerate them, but they do exist. The most obvious of those risks lies in our foreign trade; within two years the great flow of American aid will come to an end, and at very much the same time we shall probably find that what is called the sellers' market will also come to an end, that is, the state of affairs in which we and other countries find little difficulty in selling abroad what we can produce. Devaluation will have helped to give us a start in these conditions, but we may find ourselves in about two years' time fighting for our lives in the world's market, and we are not, I fear, in very good condition for that.

The risks at home are not so obvious as those abroad, but they are no less real. If you look round the industries of the country you will find in a great many of them—not in all, but in a great many—that the prices at which goods are sold have risen more than the incomes of the people who buy them. The outstanding case is that the building worker cannot now afford to live in the house that he is building, and it is obvious when you have that state of affairs that those industries will not indefinitely be able to maintain their present high level of activity.

Last week I inquired how this state of affairs had come about, and the answer that I gave was that for a whole genera-tion we have neglected the efficiency of our economic machine. We have concentrated on stability and security, which are indeed good things to concentrate on, but we have done so to the exclusion of the efficiency of our economic mechanism, with the result that to-day there is hardly another country in the world where less emphasis is placed on economic efficiency than here.

What can be done about it? The obvious short answer is we should start paying attention to the efficiency of our arrangements, and bringing efficiency back into the front rank as an object of policy. Something can be done simply by paying attention to the matter of efficiency, by exhortation, by educating the public, but the effects of those are likely to be limited. I think what you can get by exhortation is limited at any time, and perhaps particularly now in this country when for ten years we have had a steady diet of exhortation and have had about enough of it. Moreover the particular problem of increasing efficiency that we are confronting now is one where exhortation is not likely to be very effective, because if we are to succeed in restoring our efficiency, we are going to have to do some very difficult and unpleasant things. We are going to have to show ourselves a willingness to change, which is something that no human being likes to do. We shall have to allow the more efficient method of doing things to supersede the less efficient, and the more efficient man to supersede the less efficient man. In fact a resuscitation of efficiency involves two of the things that human beings find hardest in the world to achieve, that is constant mental effort, and a continuous disturbance of settled habits. I do not believe that you can get that sort of thing by exhortation alone. You have got to make it worth people's while. That is a familiar phrase and, if you analyse it, to say that you must make it worth people's while means this: that you must see that they are better off if they do make themselves more efficient, and that they are worse off if they do not make themselves efficient. In short, you should do what you can by leadership and by inspiration, but I do not believe you will get any significant return to efficiency unless you also get a return to competition.

Competition, I know, is a fighting word, and nothing has

had more abuse in recent years than the word and the concept of competition. The trouble is that people will talk in extremes, and when you say that you want more competition they will jump to the conclusion that you want to go back to the old nineteenth-century days of cut-throat competition and devil-take-the-hindmost; they will talk as if the choice were between no competition at all and completely unbridled competition. But that is not the case at all; it is a matter of degree. There is always some degree of competition in every economy and in every country; what I am saying is not that I want to go back to the nineteenth century, but that the element of competition that we have to-day in our economy is too small and that we should be better off if we enlarged it.

Once or twice in these talks I have compared our state of affairs with that in America. America is a country where to my mind they have too much competition. It does indeed make them rich; much of their very high standard of living is due to the competitive nature of their society. But every time I go there I am struck again by how much personal instability and unhappiness comes with the heavy competition. It shows up, I think, in the greater incidence of things like suicides, of nervous breakdowns, of alcoholism; very few people there can feel economically secure. So I am not suggesting that we should go to the American extreme and imitate their degree of competition. They pay too high a price for their wealth. But if they have too much competition, we have too little; we have something to learn from the Americans, and we ought in this respect to move some way in their direction—perhaps not even half way, but we must retrace some of the steps that have been taken in the past generation in this country in suppressing competition, and in neglecting efficiency.

Let me give you a couple of examples of the sort of thing that we can do to bring back a somewhat larger element of competition. In the first place, I think we should try to get rid, once and for all, of the inflation that still remains in the

British economy. What I am suggesting to you is that there is still in this country too much money chasing too few goods. I know that is very difficult to believe. I have not got too much money, and I am sure you have not got too much money. In fact I have never come across anybody who would admit, even to himself, that he had too much money. But nevertheless, there is too much money about. If you do not believe that, I invite you just to look at some of the official figures of the colossal sums that the British people are spending on tobacco, on alcohol, and on sports and entertainments—21·4 per cent. of the total expenditure of the British people, 4s. 3d. in every pound that we spend—goes at present on those things; tobacco, alcohol, sports, and entertainments. And I am not even bringing in the gambling that goes with the sports and the entertainments.

I am not saying that tobacco and alcohol and sport are bad things, very far from it; but before the war we spent on those things only 11·4 per cent. of our total expenditure, 2s. 3d. in the pound. Now it is 4s. 3d. in the pound; and that is to my mind conclusive evidence that there is far too much loose money about. I know the figures are inflated by the tax that is in those things; but the point I am making at the moment is—look at the enormous sums of money that people do find somewhere to spend on these things. Even if there is not too much money, it is certainly true to say that money is still too easy to get. Lest you think that I am trying to hit at one class of the people, let me say that to my mind the most striking proof of that fact to-day is the great ease with which business firms of all kinds make large profits—which are, of course, later taxed away, but that again is not the point that I am making at the moment.

Why should anyone bother to make himself efficient, whether he be profit earner or wage earner, when it is easy to get a living without being efficient? I think if we are to restore efficiency, we must reintroduce some sort of penalty for inefficiency, not the old severe penalty of starvation, but we must make it not worth a man's while to be inefficient. And on the other hand I think we must pay some attention to the rewards that our society gives to those who are efficient. At present we do not, it seems to me, allow the man who does make himself efficient to derive enough advantage for himself from so doing.

This is partly, but only partly, a result of the very high level of taxation in this country. But I am not simply asking, as you may think, for lower taxes on the rich. In fact, I am not mainly thinking about the rich at all. I am thinking about the skilled man as against the unskilled man. I am thinking about the trained and educated man or woman as against the untrained and uneducated man or woman. We have in the last thirty or forty years severely narrowed the margin of advantage that a man can get by acquiring a skill or having some education and I think if we need skill and efficiency and education—and we do need them as never before in our history—then we must see that the margin of personal advantage that a man or a woman gets by acquiring those things is wider than it is to-day. Do not think that I am arguing against fair shares. On the contrary, I am arguing for fair shares, because equal shares are not fair shares. If a man has contributed more to the community, then the community ought to allow him more for himself.

Those are only examples of the sort of thing that is meant by making the society more competitive. And I would remark in passing that they are carefully selected so that they could be applied whether industry was privately or publicly owned. The argument of socialism versus anti-socialism simply does not come in. But all these devices for increasing efficiency have one thing in common. They are all more or less unpleasant because they all, in greater or less degree, disturb somebody's security or complacency. I think that we must face the fact quite squarely, that in the short run there is some antagonism between efficiency and security. After all, nothing is more secure than an absolutely rigid state of affairs, and if you are aiming to break down that rigidity you must be disturbing somebody. But this conflict, this antagonism is true only in the short run. In the longer run, for this country at any rate, there is no antagonism at all between efficiency and security. Quite the contrary. If we do not look to our efficiency, we shall soon lose our social security, and our full employment. We cannot have security until we first pay our way.

In fact the choice before this country is a perfectly simple and clear one. We can choose between two courses— either on the one hand we will deliberately make up our minds to shift the balance of emphasis back to efficiency under conditions in which we can safeguard full employment and social security: or, on the other hand, we can wait until we get into really serious trouble and then we shall have to go all out for efficiency at all costs, and let the rest go hang. For myself, I want to preserve all three. I do not want to abandon any of the gains in full employment and social security of this past generation. But the only chance of keeping them is to put efficiency back into its place of primacy, and to do so quickly. Let us not go on dodging unpleasant necessities until history once again has to say of the British people that they did too little and too late.

From Alfred Marshall onwards our leading economists have been careful to stress the fact that economic laws are not, like the laws of physical science, immutable and inescapable. There is an " If " in most of them. They tell us that if certain conditions exist, then certain results must follow; and that if we alter those conditions in certain ways, then certain other consequences will follow.

Economics is a branch of Sociology, the study of human society, and to the ultimate welfare and happiness of man we must return. That is our rallying point. Now the study of Economics has one great value: it enables us to see more clearly how incompatible are many of our quite legitimate aims. As Professor Robbins says, in *The Nature and Significance of Economic Science,* " It may well be that there may exist differences as regards ultimate ends in modern society which render some conflict inevitable. But it is clear that many of our most pressing difficulties arise, not for this reason, but because our aims are not co-ordinated. As consumers we will cheapness, as producers we choose security. We value one distribution of factors of production as private spenders and savers. As public citizens we sanction arrangements which frustrate the achievement of this distribution. We call for cheap money and lower prices ; fewer imports and a larger volume of trade. The different ' will-organizations ' in society, although composed of the same individuals, formulate different preferences. Everywhere our difficulties seem to arise, not so much from divisions between the different members of the body politic, as from, as it were, split personalities on the part of each one of them.

"To such a situation, Economics brings the solvent of knowledge. It enables us to conceive the far-reaching implications of alternative possibilities of policy. It does not, and it cannot, enable us to evade the necessity of choosing between alternatives. But it does make it possible for us to bring our different choices into harmony. It cannot remove the ultimate limitations on human action. But it does make it possible within these limitations to act consistently."

We can only strive for consistency if we have some final goal clearly in view. So our final question must be, *What's it all for?* Sir George Schuster's answer will put minor material considerations in their right place and take us back to our rallying point.

SIR GEORGE SCHUSTER

WHAT'S IT ALL FOR?

I WONDER how many million words have been written and spoken about our so-called "crisis" and how to increase production. I want to get away from that here and ask the deeper question, "What's it all *for*?" Are we going to become so worried with our material tasks that we forget the values that matter infinitely more? Or are we going to use the urge of these times to get on the road of true human progress?

What is true progress? What is the kind of society we are aiming at? These are elementary questions. But it is a good thing sometimes to check up on the elements of our faith and purpose. My first answer is that a society must be judged by the lives of its individual members. It should be a society which offers, at least to everyone who plays his part as a member, the chance of a " good life " in the highest sense. But that only brings me to another question, " What is meant by a ' good life ' ? "

On matters like this I think one's best contribution is to trace out one's own experience and lines of thought. So forgive me if my next remarks are a bit personal and element-ary. I start from the impression made on me at Oxford by a passage in Aristotle's *Ethics*. I take as my foundation his conception of the good life or happiness as a form of activity— intense activity at something which one does well. To that I add a second factor—personal freedom as the essential condition for personal responsibility. There must be sufficient freedom in the exercise of one's activities. And thirdly I come to a still more vital point. Mere excellence in a personal activity is not enough. Taken alone that is a cold intellectual idea. One's activities must be warmed by affection: they must be exercised in a setting of human comradeship and love.

I believe that this very simple conception of good work well done in conditions of liberty and in an atmosphere of human love and comradeship gives a clear working guide to what is worth going for in this worldly life. At least I see these three factors as the three foundation stones. I do not say they are all. To go back to Aristotle again, he says that one's life must have an adequate material setting—" the stage properties for the play of life " as he calls it. Of course that is true, and in our modern life all the material conditions— housing, health services, and so on—are of great importance. But they are no more than conditions—means to an end. (For example, it is terribly important that every family should have a good house. But a good house does not necessarily mean a happy home.) These things can ne er replace the true ends.

So I come back to my three " foundation stones ". Take the first: the active exercise of one's best faculties. As I see it, nobody can have a happy life unless he feels that he is doing good work, work which has a meaning for him, and is of recognizable benefit to society. There is no more certain cause of misery than inactivity, aimlessness, feeling that you are not wanted. But here in the case of industrial work we get up against one of the main difficulties. The whole field is bedevilled by past memories. Our curse to-day is that, owing to the way in which the Industrial Revolution came in this country, in which work became identified with factory labour in bad conditions, excessive hours, and fears of exploitation, work itself has come to be regarded as a bad thing, as something to be reduced as far as possible, instead of, as it should be seen, the very foundation of human happiness. The most distressing feature in modern industrial life is the loss for so many of the joy of creation. Nothing matters more than to restore that. And I am not thinking of material results—important though they are. I am thinking of the spiritual value—the satisfaction of work well done, backed by the feeling that you are playing your part, putting in more than you are taking out. To give everyone the chance of that is not easy. Much depends on how my other two points are handled. So I will turn to the next—freedom.

When people talk about freedom they generally mean political freedom. But I am concerned here with an aspect equally important, but often forgotten: freedom in work. And this means not merely freedom in the choice of a job—whether a man will be a coalminer or a bricklayer or a docker or an engineer—but, more important, that he should have the chance to express himself in his work, have some share in saying how it is to be done, not to be treated as a mere automatic piece of machinery which " is not paid to think ". That is easy to say, but not so easy to work out. Full freedom of this kind depends on full co-operation. Anyhow I am sure this is a key point. Freedom of this kind can help enormously to create happiness and interest in work.

But more important still is my third " foundation stone " —what I have called an atmosphere of human love and comradeship. I feel in a difficulty in speaking about this. I do not want to preach a sermon. Yet I cannot disguise my own profound belief, which grows stronger every day, that the key to all our problems can be found in Christian ethics, supported by religious faith. Brotherly love in the Christian sense, treating each individual as a personality of infinite value, family affection, comradeship, kindliness, tolerance—all these conceptions cover manifestations of the same spirit.

Of course I know some people say you cannot have this in business life. I am convinced that they are wrong. Others say that our present economic system of private profit-making makes it impossible. But in my belief it is not a matter of system, but of the way men behave to each other. I wish I had time to argue all this out. I can only state my own convictions. And do not imagine that I am thinking of any kind of sloppy sentimentality or ignoring the realities of accounting. You cannot do that. We must all really earn our daily bread. But what I do say is that in a country of free educated people, and not slaves, even to get the best material results you must have the right human relations in industry and that you cannot have them without faith in your fellow-men, without love and comradeship, without treating the other fellow as of equal value to yourself.

Let me sum up what I have been trying to say. It is that the greatest need in our modern society is to create the chance for all to find happiness in work well done as something of spiritual value—an end in itself—and that for this two things are necessary: first, that all should be given the chance to feel personal responsibility, and, secondly, that our human relations should be governed by the right spirit—equal comradeship, love, faith in our fellow-men. Are these ideas satisfying

Are they practicable? I can imagine many criticisms. I have said nothing of culture, intellectual pleasures, the joy of beauty in art and nature. I have said nothing of the use of leisure, the pleasure of relaxation—sport and all that goes to make a Merrie England. I profoundly value all these things. They are all necessary parts in a balanced structure of a good life. But my point is that the structure itself cannot stand firm without my three " foundation stones ", and I have also got this in mind. Our modern society, whether we like it or not, is essentially an industrial society. We cannot put its pattern right by mere escape, by trying to find all the values and compensations outside people's normal working lives. Others may think I have ignored the difficulties—the sordid drudgery of many jobs, the difficulty of evoking true co-operation; the fact that, as men are, the fear of want may for some be the only spur to work.

Certainly I do not belittle the difficulties. There is an immense load of old habits and suspicions to be shaken off. I know all that. I see it when I watch the efforts of those who are working on the lines I am advocating. I have just been at a week-end conference organized for its workers by an industrial company which is genuinely attempting to create common interest and responsibility among all ranks. At this conference every aspect of organization and daily work was discussed with complete frankness. The conception of pride in the job, pride in the firm, pride in the country, was freely voiced and applauded. But equally there were signs of difficulty—questions whether joint consultation was not an attempt by management to shirk its own responsibilities, questions of conflict between loyalty to the firm and the trade union, and so on. I need not elaborate the difficulties. Nevertheless I left that conference filled with hope and strengthened in my conviction that this is the way of progress and that we must go forward.

And that points to the issue of our time. We stand at a choice of ways when each of us must ask himself crucial questions. Have I faith in my fellow-men and the courage to appeal to the best and not the worst of motives? Do I believe in the rules of conscience? Do I believe that human life has a purpose and meaning and that there is an end worth striving for? My faith is that this country above all others must stand before the world as the country which says "Yes" to these questions. And now is the time.

There has never been a time when it mattered more how *we* go—whether we can stand firm as a rallying point for all that is good in the traditions of European culture and Christian civilization. That is the one effective way for us to counter the threat of war. But I am not thinking only of the threats of militant communism. There is a more subtle threat in the pessimism and disillusionment of Europe—shown, for example, in the astonishing support for nihilistic philosophies like Existentialism. It is for us above all peoples, by the vigour of our own healthy ideas, to counter these disintegrating thoughts and forces. We have not been through the terrible experiences which have fostered European pessimism. Nor is our country the spiritual home for this kind of torturing self-examination or for the confusing tangles of what my friend Will Lawther calls " intellectual tap-dancing on the ideological staircase ".

The world needs a renewal of a simple optimistic faith. And we can give it. But to do that we must live according to that faith and make a success of our society. We must face realities too. I have talked of " optimism ", but I do not mean the foolish optimism which comforts itself by ignoring the facts. Just now all our values are in deadly peril. But that should not make us question the validity of these values. It should only make us appreciate them more keenly and rally us more strongly to their defence. It is in that sense that we must be optimists—optimists in the belief that there is something worth striving for.

I am an optimist too in another sense. I see the present time as an occasion not for depression and pessimism but for thrill and inspiration, because never, at least in the fifty-odd years of my own working life, has there been for all who have the chance to work so clearly a worth-while job to do. And that, as I have urged, is the foundation of happiness in life.

BIOGRAPHICAL NOTES

A. NEVILLE CHAMBERLAIN (1869-1940) will always be remembered as the man who faced the impossible task of maintaining peace in a Europe dominated by Nazi aggression. One of the two famous sons of Joseph Chamberlain, he was educated at Rugby and at Mason College, Birmingham, and then spent seven years in the Bahamas as manager of a fibre plantation. On his return to Birmingham he settled down in industry, and his public career did not begin until 1910. In that year he entered the City Council and played an active part in improving the housing and transport arrangements, and in the formation of the Municipal Bank. In 1918 he entered Parliament and was quickly given Cabinet rank. As Minister of Health he introduced the famous " De-rating " Act of 1928. Three years later he became Chancellor of the Exchequer, and as such was able to introduce the protective tariff which had been his father's dream. On the resignation of Mr. Baldwin in 1937 he was an automatic choice for the Premiership. Storm-clouds quickly gathered. The Nazi Anschluss (union) with Austria came in March 1938, followed by trouble in Czechoslovakia. As Hitler's demands grew more and more ambitious so did Chamberlain's efforts to preserve peace become more and more energetic. Two flying visits were paid to Hitler, but war seemed inevitable until the sudden relief of Munich came on September 30. It was only temporary. The agreement was soon broken, but Munich did give us a year for rearmament and A.R.P. organization. Poland was marked as Hitler's next victim, and Chamberlain introduced conscription in April 1939. He still tried to preserve peace, but the task was obviously impossible. Poland was invaded on September 1, and two days later Chamberlain broadcast the news that Great Britain was again at war—not with the German people, but with their irresponsible government. Following the German advance in 1940, Chamberlain resigned on May 10, after which his health rapidly failed, and he died on November 9.

STANLEY PAUL CHAMBERS (1904-   ), Companion of the Bath, and of the Order of the Indian Empire, played a leading part in the introduction of Pay As You Earn into the British income-tax system. He was educated at the City of London College, and the London School of Economics, where he took a commerce degree and an Economics

305

M.Sc. He was a member of the Indian Income Tax Enquiry Committee in 1935, and Income Tax Adviser to the Government of India from 1937 to 1940. As Commissioner on the Board of Inland Revenue from 1942 to 1947 he worked first in the Statistics and Intelligence department and then as Chief of the Finance Division of the Control Commission for the British Zone of Germany. He is a Deputy Chairman of I.C.I.

GEORGE DOUGLAS HOWARD COLE (1889-   ), Chichele Professor of Social and Political Theory in the University of Oxford, 1944-57, and Research Fellow of Nuffield College since 1957, has the rare gift of making books on economic and social problems as interesting as novels. He combines a clear and effortless style with a complete grasp of his subject, and the ability to see, and to state fairly, all sides of any question.

After attending St. Paul's School and Balliol College he was appointed a Fellow of Magdalen College, Oxford, in 1912, and University Reader in Economics in 1925. He has written biographies of Cobbett, Robert Owen, and Samuel Butler, and a great number of books on economic subjects, of which the most important are possibly the following: *World of Labour*; *Principles of Economic Planning*; *The Means to Full Employment*; *Some Relations between Political and Economic Theory*; *The Meaning of Marxism*; *The Means to Full Employment*; *Money, Its Present and Future*; *Local and Regional Government*; *The Intelligent Man's Guide to the Post-war World*; *Socialist Economics*; *Essays in Social Theory*, and *Socialist Thought* (3 vols.).

SIR STAFFORD CRIPPS (1892-1952) was appointed Chancellor of the Exchequer in November 1947, when Mr. Hugh Dalton resigned following the leakage of Budget secrets. His austere and cautious financial policy matched the gravity of the situation in the post-war years.

Educated at Winchester and University College, London, he then studied law in the Middle Temple, and quickly came to the front rank as a barrister. He was appointed a K.C. in 1927 and a knighthood followed in 1930. Elected M.P. for East Bristol in 1931, he continued to represent that constituency until his resignation, through overwork and ill-health, in October 1950. In 1940 he was given the delicate post of Ambassador in Moscow, and in 1942 returned and took office as Lord Privy Seal, going to India to put the proposals for self-government after the war before the Indian political leaders. On his return he became Minister of Aircraft Production, and was President of the Board of Trade in the Labour Government of 1945. He there had the difficult task of organizing the recovery of British industry after six years of war, and as Chancellor he faced the equally difficult problem of putting the country's finances back on a sound basis.

SIR GEOFFREY CROWTHER (1907-), Managing Director of The Economist Newspaper Ltd. since 1956, was educated at Leeds Grammar School, Oundle, and Clare College, Cambridge, and then at Yale and Columbia universities. He was President of the Cambridge Union in 1928. After some practical experience of financial work in New York and London he joined the staff of *The Economist* in 1932, and became assistant editor in 1935. He was also assistant editor of the *News Chronicle* from 1936 to 1938, when he became editor of *The Economist*. His post-war editorials have aroused immense interest. Even people who disagreed most violently with the views expressed have felt that they just had to read them. Crowther is a director of some publishing companies, and a member of the governing bodies of Charterhouse and Haileybury public schools, and of the London School of Economics.

His main publications are *An Introduction to the Study of Prices* (with Lord Layton) ; *Ways and Means* ; *Economics for Democrats* ; and *An Outline of Money*.

STANLEY RAYMOND DENNISON (1912-), C.B.E., and Fellow of Gonville and Caius College, is University Lecturer in Economics at Cambridge. He was born at North Shields, and educated at Durham University and at Trinity College, Cambridge. From 1935 to 1939 he was Lecturer in Economics at Manchester University, and Professor of Economics at Swansea from 1939 to 1945. He also served as Chief Economic Assistant to the War Cabinet Secretariat from 1940 to 1946, and was a member of the Scott Commission on Land Utilization in Rural Areas. He has published many articles on economic subjects, and a penetrating study of *The Location of Industry and the Depressed Areas*.

EVAN F. M. DURBIN (1906-48) the protagonist of state planning, won his way by means of scholarships to New College, Oxford, where he later gave his first lectures. He won the Ricardo Fellowship at London University, and became Senior Lecturer at the London School of Economics, where, in Mr. Attlee's words " he proved an able and inspiring teacher ". In 1940 he joined the Economic Section of the War Cabinet Secretariat. and in 1942 was Mr. Attlee's personal assistant.

After two earlier disappointments he was returned to Parliament in 1945 as member for Edmonton. He served for a time as Parliamentary Private Secretary to the Chancellor of the Exchequer, and in 1947 became Parliamentary Secretary to the Minister of Works. As a man of generous sympathies and wide understanding, he believed it the duty of every government department to be of the utmost service to the public. It was a great shock to his many friends when he was drowned on September 3, 1948, near Bude. Going to the assistance of his children, who were in difficulties on the rocks, he was caught by the fierce undertow of a heavy sea and swept away. His chief works are *Politics of Democratic Socialism*; and *Problems of Economic Planning*.

WALTER E. ELLIOT (1890-1958), C.H. (1952), P.C., Fellow of the Royal Society, and sometime Rector of the Universities of Aberdeen and of Glasgow, played many parts with distinction. Educated at the Academy and University of Glasgow he qualified as a doctor in 1913, and served throughout the war of 1914-18 in France, winning the Military Cross and a bar to it. He then took to politics, entered Parliament in 1918, and his absences after that time were very brief indeed. He was Under-Secretary of State for Scotland in 1923, and again from 1924 to 1929, and Financial Secretary to the Treasury in 1931. In the following year he was given the task of protecting agriculture and seeing that the British farmer received a fair price for his produce without raising the cost of living, offending the taxpayer, or discriminating against farmers in the Dominions. His work as Minister of Agriculture no doubt helped to lay a sound foundation for the country's increase in its home production of food during the anxious days of the Second Great War. In October 1936 he took over the office of Secretary of State for Scotland; from 1938 to 1940 he was Minister of Health, and in the following year he became Director of Public Relations at the War Office. *Long Distance* (1943) gives the speeches which he made to Canada and the United States through the B.B.C. Overseas programme. He received honorary degrees from a number of universities, and in 1938 he was awarded the Freedom of the City of Edinburgh.

P. SARGANT FLORENCE (1890-   ) is one of the modern school of economists who delight in the statistical approach to the subject if only because the inquirer must then be " quite certain what he is discussing ". This certainty about the point at issue is very desirable at any time, and more so when the economists are called in by the politicians to advise on the planning of industry. He was educated at Rugby and Caius College, Cambridge, where he took a First in Economics in 1914. During the first War he was occupied with research work on health and problems of fatigue among munition workers. He crossed the Atlantic to work in America, and took his Ph.D. at Columbia, returning to Cambridge in 1921 as University Lecturer in Economics. He held the Chair of Economics at Birmingham University from 1929 to 1955, and was appointed Dean of the Faculty of Commerce and Social Science 1947-50. Among his publications we may mention *Economics and Human Behaviour*; *The Statistical Method in Economic and Political Science*; *The Logic of Industrial Organization*; *Investment Location and Size of Plant*; *Industry and the State*; and, in collaboration with Professors Carr-Saunders and Peers, *Consumers' Co-operation in Great Britain*.

SIR THEODORE GREGORY (1890-   ), Economic Adviser to the Government of India from 1938 until the formation of the Dominions, studied at Owen's School, Islington, at Stuttgart, and at the London School of Economics. He lectured at the L.S.E. from 1913 to 1919, and was Sir Ernest Cassel Professor of Economics in the University of London from 1927 to 1937. He was a member of the 1929 Macmillan Committee on industry and finance, economic adviser to the Niemeyer Mission which showed Australia and New Zealand the way to recovery in 1930, and a member of the Eire Banking Commission 1934-37. He has written many books on financial topics, notably *Tariffs*; *Foreign Exchange*; *The Return to Gold*; *The Gold Standard and its Future*; and *Gold, Unemployment, and Capitalism*.

FRIEDRICH AUGUST (VON) HAYEK (1899-   ) has been Professor of Social and Moral Science in the University of Chicago since 1950. He was formerly Dean of the Faculty of Economics at London. He was born in Vienna, and from 1927 to 1931 was Director of the Austrian Institute for Economic Research. He became a British subject in 1938, and was elected a Fellow of the British Academy in 1944. Professor Hayek (he has dropped the " von ") has written a number of important books on economics, and he is a staunch defender of private enterprise. The chief titles are: *Prices and Production*; *Monetary Theory and the Trade Cycle*; *Monetary Nationalism and Economic Stability*; *Profits, Interest and Investment*; *The Pure Theory of Capitalism*; *The Road to Serfdom*; and *Individualism and the Economic Order*.

JOHN RICHARD HICKS (1904-   ), Professor of Political Economy at Oxford since 1952, is another of the distinguised band who have lectured for a time in the London School of Economics. Educated at Clifton College, and Balliol College, Oxford, he lectured at London from 1926 to 1935, and then took up a Fellowship at Gonville and Caius College, Cambridge. From 1938 to 1946 he held the Chair of Political Economy at Manchester University. He has written a large number of papers and books on economic subjects, many of them in collaboration with his wife, URSULA K. HICKS. Among them may be mentioned *The Theory of Wages*; *Value and Capital*; *The Social Framework*; and (with his wife) *Standards of Local Expenditure*; *The Problem of Valuation for Rating*; and *The Incidence of Local Rates in Britain*. Mrs. Hicks is the author of *The Finance of British Government*, and of *Public Finance*.

JOHN ATKINSON HOBSON (1858-1940) was born at Derby and educated at the local school, and at Lincoln College, Oxford. After seven years as classical master at Faversham and Exeter schools he became a University Extension Lecturer for the next decade, and then devoted all his time to journalism and writing books on economic and social topics. His most important works are *Imperialism*; *The Evolution of Modern Capitalism*; *The Industrial System*; and *The Economics of Unemployment*. He wrote as a " humanist ", and he had much in common with Lord Keynes. He thought that the maintenance of a correct balance between expenditure on consumption goods and on capital goods was necessary to keep the wheels of trade and industry turning, and he strongly criticized the tendency of the rich to save too much. He wrote, of course, in the days when it *was* possible for very wealthy people to save a large proportion of their income.

JOHN MAYNARD KEYNES, First Baron Keynes of Tilton (1883-1946), the most original, and probably the greatest of the twentieth-century economists, was for many years the leading British authority on the intricacies of international finance. After Eton and King's College, Cambridge, he entered the Civil Service and worked first in the India Office and then in the Treasury. At the Paris Peace Conference in 1919 he saw more clearly than any other Allied councillor the inevitable effect of the Reparations claims on German economy. He resigned his position in order to write *The Economic Consequences of the Peace* and from this time onwards his reputation as a far-sighted critic of the orthodox financiers and economists steadily grew. His most important works are

A Treatise on Money and *The General Theory of Employment, Interest and Money*. Lord Keynes held that if only one looked below the surface of a subject one was bound to find it fascinating, and he certainly made economics fascinating for many people. He held that economics should be more than a merely descriptive science. It should be made an instrument of social progress, and its theories should be given practical application so that such things as full employment, which would not come of themselves under modern conditions, should be achieved by a central control and direction of the vital factors. But he preferred to leave all the details of production and trade to private enterprise.

Keynes had a very poor opinion indeed of Karl Marx and the class struggle. He loved the good things of life himself, and he did not see why the passage of years should not see a steady improvement in the standard of living of the workers until they, too, could enjoy and appreciate such refinements.

In his last years he was the chief advocate of a scheme to facilitate international trade and investment by the creation of a new international currency called *bancor* to be issued by a World Bank. He played a leading part at the Bretton Woods Conference and his untimely death undoubtedly helped to retard the recovery of trade.

JOHN RAMSAY M'CULLOCH (1789-1864) was a disciple of Ricardo, and it was only natural that when a Memorial Lectureship was established by public subscription in the year following Ricardo's death M'Culloch should be appointed. He had studied Political Economy at Edinburgh University, and he first became known as a contributor of articles on economic subjects to the *Scotsman* and the *Edinburgh Review*. He was appointed Professor of Political Economy in London University in 1828, but he resigned to become Comptroller of the Stationery Office in 1838. He wrote a large number of books, of which the best known is his *Principles of Political Economy*, and while he was at the Stationery Office he produced a number of important statistical compilations. He was a great friend of James Mill.

ALFRED MARSHALL (1842-1924), a student of Merchant Taylors' School and St. John's College, Cambridge, was second wrangler in 1865, and elected a Fellow of his College. After being the first Principal of University College, Bristol, and Lecturer in Political Economy at Balliol, Oxford, he returned to Cambridge in 1885 as Professor of Political Economy.

In 1890 the famous *Principles of Economics* appeared and many editions were called for in the next few years. Marshall served on a large number of government commissions inquiring into financial and industrial problems. His *Industry and Trade* was published in 1918, and *Money, Credit and Commerce* in 1923. Writing at a time when "six economists meant seven different opinions ", at least on the theory of value, he did succeed in reconciling various schools of thought, and it is probable that in the future he will come to be regarded as the main founder of the modern outlook on economics. He always insisted that economic " laws " should be regarded as only a means of discovering the real truth about a problem.

KARL MARX (1818-83) and FRIEDRICH ENGELS (1820-95) met in Paris in 1843. They found themselves in agreement on all essential points in their views on politics and philosophy, and the close friendship and collaboration which they then established continued until Marx's death.

Marx was born at Trier in the Rhineland, the son of a Jewish lawyer, and he studied law, history, and philosophy at the universities of Bonn and Berlin. He became the editor of a Radical newspaper, the *Rheinische Zeitung*, but the socialist doctrine which began to appear in its pages led to its suppression in 1843, and he went to Paris and joined the staff of another Radical paper.

Engels was the son of a wealthy German cotton-spinner, and as the family had business interests in Manchester he had spent some time in England, where he had come in touch with Owenites and Chartists.

At the request of the Prussian government Marx was expelled from France, and he and Engels went to Brussels where they joined the League of Communists. For this propagandist body they drew up the famous Communist Manifesto of 1848. This was the year of revolutions in Europe. The rising in France was quickly followed by an upheaval in Germany, and Marx and Engels went to Cologne and founded a political newspaper. The Conservative reaction soon followed, however, and after being charged with high treason Marx was expelled from Prussia. France would not receive him so he went to London, where he spent the rest of his life.

The first volume of his great work appeared in 1867 under the title of *Das Kapital*. The main theme is that of " surplus value ". It is the labour of the workers which gives the finished product its value, and therefore, says Marx, the labourer should have the right to the whole produce of his labour. The capitalist who provides the machine and the raw material and the land, deserves nothing.

After Marx's death Engels compiled and published three more volumes of *Das Kapital* from material which he had left. He himself put his most important writing into the *Anti-Dühring* and the *Feuerbach*, the latter being an exposition of the philosophy of Dialectical Materialism.

J. MIDDLETON MURRY (1889-1957), editor of *The Adelphi* from 1923 to 1948, has been one of the moral reformers of the age. He was educated at Christ's Hospital and Brasenose College, and he married Katherine Mansfield while at Oxford. On coming down he worked as a journalist for the *Westminster Gazette*, and then as a reviewer for *The Times Literary Supplement*. He was found unfit for active service when he volunteered in the first World War, and was attached to the Political Intelligence Department of the War Office. He became Chief Censor, and was awarded the O.B.E. Only a few of his numerous publications can be mentioned here: his books on Keats and Shakespeare as examples of his literary appreciation, his *Life of Jesus* on the religious plane, and his *Defence of Democracy* and *The Free Society* on the political and social side.

DAVID RICARDO (1772-1823) was born in London of a Jewish family, and at the age of 14 he entered the office of his stockbroker father. At the age of 21 he abandoned the Jewish faith in order to marry a Christian girl, and quitted his father's office. He set up on his own account on the Stock Exchange and soon made a fortune.

He now turned to scientific studies, and having read *The Wealth of Nations* he became deeply interested in political economy. He wrote a number of tracts on financial matters, and his main work, *Principles of Political Economy and Taxation*, appeared in 1817. The foundation of his theory is that the exchange value of any commodity is determined by the amount of labour which has to be used to produce it. His main contributions to economic thought are the analysis of rent which we have given, his theory of foreign trade being controlled by comparative costs, and his study of the incidence of taxation.

SEEBOHM ROWNTREE (1871-1954), Companion of Honour, was deeply interested in social problems throughout his long and active life. He made two detailed studies of working-class life in his own city of York, the first, published in 1899, carrying the title of *Poverty: A Study of Town Life*, while the second, begun in 1936, led to the brighter title of *Poverty and Progress*. But the economic progress which has undoubtedly been made has not been paralleled by moral and spiritual progress. "A democratic state " he declares at the end of the second survey " can only flourish if the level of intelligence of the community is high, and its spiritual life dynamic."

Seebohm Rowntree was educated at the Friends' School in York and at Owen's College, after which he worked his way up to the top of the well-known cocoa firm. He was Chairman of the company from 1925 to 1941. Practical experience is united with warm sympathy and clear thinking in his books, which include, in addition to those mentioned above, *The Human Factor in Business*; *The Human Needs of Labour*; *The Way to Industrial Peace*; and *Betting and Gambling, a National Evil*.

SIR GEORGE SCHUSTER (1881-   ), scholar, barrister, banker, soldier, administrator, and financial adviser, has exercised his brilliant talents to the full. From Charterhouse (of which he is now Vice-Chairman of the Governing Body) he went to New College, Oxford, where he took a First in Greats in 1903. Two years later he was called to the Bar, and then entered the family banking business and soon became a director of many important firms. In the first World War he won the M.C. and the C.B.E. and was four times mentioned in despatches. When peace returned, his financial genius soon found congenial employment again both in London and with a number of Colonial governments. He was a member of the Select Committee on National Expenditure, 1939-45. He is Treasurer of the Medical Research Council, a Director of the Westminister Bank, and a member of many important business associations. In *India and Democracy* he gives a thoughtful study of that country's political problems.

ADAM SMITH, probably the greatest political economist who has ever lived, was born at Kirkcaldy in 1723, and his education began at the school in that town. From there he went to Glasgow University in 1737, where he remained for four years, and it was here that he met Francis Hutcheson, whose teachings on moral and economic questions were later to exert a great influence. In 1740 Smith won an exhibition to Balliol College, Oxford, where he stayed until 1746.

He soon acquired a reputation for his lecturing ability, which led to his election as Professor of Logic at Glasgow in 1751, and the following year to the Chair of Moral Philosophy.

In 1763 he resigned from this position to accept a travelling tutor-ship to the young Duke of Buccleuch, and they toured France together from 1764-66 during which time Smith met many of the leading French philosophers. In 1767 he was elected F.R.S., and from this time until its publication in 1776 was occupied with his great work, *Inquiry into the Nature and Causes of the Wealth of Nations*. Shortly after this he was appointed Commissioner of Customs in Scotland and in 1787 was elected Lord Rector of Glasgow University. His health had rapidly declined after the death of his mother in 1784 and in 1790 he died.

Smith's greatest work is undoubtedly the *Wealth of Nations*, in which he sets out to show that the wealth of a nation springs from its labour supply, and it is on this basis that he discusses the factors of production, and their most effective use. Though Smith can hardly be said to have been the founder of Political Economy, he rendered all previous theories obsolete, and set out from an observation of facts to make economics a science.

P. H. WICKSTEED (1844-1927) was born in Leeds and educated at Manchester and London. After some years as a Unitarian minister he resigned in 1887 and devoted all his energies to University Extension lecturing and to writing. His main interests lay in ethics, sociology, and economics and he wrote a number of books and pamphlets on these subjects. His greatest work, *Commonsense of Political Economy*, appeared in 1910. In this he attempted a systematic exposition of the utility theory of value, and applied the idea of the " marginal " product to many practical problems. He was President of the British Association in 1913.

BIBLIOGRAPHY

HERE is a short list of books suitable for study by readers who, without special training in Economics, wish to carry their knowledge beyond what they may find in this volume.

(A) GENERAL INTRODUCTORY BOOKS

J. R. Hicks. *The Social Framework.*
[*Not* a text-book of Economics, but an excellent realistic introduction to the subject dealing with the structure of the economic system.]

F. Benham. *Economics.*
[A widely used text-book, covering the main ground of elementary Economics as it is taught to University economic students.]

A. Cairncross. *Introduction to Economics.*
[A shorter alternative to Benham.]

Sir D. H. Robertson. *Lectures on Economic Principles.*

(B) MORE SPECIALIZED OR ADVANCED WORKS

G. D. H. Cole. *Money, Present and Future.*
[Includes both the theory and a discussion of current monetary problems.]

Sir G. Crowther. *An Outline of Money.*
[Useful elementary introduction.]

U. K. Hicks. *Public Finance.*
[The best introduction.]

Lord Beveridge. *Full Employment in a Free Society.*

G. D. H. Cole. *The Means to Full Employment.*

A. Lewis. *The Principles of Economic Planning.*

J. E. Meade. *The Control of Inflation.*

J. K. Galbraith. *The Affluent Society.*

A. J. Brown. *Applied Economics.*

B. S. Rowntree. *Poverty and Progress* (A Study of York) (1941).

N. Barou. *British Trade Unions.*

R. S. Sayers. *Modern Banking.*

T. Balogh. *The Dollar Crisis.*

R. S. Edwards and H. Townsend. *Business Enterprise: Its Growth and Organisation.*

Lord Keynes. *The General Theory of Employment, Interest and Money.*

E. Chamberlin. *The Theory of Monopolistic Competition.*

G. Haberler. *Prosperity and Depression.*
   [On trade fluctuations and their causes.]
J. P. Davison, P. S. Florence and others. *Productivity and Economic Incentives.*
C. Gide and C. Rist. *History of Economic Doctrines.*
R. L. Heilbroner. *The Great Economists.*

ACKNOWLEDGMENTS

FOR permission to include copyright material in this volume our acknowledgments and thanks are due to the following:

To Sir George Schuster for " What's It All For? "; to Seebohm Rowntree for " The Price of Full Employment "; to Professor Sargant Florence for " Desirable Site for Factory"; to S. P. Chambers for " Taxation, Incentives, and Social Insurance "; to S. R. Dennison for " Does Bigness make for Efficiency? "; to Sir Geoffrey Crowther for " The Way Back to Solvency " from his broadcast talks on " Wealth and Welfare "; and to the late Lord Keynes for " How much does Finance Matter? "

To Professor G. D. H. Cole and his various publishers for " What Happens in Slumps " from *The Intelligent Man's Guide to the Post-War World* (Victor Gollancz, Ltd.), for " Politics and Economics " from *What Marx Really Meant* (Victor Gollancz, Ltd.), for "A Planned Monetary Policy " from articles on *The Future of Money* (*New Statesman and Nation*), and for " Money in the Bank " and " The Supply of Money " from *Money, Its Present and Future* (Cassell & Co., Ltd.).

To Sir Geoffrey Crowther and Nelson & Sons for "Exchange Rates" from *An Outline of Money*; to Sir Theodore Gregory and P. S. King & Sons for " Rationalization and Technological Unemployment "; to the Right Hon. Walter Elliot and Philip Allan & Co. for "The Endless Adventure "; to J. R. Hicks and the Clarendon Press for " The National Income" from *The Social Framework*; to Ursula K. Hicks and the Cambridge University Press for " The Development of Modern Tax Ideals " from *Public Finance*; to the Oxford University Press for " International Trade " from *The Science of Wealth* in the Home University Library series, and to the United Nations Department of Economic Affairs for " The Key to the Problem of Unemployment " from *National and International Measures for Full Employment*.

To the Executors of the late Lord Keynes and to Macmillan & Co., Ltd., for " The General Theory of Employment " from *The General Theory of Employment, Interest and Money*, and for " Inflation and Deflation " from *Essays in Persuasion*; to the Representatives of the late Alfred Marshall and to Macmillan & Co., Ltd., for " Human Wants ", " The Principle of Substitution ", and "The Distribution of

318

Wealth ", all from *Principles of Economics*; to Professor Hayek and to Routledge and Kegan Paul, Ltd., for " Is Planning Inevitable? " from *The Road to Serfdom*; to the Representatives of the late E. F. M. Durbin and to Routledge & Kegan Paul, Ltd., for "The Case for Planning", from *Problems of Economic Planning*; to the Representatives of the late P. H. Wicksteed and to Routledge & Kegan Paul, Ltd., for " Interest " from *The Commonsense of Political Economy*.

Indulgence is craved for any inadvertent failure to express due acknowledgments.

INDEX

(Titles of Lectures are in Black Type)